Problems in Modern
Latin American History

LATIN AMERICAN SILHOUETTES

Series Editors: William H. Beezley and Judith Ewell

Recent Titles in the Series

For a complete listing of titles, visit www.rowmanlittlefield.com/series.

Problems in Modern Latin American History

Sources and Interpretations

Fourth Edition

JAMES A. WOOD

ROWMAN & LITTLEFIELD
Lanham • Boulder • New York • Toronto • Plymouth, UK

Published by Rowman & Littlefield
4501 Forbes Boulevard, Suite 200, Lanham, Maryland 20706
www.rowman.com

10 Thornbury Road, Plymouth PL6 7PP, United Kingdom

Copyright © 2014 by Rowman & Littlefield

British Library Cataloguing in Publication Information Available

Library of Congress Cataloging-in-Publication Data

Problems in modern Latin American history : sources and interpretations / James A. Wood. — Fourth edition.
    pages cm. — (Latin American silhouettes)
  Includes bibliographical references and index.
  ISBN 978-1-4422-1859-8 (cloth : alk. paper) — ISBN 978-1-4422-1860-4 (pbk. : alk. paper) — ISBN 978-1-4422-1861-1 (electronic) 1. Latin America—History—1830– 2. Latin America—Social conditions. I. Wood, James A., editor.
 F1413.P76 2014
 980.03—dc23

2013028271

♾️™ The paper used in this publication meets the minimum requirements of American National Standard for Information Sciences—Permanence of Paper for Printed Library Materials, ANSI/NISO Z39.48-1992.

Printed in the United States of America

Contents

Preface to the Fourth Edition

Like everything else that touches our lives, this book has a history. That history began forty years ago when Joseph S. Tulchin, a professor of Latin American history at the University of North Carolina Chapel Hill (UNC-CH), put together a book titled *Problems in Latin American History: The Modern Period* (New York: Harper & Row, 1973). Tulchin called upon noted experts in the field to put together selected readings covering ten chronological and thematic chapters that "aimed at conceptualization." Twenty years later, Tulchin and his former advisee, John C. Chasteen, who was also a professor of Latin American history at UNC-CH, coedited a new edition of the book, which was retitled *Problems in Modern Latin American History: A Reader* (Wilmington, DE: Scholarly Resources, 1994). The Chasteen and Tulchin edition, which followed the model of having experts in the field handle individual chapters, was the one I used as a UNC-CH graduate teaching assistant under Chasteen in the 1990s. After receiving my first academic position in 1999 at North Carolina A&T State University in Greensboro, I proposed to Chasteen that we do another update of the book but this time to edit all of the chapters by ourselves. Our close collaboration resulted in the publication of *Problems in Modern Latin American History: Sources and Interpretations* (Wilmington, DE: Scholarly Resources, 2004). We then did yet another edition of *PMLAH* five years later, this time published by Rowman & Littlefield in 2009. This is therefore my third experience in editing a version of this book. I explain all of this now not because it is important to students who might study the book's contents but rather because I am truly humbled to have been entrusted with the editing of such a historically significant teaching resource. I want to thank John, my pal for over twenty years, and Joe, whom I have only recently gotten to know, for this opportunity to usher the book into a new decade.

In editing this edition of *PMLAH* I have tried hard to keep my students in mind. In some ways I imagine that A&T students are much like students at any midsized, regional university. They do not necessarily come into my modern Latin American history classroom with much background knowledge of the region's history, but they often come with a curiosity about this fascinating place that they know about through music, film, travel, or friendships. In other ways, however, A&T students are probably a little different from students at most institutions. NC A&T State University is a public, historically black university, which means that in general my students have a fairly high level of awareness about issues of race and racism. Undoubtedly, their awareness has influenced the way I teach the history of modern Latin America, which, in turn, is reflected in this book.

It is my firm belief that the "problems" approach followed in this book helps students in two important ways. First, they learn the content of modern Latin American history—its chronology, periodization, and some of its essential themes—by working through the more than sixty primary and secondary source selections that cover a wide range of topics, from political independence to globalization. Second, they develop skills that make them better students regardless of their majors. Most of my students are not history majors; many of them take my course as a way of satisfying general education requirements. I have thus learned to place greater emphasis on the development of critical thinking and communication skills, which have become a fundamental part of the university's educational mission. In this edition I have tightened the interpretive problems in each chapter and given each a specific learning objective. When worked through collaboratively, with a good mix of oral and written communication assignments, the problems approach is highly conducive to students learning to think critically.

New in this edition are several key features. I would like to thank Susan McEachern and three anonymous reviewers of the previous edition, whose insights and ideas have most definitely been incorporated into this one. Specifically, the number of chapters has been reduced from thirteen to twelve, making it easier to fit the whole book into a sixteen-week semester. I have added some classics to this edition: José Martí, Octavio Paz, Joaquim Nabuco, Justo Sierra, and more. Two chapters from the previous edition, "Neocolonialism" and "The New Left Turn," have been dropped, although they live on in merged form in the current chapters "Race and Nation Building" and "The Global Economy." Also, a new chapter, "Historical Memory," has been added to this edition. This new final chapter of the book takes us back to the period of the Cold War, which is explored in chapters 9 and 10 ("Social Revolution" and "The Cold War"). Creating this new chapter was a major departure for me. Reading Steve Stern's brilliant trilogy *The Memory Box of Pinochet's Chile* led me to the concept. In addition, in revising the introductions and headnotes to each chapter, I have tried to create more connections between them. This was one of the many useful suggestions I got from reviewers.

Finally, I have to say that this is the first edition of the book I have done without my coeditor, John Chasteen. John has decided to step away from this book project, focusing his attention instead on his other writing and translation plans. The success of John's work speaks for itself, but it is worthwhile to mention the (probably obvious) influence of John's highly regarded textbook *Born in Blood and Fire* on this book. I have rewritten all of the introductions and headnotes that were written by John in the last edition. I am grateful to him for allowing me to continue to use some of the translations he has so graciously done for this book over the years.

James A. Wood
Greensboro, North Carolina

I

Independence

When the nineteenth century began, Europe and the Americas were in a state of transition. It was a revolutionary moment in the political history of the Atlantic world. Europe was in the middle of dealing with the French Revolution of 1789 and the subsequent rise of Napoleon Bonaparte. Only two decades earlier the British colonies of eastern North America had won their independence, establishing the Americas' first constitutional republic. The French colony of Saint–Domingue followed suit in the 1790s when an army of rebel slaves led by Toussaint L'Overture overturned slavery and colonialism in what became known as the Republic of Haiti. Though it was thoroughly shaken by these vivid examples of anticolonial rebellion and revolution, colonial rule in Latin America was still in good shape in 1800.

Yet by 1825, just a quarter-century later, every one of the Spanish and Portuguese colonial possessions in the Americas (with the notable exceptions of Cuba and Puerto Rico) underwent a process of separation from their imperial mother countries. In the Spanish American colonies, that process of separation was extremely violent and required more than a decade of war between royalists (defenders of the continuation of imperial rule) and patriots (those who sought to break with imperial rule) to be achieved. In the Portuguese colony of Brazil, the process was less violent and only lasted about a year.

Historians have identified some commonalities in the achievement of political independence in both cases. First and foremost, the great impetus behind the process of separation in both Spanish America and Brazil was the historic crisis brought on by the Napoleonic wars in Europe. In 1807, Napoleon's forces invaded the Iberian Peninsula. The Peninsular War of 1807–1814 (as it was known) resulted in the capture of both the Spanish king Charles IV and his son, the heir apparent, Prince Ferdinand, who were held by Napoleon's forces in France, leaving Spain without a king. The Portuguese prince regent (soon to be king) Joao VI fared better; he fled by ship to Brazil with his family and royal entourage, and reestablished the empire there. By 1808, French forces had taken control of Spain and Portugal, and Napoleon placed his brother Joseph on the Spanish throne.

The other thing that the Latin American movements for independence shared was a common philosophy that came out of the European Enlightenment and that was based on the concepts of liberalism, republicanism, and nationalism. Liberalism, in theory, meant the legal equality of all citizens (though it did not work that way in practice). Republicanism meant a form of constitutional government with representatives elected by the people (though, again, in practice this right did not apply to all of the population). Nationalism meant a sense of shared history and common identity, which in the American colonies was complicated by the legacies of conquest and slavery. While there was plenty of disagreement within the independence movements over the meaning of these concepts, there is no denying that they were central to the debates and discussions that independence generated.

The Peninsular War posed a dilemma for all politically active individuals living in the Spanish dominions. Should we recognize the authority of this false king? How long should we wait for our true king's restoration? Do we really need a king at all? While the French regime of occupation had some Spanish support, most politically active Spaniards chose to resist it. Spanish rebels initiated a strategy of guerrilla warfare against the French while temporary governing bodies called juntas sprouted up throughout Spain and its American colonies. These juntas would become the basis of the independence movements in Spanish America. The Spanish Constitution of 1812, written mostly by anti-French liberals who were holding out in the southern city of Cádiz, further legitimized the juntas.

In the colonies, the juntas that formed in places like Buenos Aires and Caracas seized on this opportunity to declare independence from Joseph Bonaparte. But when Napoleon's forces were finally defeated in 1814 and Ferdinand returned to the Spanish throne as King Ferdinand VII he refused to accept the Cádiz constitution's provisions and launched a military campaign to regain control of the American colonies. From 1815 until 1825, battles were fought across Mexico and the South American continent between royalist and patriot armies (this did not include Brazil, which avoided the bloodshed by splitting the Portuguese empire into two parts, Portugal and Brazil). By 1825, a host of new American republics arose from the ashes of colonial rule.

The Wars of Independence in Spanish America introduced a number of important political innovations, such as the writing of constitutions and the holding of elections. It also brought notions of national identity and racial equality to the fore. Political life would never be the same. There is no doubt that independence also had an impact on economic and social life in the former colonies. Traditional barriers to international trade, for example, were lifted by the newly independent governments. What is more difficult for historians to assess is the extent to which the changes that flowed from political independence had any tangible effect on the everyday lives of ordinary Latin Americans. How far down into society did the political revolution of independence reach? By the end of this chapter, students will be able to formulate their own answer to this important question.

QUESTIONS FOR ANALYSIS

1. Describe the political philosophy underlying the documents excerpted in this chapter? What were its defining elements?
2. Did the movements for independence challenge the colonial conception of racial hierarchy?
3. How did slaves and women use the disruption of independence to their advantage? How did it work against their interests?

1. The Political Constitution of the Spanish Monarchy ⁓ Cortes of Cádiz*

In 1808, as the French occupation was being implemented, the juntas that were forming throughout the Spanish empire came together in the city of Aranjuez. This Supreme Central Junta called for the convening of what was known in Spanish history as the Cortes, *an assembly of representatives of the entire Spanish nation, including its American colonies. The Cortes was charged with producing a new government and writing a new political constitution, all while maintaining the resistance to the French regime. Due to setbacks on the battlefield in 1810, the rebel government was forced to withdraw to the only safe place left to them, the southern port city of Cádiz. That is where they wrote the document that is excerpted below. The Spanish Constitution of 1812 is often regarded as liberal in orientation. What evidence do you see of that?*

In the name of God Almighty, Father, Son, and Holy Spirit, author and supreme legislator of society.

The General and Extraordinary Cortes of the Spanish Nation, well convinced, after the most minute examination and mature deliberation, that the ancient fundamental laws of this Monarchy, aided by every appropriate precaution and measure, that can assure their complete fulfillment in a stable and permanent manner, are properly calculated to fulfill the grand object of promoting the glory, prosperity, and welfare of the nation, decree the following Political Constitution for the good governing and right administration of the State.

Of the Spanish Nation

Article 1. The Spanish nation is the gathering together of all the Spaniards of both hemispheres.

---

*From "Constitución Política de la Monarquía Española Promulgada en Cadíz el 19 de Marzo de 1812," trans. James A. Wood, accessed May 1, 2013, www.cervantesvirtual.com/.

Article 2. The Spanish nation is free and independent, and neither is nor can be the property of any family or person.

Article 3. Sovereignty belongs to the nation; consequently it exclusively possesses the right of establishing its fundamental laws.

Article 4. The nation is obliged, by wise and just laws, to protect the liberty, property, and all other legitimate rights of every individual which composes it.

Of Spaniards

Article 5. Spaniards are [defined as]:

1. All free men born and raised in the Spanish dominions, and their sons;

2. Foreigners who have obtained letters of naturalization from the Cortes;

3. Those foreigners who, without such letters, have resided ten years in any town or village in Spain, and acquired thereby a right of residence;

4. Slaves who receive their freedom in the Spanish dominions.

Article 6. Love of country is one of the principal duties of every Spaniard, as well as being just and charitable.

Article 7. Every Spaniard is obliged to be faithful to the Constitution, obey the laws, and respect the established authorities.

Article 8. Every Spaniard, without exception, is also obliged to contribute a proportion to his assets to the finances of the State.

Article 9. It is also the duty of every Spaniard, without exception, to bear arms in defense of the country, when called for by law.

Of the Cortes

Article 27. The Cortes is the gathering together of all the deputies who represent the nation, named by the citizens in the manner hereafter to be explained.

Article 28. The basis of national representation is the same in both hemispheres.

Article 29. This basis is the people composed of those inhabitants who, by both family lines, are natives of the Spanish dominions; [and] of those who have letters of citizenship from the Cortes.

Article 31. For every seventy thousand souls, consisting of those expressed in Article 29, one deputy shall be sent to the Cortes.

Article 34. For the election of deputies to the Cortes, *juntas* shall be held in the parishes, districts, and provinces.

Article 35. The parish electoral juntas shall be composed of all the citizens and residents within the bounds of the respective parishes, including the secular clergy.

Article 36. These juntas shall meet in the Peninsula and Islands* and possessions adjacent the first Sunday in October the year preceding that in which the Cortes is to meet.

---

*The document refers to the Iberian Peninsula and the Canary Islands. Spain had earlier colonized the Canary Islands, and thus the islanders were, in effect, Spaniards.

Article 37. In the overseas provinces the juntas shall meet the first Sunday of December, fifteen months preceding the meeting of the Cortes, in order to insure sufficient time for them to exercise their rights in advance.

Of the National Militias

Article 362. There shall be national militia units in each province, composed of the inhabitants thereof, in proportion with its population and other circumstances.

Article 363. The mode of the militia's formation, its number, and its composition shall be arranged by a separate ordinance.

Article 364. Militia service shall not be continuous, and will only occur when circumstances demand it.

Of Public Education

Article 366. Elementary schools shall be established in every town throughout the kingdom, in which children shall be taught reading, writing and counting, the catechism of the Roman Catholic religion, [and] that will include a brief exposition of civil obligations.

Article 367. Measures shall also be immediately taken to found a competent number of universities and other establishments for the promotion of science, literature, and the fine arts.

Article 368. The plan of general instruction shall be the same throughout the kingdom; the Political Constitution of the monarchy shall be expounded in all the universities and literary establishments where the ecclesiastical and political sciences are taught.

Article 371. Every Spaniard possesses the liberty to write, print, and publish his political ideas without any previous licence, revision, or permission needed under the restrictions and responsibility established by law.

---

2. War to the Death ~ Simón Bolívar*

Among the many leaders of the Latin American movements for independence, Simón Bolívar stands out. A member of one of colonial Caracas' leading families, Bolívar led the sort of patriot movement that existed in most other parts of Spanish America—a movement dominated by criollos *(creoles, or Spanish people born in the Americas) but that needed the support of the nonwhite majorities. Bolívar's early career as a patriot military commander featured battles to defend*

---

*From *Simón Bolívar: Selected Writings, 1810–1830*, comp. Vicente Lecuna, ed. Harold A. Bierck Jr., trans. Lewis Bertrand (New York: Colonial Press, 1951), 31–32.

the independence of his home territory of Venezuela as well as battles to liber-
ate neighboring New Granada (present-day Colombia) from the royalists. The
following selection comes from an 1813 proclamation given by Bolívar in the
western Venezuelan town of Trujillo. In it, he famously drew a rhetorical line in
blood separating all American-born people from all Spanish-born. What purpose
did such rhetoric serve in the struggle for independence?

Venezuelans: An army of your brothers, sent by the Sovereign Congress of New Granada [present-day Colombia], has come to liberate you. Having expelled the oppressors from the provinces of Mérida and Trujillo, it is now among you. We are sent to destroy the Spaniards, to protect the Americans, and to reestablish the republican governments that once formed the Confederation of Venezuela. The states defended by our arms are again governed by their former constitutions and tribunals, in full enjoyment of their liberty and independence, for our mission is designed only to break the chains of servitude which still shackle some of our towns, and not to impose laws or exercise acts of dominion to which the rules of war might entitle us.

Moved by your misfortunes, we have been unable to observe with indifference the afflictions you were forced to experience by the barbarous Spaniards, who have ravished you, plundered you, and brought you death and destruction. They have violated the sacred rights of nations. They have broken the most solemn agreements and treaties. In fact, they have committed every manner of crime, reducing the Republic of Venezuela to the most frightful desolation. Justice therefore demands vengeance, and necessity compels us to exact it. Let the monsters who infest Colombian* soil, who have drenched it in blood, be cast out forever. May their punishment be equal to the enormity of their perfidy, so that we may eradicate the stain of our ignominy and demonstrate to the nations of the world that the sons of America cannot be offended with impunity.

Despite our just resentment toward the iniquitous Spaniards, our magnanimous heart still commands us to open to them for the last time a path to reconciliation and friendship. Spaniards are invited to live peacefully among us, if they will renounce their crimes, honestly change their ways, and cooperate with us in destroying the intruding Spanish government and in the reestablishment of the Republic of Venezuela.

Any Spaniard who does not, by every active and effective means, work against tyranny on behalf of this just cause, will be considered an enemy and punished. As a traitor to our nation, he will inevitably be shot by a firing squad. On the other hand, a general and absolute amnesty is granted to Spaniards who come over to our army with or without their arms, as well as to those who render aid to the good citizens who are endeavoring to throw off the yoke of tyranny. Army

---

*Colombia here is not yet the name of a particular nation. Rather, it refers generally to the Americas, the lands discovered by Columbus.

officers and civil magistrates who proclaim the government of Venezuela and join with us shall retain their posts and positions. In a word, those Spaniards who render outstanding service to the State shall be regarded and treated as Americans.

And you Americans who, by error or treachery, have been lured from the paths of justice, are informed that your brothers, deeply regretting the error of your ways, have pardoned you, as we are profoundly convinced that you cannot be truly to blame, for only the blindness and ignorance in which you have been kept up to now by those responsible for your crimes could have induced you to commit them. Fear not the sword that comes to avenge you and to sever the ignoble ties with which your executioners have bound you to their own fate. You are hereby assured, with absolute impunity, of your honor, lives, and property. The single title, "Americans," shall be your safeguard and guarantee. Our arms have come to protect you, and they shall never be raised against a single one of you, our brothers.

This amnesty is extended even to the very traitors who most recently have committed felonious acts, and it shall be so religiously applied that no reasonable cause or pretext will be sufficient to oblige us to violate our offer, however extraordinary and extreme the occasion you may give to provoke our wrath. Spaniards and Canary Islanders, you will die, though you be neutral, unless you actively espouse the cause of America's liberation. Americans, you will live, even if you have trespassed.

General Headquarters, Trujillo, June 15, 1813

---

3. The Vision of Father Morelos ~ Enrique Krause*

In 1811, Father José María Morelos took up the banner of the man who initiated the Mexican movement for independence, Father Miguel Hidalgo, after Hidalgo was executed by a firing squad. It had been Hidalgo's famous "Cry of Dolores" in September 1810 that started the independence struggle in the colony of New Spain (modern Mexico). The fact that Morelos (and Hidalgo before him) were priests demonstrates the complex nature of the intellectual sources of the Latin American movements for independence. Morelos's beliefs were most famously expressed in the 1813 document "Sentiments of the Nation," which is discussed in the following selection from Mexican historian Enrique Krause. "Sentiments" was essentially a list of twenty-three points presented by Morelos to the representatives of the Congress of Chilpancingo, which by endorsing the document was, in effect, declaring Mexico's independence from Spain. How does Morelos's Christianity show through in the following selection?

---

*From Enrique Krause, *Siglo de Caudillos: Biografía política de México (1810–1910)* (Barcelona: Tusquets Editores, 1994), 77–80 (trans. John Charles Chasteen).

More than his notable but ultimately fruitless military campaigns and victories, the greatest contribution of Father Morelos was ideological. Morelos brought with him to the struggle for Mexican independence a highly original body of arguments to legitimate it. Their overall thrust was moral, but they also included quite modern economic, social, and political prescriptions—albeit sprinkled here and there with touches of old-fashioned messianic vision. The occasion in which Morelos expounded upon these ideas, giving them legal and sometimes even constitutional form, was the Congress of Anáhuac. Morelos's role as prophet and legislator revealed that he viewed the struggle for Mexican independence as more than a worldly political contest of arms. He also considered it as a *mission*, in the Christian sense of the term.

Possibly because his social position was humbler than Father Miguel Hidalgo's, and because of his ethnically mixed origins, as well, the doctrine espoused by Morelos granted as much importance to social equality among Mexicans as it did to Mexican independence from Spain. To alleviate the condition of the indigenous people who, in the words of Bishop Abad y Queipo, lived in "ignorance and misery," and the plight of the castas (of variously mixed African and indigenous descent) who bore "the indelible mark of slavery," Morelos advanced proposals similar to those that the bishop had proposed to the Spanish crown in 1799. Among them were the right to move from place to place, freedom of contract, cancelation of tributes paid by Indians and castas, and abolition of their legal inferiority. "In Mexico," the bishop had written, "all are either rich or poor, noble or infamous, with no gradations in between." Four years later, the traveler Alexander von Humboldt, who met with Abad y Queipo during his stay in Mexico, repeated the same verdict: "Mexico is the country of inequality. Possibly no other country exhibits such shocking inequality in its distribution of wealth, civilization, population, and arable land. The color of a man's skin determines the rank he will occupy in society. A white man, even barefoot, counts himself among the nobility of the country." Daily experience in the modest ecclesiastical offices exercised by Morelos shaped his attitude toward this inequality. Unlike Hidalgo, Morelos did not call for conflict among classes. His was a constructive project of concord for all the inhabitants of Mexico except for Peninsular Spaniards. Three years before the Congress of Anáhuac, in November 1810, Morelos had issued a regulation for his army that prefigured his vision of an ideal society:

> If any movement is detected among the Indians and castas to attack whites, for example, or among whites to attack pardos, whoever tries to begin such a movement will be immediately punished. Our constituted officials [of all ethnic origins] must act in complete harmony . . . in complete accord and brotherhood . . . to punish public misdeeds committed against anyone.

A year later [referring to the possibility of interethnic conflict] Morelos clarified that it would be "the gravest of errors" to instigate "horrible anarchy" among the inhabitants of the area where his army operated. He therefore declared that the only purpose of his struggle was to transfer the reins of government from Peninsular to Creole hands, believing that a newly harmonious social, economic, and ethnic order would result:

> Let there be no more ethnic distinction made among our people, but rather, we shall all be called simply *americanos*. Regarding each other as brothers, we shall all live in the holy peace that our redeemer, Jesus Christ, bequeathed us when he rose triumphantly into heaven. Let there be no motive for fighting among those who were called castas, nor between whites and blacks, nor between blacks and Indians. Such fighting would be the greatest error that those in our situation could commit, leading to our total destruction, both spiritual and temporal. The whites are our leading representatives. They were the first to take up arms in our struggle. They therefore deserve our gratitude and should not be the targets of the sort of hatred that some have tried to foment against them. It is not our way to attack the rich merely for being rich, so no one should loot the possessions of even the richest among us.

In 1812, in Oaxaca, Morelos declared with greater succinctness, in his typically ironic style: "The lovely nonsense that divided Indians, mulattoes, and mestizos into distinct 'qualities' of human beings is henceforth abolished. From now on, all are to be called *americanos*."

A day before the Congress of Chilpancingo, Morelos outlined his personal utopian vision for a trusted associate, the lawyer Andrés Quintana Roo, who was quite moved by what he heard:

> I want us to declare formally that there shall be no sort of nobility in our society except for the nobility conferred by virtue, wisdom, patriotism, and brotherly love; that we all spring ultimately from the same origin and are all equal; that prestige and privilege shall no longer come from ancestry; that slavery is not right, nor rational, nor humane because the color of people's skin does not change the content of their hearts and minds; that the sons of a farm worker or miner should receive the same education as the sons of the richest landowner; that the courts should hear and defend all complainants against the injustices of the powerful. . . . Let us declare that this land is ours and our children's, so that all will have a faith, a cause, a banner for which to die before seeing it trampled as it is now.

The following day, writes Mexico's important nineteenth-century historian Lucas Alamán, Morelos said Mass, and "from the pulpit exhorted [the representatives of the Congress] to put aside their personal interests and desires and think only of the good of the Nation." A secretary then read "a document written by Morelos manifesting his principles for ending the war and laying the bases for a future national constitution." The document became known as *The Sentiments of the Nation*. The following are the most notable of its twenty-three articles:

ARTICLE ONE. America shall be free and independent of Spain or any other European nation, government, or monarchy. Let its independence be sanctioned and justified before the entire world.

ARTICLE TWO. Roman Catholicism shall be our official religion and no others shall be tolerated.

ARTICLE FIVE. Sovereignty emanates directly from the People, who shall delegate it to their representatives, observing a separation of legislative, executive, and judicial powers. National representatives shall be chosen by provincial representatives, all to be wise and moral individuals.

ARTICLE NINE. Only the American-born shall be eligible to receive public employment or become government officials.

ARTICLE TWELVE. The Laws, which shall apply to everyone, should impel patriotism and mitigate against both wealth and poverty. Let our Laws work to augment the earnings of the humble and improve their habits, banishing ignorance, theft, and robbery.

ARTICLE FOURTEEN. New laws shall be debated in the Congress and approved by a plurality of votes.

ARTICLE FIFTEEN. Slavery shall be forever abolished along with caste distinctions. All are henceforth equal. Americanos shall be distinguished from one another only by their personal vice or virtue.

ARTICLE NINETEEN. The Constitution shall establish 12 December, the day of Our Lady of Guadalupe, patron saint of our liberty, as a holiday to be celebrated throughout the country.

ARTICLE TWENTY-THREE. In a like manner, 16 September shall be commemorated yearly as the anniversary of the beginning of our movement for independence. . . .

Decades later, historian Lucas Alamán believed that he detected "communist and socialist" ideas in the creed of Morelos. But what really predominated in the ideology of Morelos—for all of its supremely modern social, political, and economic elements—was a much older concept, a desire to return to roots, envisioned as the kingdom of Christian equality.

---

4. Declaration of Independence ⁓ Congress of Tucumán*

In May 1810, the leading citizens of Buenos Aires became one of the earliest colonial groups to form a governing junta. The May Revolution, as the event was known, overthrew the colonial viceroy and initiated the process of independence in what would become Argentina, Uruguay, and part of Bolivia. Over the next eight years the struggle for control of South America's Southern Cone

*From *Acta de la Independencia de la Provincias Unidas en Sudamérica*, trans. James A. Wood, accessed March 11, 2013, www.me.gov.ar/efeme/9dejulio/acta.html /.

produced a varied cast of leaders, including José de San Martín, the chief organizer of the Army of the Andes, which liberated Chile and contributed to the ultimate defeat of the royalists in Peru. In 1816, in the midst of an ongoing war with the royalists, representatives of the colony's provinces held a congress in the northern Argentine city of San Miguel de Tucumán. On July 9, the Congress of Tucumán issued the following declaration, speaking in the name of the United Provinces of South America. Notice that King Ferdinand VII is addressed directly in this document.

In the most worthy and well deserving city of San Miguel de Tucumán on the ninth day of July 1816: having ended its ordinary session, the Congress of the United Provinces resumed its previous deliberations about the grand, august, and sacred object of independence for the peoples of which the congress was formed. The cry of the whole territory was universal, constant, and decidedly in favor of its solemn independence from the despotic power of Spanish kings; the Representatives nevertheless dedicated themselves to this arduous affair with the full extent of their talents, the rectitude of their intentions, and the interest that demands their personal commitment, that of the Peoples represented, and of posterity. At the end [of these deliberations] the question was asked: "Do [the Representatives] want the Provinces of the Union to be a free nation and independent of the kings of Spain and its capital?" Filled with the holy ardour of justice, they acclaimed firstly in the affirmative and then one by one reiterated successively their unanimous, spontaneous, and firm votes for the independence of the country, and in virtue thereof they established the following declaration:

We the Representatives of the United Provinces of South America, brought together in this Congress, invoking the Supreme Being who presides over the universe, in the name and by the authority of the peoples that we represent, protesting to Heaven, and to all the nations and inhabitants of the globe, the justice that rules our votes: we solemnly declare on the face of the Earth that it is the unanimous and undoubtable will of these Provinces to break the violent chains that bound them to the kings of Spain, to recover the rights that were stripped away from them, and invest themselves with the high honor of being a free nation and independent of Ferdinand VII, his successors, and territories. In consequence thereof, [the Provinces] in fact and in law, possess full and ample power to create for themselves the forms of government that justice may demand, and that the accumulation of actual circumstances may demand. All [the Representatives] and each one individually, make public, declare, and ratify this through our means, and commit themselves to fulfill and sustain its will, under the standing and guarantee of their lives, assets, and good name.

Let this declaration be communicated for publication and, in honor of the respect owed to all nations, let a separate manifesto detail the grave and compelling foundations behind this solemn declaration.

Sworn in the session hall, signed by our hands, stamped with the seal of the Congress, and endorsed by our elected secretaries.

5. Independence and Slavery ~ George Reid Andrews*

How disruptive were the Spanish-American Wars of Independence to the fabric of everyday life? The following selection from historian George Reid Andrews helps us think about that question from the perspective of enslaved Afro-Latin Americans. As we have seen in some of the other documents in this chapter, the leaders of the Spanish American struggles for independence often embraced the language of "Americanism" and racial equality in their proclamations. Standing up for the immediate abolition of slavery, though, was another matter. Some leaders, like Morelos, did advocate abolition openly. Bolívar offered freedom to any slave that would join his army, and then later proposed free-womb laws and eventually immediate abolition. But, overall, independence did not threaten the existence of the institution in Latin America. Andrews argues here that warfare had several effects on the lives of slaves. What were they?

For slaves throughout the Americas, national independence and chattel slavery were mutually exclusive concepts. For them it was self-evident that nations that had fought and suffered for freedom could not now deny that right to their slaves. As a French visitor to Brazil observed in 1822, "liberty" is a word "that has much more force in a country of slaves than anywhere else." Thus when independence came to Spanish America and Brazil, many slaves concluded that their own freedom could not be far behind. In 1818, as the Spanish viceroy in Peru awaited the invasion of the colony by rebel forces massing in Chile, he informed his superiors in Madrid that the local slave population was "openly decided for the rebels, from whose hands they expect liberty." When the victorious invaders declined to declare immediate emancipation, slaves denounced the contradiction between national freedom and the continuation of slavery. "If our liberal constitutions have any meaning at all," argued the lawyer for Lima slave Juana Mónica Murga in 1826, "it is the freedom of every man to no longer be a slave."

In Brazil, where slavery had sunk especially deep roots, independence leaders themselves cultivated the rhetorical connection between independence and freedom, condemning colonial rule as a form of national enslavement. Thus when colonial rule came to an end in 1822, so, presumed the slaves, would slavery. In Minas Gerais, thousands of slaves gathered in the mining towns of Ouro Preto and São João do Morro to await news of their liberation, as did smaller groups in Espírito Santo. In the Bahian capital of Salvador, a French visitor reported that "not only do the free and Creole Brazilians want political independence, but even the slaves,

---

*From George Reid Andrews, *Afro-Latin America, 1800–2000* (New York: Oxford University Press, 2004), 55–57, 60–62. © 2003 by Oxford University Press, Inc. Reprinted by permission of Oxford University Press.

born in the country or imported twenty years ago, claim to be Brazilian Creoles and talk of their rights to freedom." When those rights failed to materialize, slaves in the Bahian city of Cachoeira petitioned the Portuguese Cortes (Parliament) in 1823 for their freedom. They may not have realized that Portugal no longer held authority over Brazil; more likely they were signaling their discontent with the new Brazilian government's refusal to even consider the question of abolition.

Some Creole leaders acknowledged the contradiction between national independence and the continuation of slavery. José Bonifácio de Andrada e Silva, one of the architects of Brazilian independence, was an early exponent of emancipation, asking how a free people could condone anyone's right "to steal another man's freedom and, even worse, to steal the freedom of his children and his children's children." The two great Spanish American liberators, José de San Martín and Simón Bolívar, initially perceived no conflict between independence and slavery, but by the second half of the 1810s both men had reversed position. Bolívar dismissed as "madness [the idea] that a revolution for liberty should try to maintain slavery," and he and San Martín imposed programs of gradual emancipation on the territories they conquered—in the case of San Martín, Chile and Peru; in the case of Bolívar, Colombia, Ecuador, and Venezuela—despite opposition from local slave owners.

But the voices of anti-slavery, even when emanating from powerful individuals in positions of command, were few and far between. Other than the slave rebellions of the late colonial and early independence periods, nowhere in Latin America during the early 1800s was there a significant organized movement dedicated to opposing slavery. Pro-slavery forces were far better organized than anti-slavery, both through the kinship and business networks that permeated elite classes and through elite civic and commercial associations. Planters and merchants readily agreed that slavery was a lamentable, barbarous inheritance from the colonial past, one that would eventually have to be overturned as the region continued its march toward modernity. But even elites committed to independence insisted that current economic conditions—particularly the supposed lack of alternative sources of labor—and the property rights of slave owners made abolition impossible for the time being.

Despite this opposition, by 1825 almost every Spanish American country had banned further imports of slaves from Africa and enacted programs of either gradual or immediate emancipation. Slave owners had not weakened in their opposition to such measures. Political pressure to maintain slavery continued in the decades after independence, making emancipation an extended struggle that was not finally resolved until the 1850s and 1860s. Masters agreed to free their slaves only reluctantly, resisting every step of the way. But slaves were also skilled at resistance; and the turbulent conditions of the independence period offered unprecedented opportunities for slaves to pursue freedom, through both official and unofficial means.

War strengthened slaves' bargaining position vis-a-vis their masters and the state in three ways. First, as in Haiti, the turmoil that war brought in its wake greatly reduced owners' control over their slaves, while increasing slaves' opportunity to flee. Second, war gave thousands of male slaves the opportunity to obtain freedom through military service. Finally, the price of slave participation in the independence armies was the enactment throughout Spanish America of programs of gradual emancipation.

Throughout Spanish America, the disorder and turmoil of the wars gave slaves unprecedented opportunities for pursuing their own goals and interests. The devastation of much of the plantation sector, the weakening and impoverishing of the planters as a class, and the destruction of the Spanish state all combined to greatly strengthen slaves' bargaining power. Within this changing balance of forces, however, slaves still remained slaves. More of them than ever before sought freedom through flight; but that freedom remained precarious and uncertain, subject to revocation at any time. More permanent and secure—though also more difficult to obtain—was the freedom offered through a second opportunity created by war: that of military service.

Every New World colony that won independence through warfare faced the issue of whether or not to arm slaves. The risks of doing so were substantial: slave soldiers could just as easily turn on their masters as on their masters' enemies. Slaves also would not place their lives in jeopardy without some promise of freedom, which made their services far more expensive, in purely financial terms, than those of whites and free blacks. But as the wars ground on and free black and white recruits became harder to find, Spain and the rebels both found themselves turning to slave soldiers. Rebel governments in Argentina and Venezuela began conscripting slaves in 1813; a year later Chile followed suit. Spain did not initially resort to conscription but did offer freedom to those slaves who volunteered for service. In 1821, having been defeated everywhere else in the continent, the Spanish government in Peru drafted 1,500 slaves in a last-ditch (and unsuccessful) effort to turn back San Martin's invading army.

Owners' opposition to the recruitment of slaves is quite clear; the attitudes of the slaves themselves are more ambiguous. Some responded enthusiastically. In Chile in 1811, well before the announcement of slave conscription, 300 slaves in Santiago hired a lawyer to petition the government for the right to enlist and threatened to rebel if they were not admitted into the army. In Peru in the early 1820s, slave mothers actively sought out rebel recruiting agents to enlist their sons and make them free. On the other hand, there was also ample evidence of slave reluctance to enter the armed forces. Rebel recruiting agents in the Cauca reported that slaves joined their masters in trying to evade the draft. Recruiters in Peru found that, while on some haciendas 15 or 20 slaves would step forward, ready to sign up, on others only one or two were willing to enlist, the rest declaring "that they could not forsake their owners," one officer reported.

Bolívar complained bitterly about the slaves' refusal to serve, charging that they "have lost even the desire to be free" and threatening them with capital punishment if they did not report for duty. But of course the slaves had not lost the desire to be free. Rather, they were far from certain that military service represented the most likely way to obtain their freedom. Slave recruits did become *libertos* (freedmen) upon entering the army, but this was conditional upon successful completion of their term of military service—five years in Argentina and elsewhere, or even longer if they incurred disciplinary infractions or other punishments. Though comprehensive studies of slave losses during the wars remain to be done, it is clear that many slaves died before completing their enlistments. Of the 2,000 to 3,000 Argentine libertos who crossed the Andes into Chile with San Martín in 1817, fewer than 150 returned with him in 1823, after six years of campaigning through Chile, Peru, and Ecuador. In a different theater of operations, Argentine libertos suffered terrible losses during the early 1820s in Indian wars in southern Buenos Aires province. During the winter of 1824, slave troops fought in subffeezing temperatures without shoes or adequate rations. They returned to the capital crippled by frostbite and gangrene, many of them having lost toes, fingers, or parts of limbs. Well into the 1840s and 1850s, crippled black veterans begging in the streets were a common sight in Buenos Aires—as in Lima, Caracas, Cali, and other cities.

Census data from Buenos Aires and Montevideo make clear the terrible cost paid by those cities' black populations in the wars. Between 1810 and 1827 the masculinity index (number of males per 100 females) among the white population in Buenos Aires declined from 103 to 90. Among the black population, the index dropped by almost half, from 108 to 59, a catastrophic rate of loss. In Montevideo, the masculinity index among slaves alone dropped from 119 in 1805 to 78 in 1819. Lack of comparable data from other countries makes it unclear whether their black populations sustained comparable losses, but if slaves were being killed and disabled at even half the rates observed in Argentina and Uruguay, the effects would have been devastating.

Given these statistics, and the generally miserable conditions of life in the army, what is surprising is not that slaves sought to avoid military service but that so many agreed to serve. In Argentina, some 4,000 to 5,000 slaves joined the rebel forces between 1813 and 1818; when San Martín invaded Chile in 1817, half or more of his army was composed of liberto troops. In Colombia, some 5,000 slaves joined Bolívar's forces between 1819 and 1821. In Ecuador, an estimated one-third of his recruits were slaves.

---

6. What Independence Meant for Women ⁓ Sarah C. Chambers*

After the wars were over the new American republics needed to be constructed. Elections were held, constitutions were ratified, and occasionally civil wars broke

*From Sarah C. Chambers, *From Subjects to Citizens: Honor, Gender, and Politics in Arequipa, Peru, 1780–1854* (University Park: Pennsylvania State University Press, 1999), 200–215. © 1999 by the Pennsylvania State University. Reprinted by permission of the Pennsylvania State University Press.

out between rival political factions. Women were allowed to participate directly in none of it. In the following selection from historian Sarah C. Chambers we get a close-up view of the ways in which the daily lives of women living in the southern Peruvian city of Arequipa were impacted by independence. Chambers draws our attention to the language Peruvians used to discuss women's morality in the new republican system. Whereas Chambers saw the possibility that working-class or "plebeian" men could use the language of liberalism, republicanism, and nationalism to press their claims to citizenship in the new republic, she also argued that such was not the case for plebeian women. What, according to Chambers, was the justification given for such discrimination?

Citizenship in independence-era Peru became linked to the older Latin American concept of honor, a concept that inherently limits women's claims to political equality. Female honor underwent only subtle transformations after independence. Women continued to be judged primarily by their sexual purity and domestic virtue. When Doña María Rivera died in 1829, after supervising the foundling home for forty years, a full-page obituary praised her as an example of proper womanhood. At the age of twenty-one she had shut herself off from the world, to dedicate herself entirely to the care of infants whose mothers had secretly given them up (to save their *own* honor from public disgrace). "Austere with herself, sensitive and tender with the family given to her by Christian charity, never was there noted in her that hardness often produced by the effort of closing off the heart to the emotions of love. So it is that she has been the model, not the imitator, of maternal tenderness." Notables from the municipality and the church attended her funeral to pay their last respects to this "virtuous" woman.

Old-fashioned female virtues became women's "republican" virtues when expressed in an "enlightened" manner. Thus, one can speak of "republican motherhood." One can see this reformulation most clearly in female education. When young women from two schools demonstrated their mathematical ability before local notables in 1833, for example, the official newspaper covered the events with long and enthusiastic articles. Although the students humbly apologized in advance for the errors they might commit, the reporter was impressed by their skill and "their dedication to a difficult and abstract science which might seem reserved for the profound meditations and arduous investigations of the sex endowed with robustness and strength." Both the reporter and the students in their speeches contrasted the education of colonial women—limited to learning the rudiments of reading and writing by rote rather than "reflection"—to the new, enlightened curriculum. Nevertheless, the goal was still to prepare them to better fulfill their traditional roles. The lack of education in the colonial period, Rosa Amat pointed out, had made the weak sex a "victim of perversity" and "motive of corruption," who substituted "frivolous pleasures for the true merit of being good wives and mothers." Even arithmetic, pointed out another student, was "necessary for domestic order."

Extending a domestic metaphor into the public realm, the same reporter noted that a local official "offered to the spectators the appealing picture of a family patriarch surrounded by his children." During the colonial period, the monarch had been depicted as a father to all his subjects, but in the republic it was primarily women and children who were under the paternal care of the state. Pupil Juliana Sanches echoed the familial theme in her address to the gathered officials: "Under your auspices, the fair sex will be, not a group contemptible for its ignorance, but rather, adorned with knowledge and virtues; it will be the compass that guides the domestic ship along the path of honor, inspiring in the family sentiments of justice and religion."

Though praising their mathematical abilities, moreover, the articles dwelled more on the beauty, modesty, and purity of the students. Indeed, as noteworthy as their earlier efforts at the blackboard was their performance at the banquets given in their honor, where the young women, "with their decency and neatness, and their dexterity in the handling of the table setting, gave an idea of the care of their breeding and to their belonging to people of Quality." Such skills were more important than book learning, to many parents; in defending the disciplinary methods of the female teacher accused of whipping her students, several parents praised her particularly for teaching their daughters manners.

The role of virtuous women was now to nurture republican virtues in members of their families, and there were occasions when they were called upon to extend this inspirational role into the public sphere. The editor of Arequipa's paper, *El Republicano*, advocated the introduction of French-style salons, where "the ladies distinguish with their esteem only he who demonstrates the most ingenuity and judgment in the resolution of difficult problems." Descriptions of civic celebrations never failed to highlight the presence of the "fair sex," who cried out praises of the parading heroes, threw flowers from balconies, and—in virginal choirs—sang patriotic anthems.

Women also played a role—albeit a limited one—in political life. Once again women were, officially, to serve primarily as an inspiration to men. Soldiers were exhorted to arms with promises that their sacrifices would be "rewarded with the civic crown of laurels woven by the lovely hands of Arequipa's fair sex." Conversely, the specter of what would happen to their wives and children at the hands of the enemy was invoked to bolster the men's fighting spirit. Women were praised, if not called upon, for their financial contributions—most commonly, the symbolic as well as valuable donation of their jewels—to political causes. In rare cases, women even participated actively in military movements. In 1839, for instance, with the restoration of strongman Agustín Gamarra to power, Doña Antonia Torreblanca requested compensation for her services to his cause over the previous five years. She related how she had infiltrated enemy troops under the pretext of selling them food. Then, in spite of the supposed "weakness of her sex," she crawled on her hands and knees to avoid gunfire and crossed the river in the middle of the night in order to relay urgent information. Finally, she had solicited donations from other women in order to serve food to the wounded soldiers in the hospital. After several military commanders testified to the truth of her claims, Torreblanca was rewarded with one hundred pesos.

Antonia Torreblanca's case reveals both the potential and the limitations of women's participation in the republican public sphere. Even if it was economic need that motivated her to request compensation, her account bespeaks a pride in her services and a desire for recognition. Yet, while praised for her "ardent and praiseworthy patriotism," Torreblanca did not describe her virtues as those of republican citizenship, merely proclaiming her allegiance to "the present regime so just and beneficent to the fatherland."

The failure to identify women, even figuratively, as citizens or republicans was typical. While the female superior of the foundling home was eulogized solely for her maternal virtues, for example, the priest with whom she served was paid homage as a "good patriot" and "virtuous citizen," dedicated to national independence and republican institutions. Although some women had been involved in the wars of independence at the national level, they never called for political inclusion in the new state, and male politicians never raised the issue of female suffrage. Either it did not occur to most women to identify themselves as citizens or they realized that such claims would have fallen on deaf ears. After all, the new republican constitutions excluded women and so did the entire discourse of honorable citizenship.

Women probably realized that they could use the language of domesticity, instead, to better advantage. María Seballos, a self-declared merchant, claimed ignorance of a new regulation against distilling alcohol, "as a woman who does not deal with anyone and lives withdrawn in the refuge and care of her family." In point of fact, her account reveals that she had not heard of the new order because she was away on business, her motherly reclusion being, in this case, a rhetorical gambit. Flora Tristán, a sophisticated traveler with family in Arequipa, commented on the appearances prized by her aunt there: "Joaquina's great gift is to persuade everybody, even her husband, shrewd as he is, that she knows nothing, that she is concerned only with her children and her household. Her great piety, her humble and submissive air, the kindness with which she speaks to the poor, the interest she shows in the unimportant people who greet her in the street, all make her seem a modest woman without ambition." Republican discourse rewarded virtuous ladies, if not with citizenship, with the right to an education and a recognition of their social value as mothers and arbiters of morality.

Plebeian women were in a different situation. While plebeian men asserted their inclusion in the discourse of honorable citizenship, poor women rarely spoke the language of republican motherhood. Whereas men met and communicated in the workplace, the military corps, and the tavern, there were few opportunities, outside of household service, for dialogue among women of different classes. Only families with substantial means could afford to send their daughters to school, where they would be exposed to the new ideas. Even if plebeian women were aware of the subtle shifts in gender ideology, moreover, most forms of employment made it difficult to maintain even the appearance of being retiring keepers of the home and family. Although poor women probably did not accept elite stereotypes, challenging them within the official discourse of republicanism was not an effective strategy.

Not only was it difficult for poor women to base claims upon their rights or duties as mothers, but the mitigating factors used by plebeian men were also denied them. A work ethic failed to redeem women, since their virtue depended upon fulfilling their domestic roles. María Toledo, an "anguished mother," was denied a request for early release from imprisonment although she supported her children on the income she earned as an agricultural laborer. Just months before her request was denied, the sentence of an "honorable" man was reduced for that very reason. The role of hardworking provider was reserved for men.

Also reserved for men were the honors of military service, which (with rare exceptions, such as Torreblanca) usually *dis*honored women because of the assumption that their morals would be corrupted by a soldier's life. Despite the critical support that they provided to the troops and their occasional participation in combat, the female "camp followers" were more likely to be scorned than appreciated. This exclusion was critical because of the importance of military service in plebeian claims to honor and, by extension, to citizenship rights.

Plebeian women bore the brunt of efforts to enforce the new, stricter republican morality. While it is unlikely that their behavior changed in any significant way from that in the colonial period, their sexuality was increasingly seen as a threat to public order. When María Samudio was arrested for assaulting her lover, soldier José Valdez, even the prosecutor considered the wounds so inconsequential that the charges should be dropped. He argued, nevertheless, that Samudio should be punished for her loose morals, saying such crimes stemmed from "toleration of the public immorality of these women, who, abandoning modesty, social considerations, and family obligations, have the impudence to present themselves in public as prostituted persons." By exiling Samudio, the judges both punished her and rid the city of what they considered her immoral influence.

The transformation of the code of honor under republicanism provided a new hegemonic language but did not, by any means, create an egalitarian or democratic society. On the contrary, repressive forms of social control actually intensified after independence, and republican leaders often fell short of putting liberal principles into practice. Nevertheless, the dialectical tension between elites and plebeians forged a new republican pact, in which some working men were granted the status of citizens. The recognition of citizenship was not only contingent upon conduct, but was also based upon the exclusion of those identified as socially dependent. The legal system denied the benefits of "honorable labor" to slaves and indigenous domestic servants. Slaves and servants, like women, were legally subject to patriarchal control and so could not be free and equal citizens.

Women found their private virtues subject to increasing public scrutiny. Elite women who were able to maintain the appearance of fulfilling high republican standards of sexual purity, modesty, and maternal nurturing were still denied citizenship but were, at least, recognized as arbiters of morality within the public sphere as well as the home. Poor women, however, who often lived beyond the control of a patriarch and continued to carry out their lives in public, bore the brunt of repressive public moralism.

II

Slavery

There can be no doubt that African slavery, the same "peculiar institution" so deeply rooted in the history of the United States, had a profound impact on Latin American history. From the 1520s to the 1880s, the institution of African slavery left a lasting impression on the social relations, cultural values, and economic development of the numerous Latin American societies in which it thrived. Enslaved men, women, and children of African descent were a ubiquitous presence from the tropical islands of the Caribbean to the cane fields of Brazil to the bustling city of Buenos Aires. In all, somewhere between ten and fifteen million Africans were forced to make the horrific Middle Passage across the Atlantic to take up residence in the completely alien lands of the New World. Prior to the massive wave of European immigration to the Americas in the nineteenth century, more Africans crossed the Atlantic Ocean than Europeans.

How did enslaved Africans cope with their dreadful experience? This chapter's approach to the problem reflects two trends in the historical literature. First, the approach is cultural. In recent decades, historians in the United States and elsewhere have become more attuned to questions of culture: How is it generated? How is it transmitted? And how is meaning determined? In the case of slave culture, in particular, historians of the present generation, influenced by earlier studies of slave and peasant resistance, were not satisfied with existing interpretations. So they set out to reinterpret the role that culture—in all of its individual and collective dimensions—played in the history of American slavery. Second, the approach is transatlantic. The transatlantic approach to the history of American slavery, by emphasizing the importance of dynamics on both sides of the Atlantic Ocean, allows us to understand its true complexity. As we will see, the commonalities of slave culture throughout the Americas, brought to light by the transatlantic approach, force us to ask basic questions about the ways in which culture is carried from one place to another. Historians of slave culture often weigh the relative importance of practices brought from Africa, on the one hand, and practices invented in the diaspora, on the other.

A final point of comparison will certainly interest students. Whereas slavery in the United States was ended only by a major civil war, slavery in Latin

America declined more gradually. In 1807, the United Kingdom, bowing to reformist pressure, outlawed the commercial trade in slaves that it had dominated for a century. With the passage of this law (and the indomitable Royal Navy enforcing it on the high seas), slave importers in the Americas had to take great risks in securing their human cargoes. Some turned to smuggling operations, while others turned away from the trade altogether. In most of Spanish America, laws were passed to gradually phase out or abolish (hence the terms "abolition" and "abolitionist") the entire institution. The Wars of Independence, in which thousands of slaves earned their freedom on the battlefield, had already done much to shake up the "peculiar institution."

In two particular places, however, African slavery lived on. In Brazil, which achieved the status of an independent monarchy as a result of the Napoleonic invasion of Portugal, slavery survived until the Golden Law of 1888 freed all slaves unconditionally. Brazil was the destination for roughly 40 percent of all enslaved Africans brought to the New World after 1500; its expanding sugar and coffee plantations placed high demand on the transatlantic labor supply system. While the slave trade was choked off in many parts of the Americas after the 1807 British ban, in Brazil the first half of the nineteenth century was the time period with the largest number of newly arrived slaves—nearly 2.5 million of them from 1800 to 1850, according to the Transatlantic Slave Trade Database (an online tool created by historians of the slave trade in the United States). Yet, at the same time, an emerging Brazilian abolitionist movement with close ties to an international abolitionist network was putting pressure on the Brazilian government to reform the institution. The Brazilian Anti-Slavery Society, founded by abolitionist Joaquim Nabuco in 1880, oversaw the culmination of the movement's efforts to put an end to slavery in Brazil.

In Cuba, still part of the Spanish empire until 1898, slavery was not totally abolished until 1886. Prior to that, some gradual measures to end slavery had been introduced, and, in addition, many Cuban slaves had earned their freedom in the Ten Years' War (1868–1878), which was a key part of the Cuban struggle for independence. In its long history of involvement with the slave trade, Cuba took in roughly 8 percent of all new arrivals, most of them brought in illegally after the Spanish ban on the slave trade in 1815 to satisfy the ever-growing demand for labor on coffee and sugar plantations.

It is thus undeniable that African slavery—and the interrelated struggles to abolish it—helped to shape Latin America's modern history. And like the United States, many countries of the region still struggle with its complex legacies. After studying this chapter, students should be able to make their own assessment of the complex legacies of slavery in modern Latin America.

1. In what sorts of living and working situations did slave culture take shape? How did such situations affect the development of slave culture?

2. How did the collective experience of enslavement reshape African cultural traditions into Afro-Latin American ones?

3. What motivated abolitionists like Joaquim Nabuco to take up the struggle against slavery? What was Nabuco's main objection to the continuation of slavery in Brazil?

1. The Beginnings of African American Culture ~
Sidney W. Mintz and Richard Price*

The centuries-long ordeal of slavery had a direct and immediate impact on African American culture. According to the eminent cultural anthropologists Sidney Mintz and Richard Price, this impact began even before the arrival of the enslaved Africans in the New World. In this excerpt from their influential work (originally published in 1976 as An Anthropological Approach to the Afro-American Past*), Mintz and Price show that enslaved Africans had already begun to think and behave cooperatively on the Atlantic shores of their homeland. And this cooperative spirit continued through the terrible Middle Passage, despite its brutalizing effects on individuals. Mintz and Price also emphasize the importance of the cultural heterogeneity of the (mostly West) African slaves for the development of African American cultures. Because of the diversity of beliefs and practices brought to the Americas by slaves, they argue, African American cultures developed an extremely open attitude toward innovation and change.*

Before any aggregate of plantation slaves could begin to create viable institutions, they would have had to deal with the traumata of capture, enslavement, and transport. Hence the beginnings of what would later develop into "African-American cultures" must date from the very earliest interactions of the newly enslaved men and women on the African continent itself. They were shackled together, packed into dank "factory" dungeons, squeezed together between the decks of stinking ships, separated often from their kinsmen, tribesmen, or even speakers of the same language, left bewildered about their present and their

---

*From Sidney W. Mintz and Richard Price, *The Birth of African-American Culture: An Anthropological Perspective* (Boston: Beacon, 1992), 42–51. © 1976 the Institute for the Study of Human Issues, Inc. Reprinted by permission.

future, stripped of all prerogatives of status or rank (at least, so far as the masters were concerned), and homogenized by a dehumanizing system that viewed them as faceless and largely interchangeable. Yet we know that even in such utterly abject circumstances, these people were not simply passive victims. In the present context, we are thinking less of the many individual acts of heroism and resistance which occurred during this period than of certain simple but significant *cooperative* efforts which, in retrospect, may be viewed as the true beginnings of African-American culture and society.

Various shreds of evidence suggest that some of the earliest social bonds to develop in the coffles [slaves chained together in line], in the factories, and, especially, during the long Middle Passage were of a dyadic (two-person) nature. Partly, perhaps, because of the general policy of keeping men and women separate, they were usually between members of the same sex. The bond between shipmates, those who shared passage on the same slaver, is the most striking example. In widely scattered parts of Afro-America, the "shipmate" relationship became a major principle of social organization and continued for decades or even centuries to shape ongoing social relations.

In Jamaica, for example, we know that the term "shipmate" was "synonymous in the slaves' view with 'brother' or 'sister.' "It was "the dearest word and bond of affectionate sympathy amongst the Africans," and "so strong were the bonds between shipmates that sexual intercourse between them," in the view of one observer, "was considered incestuous." We know also that the bond could extend beyond the original shipmates themselves and interpenetrate with biological kin ties; shipmates were said to "look upon each other's children mutually as their own," and "it was customary for children to call their parents' shipmates 'uncle' and 'aunt.'"

In Suriname, to cite a different case, the equivalent term "*sippi*" was at first used between people who had actually shared the experience of transport in a single vessel; later, it began to be used between slaves who belonged to a single plantation, preserving the essential notion of fellow sufferers who have a special bond. Today in the interior of Suriname, among the Saramaka people, "sippi" (now "*sibi*") continues to designate a special, nonbiological dyadic relationship with very similar symbolic content; when two people find themselves victims of a parallel misfortune (e.g., two women whose husbands desert them at about the same time), they thenceforth may address each other as "sibi" and adopt a special prescribed mutual relationship.

Other examples of the "shipmate" relationship in Afro-America can be cited—from the Brazilian "*malungo*" and Trinidadian "*malongue*" to Suriname "*máti*" to Haitian "*batiment.*" But we have said enough already to support the following assertions. It is not surprising that same-sex dyadic ties should have loomed large in the earliest context of African-American enslavement and transport (given that such ties seem often to develop when random individuals are thrust into an institutional, depersonalized setting—such as boot camp or prison).

What may make this case unusual is the extent to which such initial bonds could develop into basic principles which probably helped to shape the institutions of such societies and which, even today, in many areas appear to retain their original symbolic content. We believe that the development of these social bonds, even before the Africans had set foot in the New World, already announced the birth of new societies based on new kinds of principles.

The initial cultural heterogeneity of the enslaved doubtless had the effect of forcing them at the outset to shift their primary cultural and social commitment from the Old World to the New, a process which often took their European masters centuries to accomplish. The quite radical cultural reorientation that must have typified the adaptation of enslaved Africans to the New World was surely more extreme than what the European colonists—with their more intact institutions, continuing contacts with the homeland, and more coherent family groupings—experienced. Even in those special situations in which some members of a particular ethnic or linguistic group could remain in close contact, such orientation must have remained a secondary focus of commitment, with the new African-American culture and its concomitant social ties being primary. All slaves must have found themselves accepting, albeit out of necessity, countless "foreign" cultural practices, and this implied a gradual remodeling of their own traditional ways of doing many things. For most individuals, a commitment to, and engagement in, a new social and cultural world must have taken precedence rather quickly over what would have become before long largely a nostalgia for their homelands. We remind ourselves and our readers that people ordinarily do not long for a lost "cultural heritage" in the abstract, but for the immediately experienced personal relationships, developed in a specific cultural and institutional setting, that any trauma such as war or enslavement may destroy. A "culture," in these terms, becomes intimately linked to the social contexts within which affective ties are experienced and perceived. With the destruction of those ties, each individual's "cultural set" is transformed phenomenologically, until the creation of new institutional frameworks permits the refabrication of content, both based upon—and much removed from—the past.

We have been suggesting that distinctive, "mature" African-American cultures and societies probably developed more rapidly than has often been assumed. The early forgings of "shipmate" ties or ritual complexes, as we have phrased them, are intended as arbitrary (though central) examples of much more general processes. Even in the realm of the arts, to choose a less likely example, it could be shown that new cultural subsystems were worked out through the interaction of slaves who had not yet set foot in the Americas. Not only was drumming, dancing, and singing encouraged for "exercise" on many of the slavers, but [John Gabriel] Stedman tells us how, at the end of the nightmare of the Middle Passage, off the shores of Suriname: "All the slaves are led upon deck . . . their hair shaved in different figures of stars, half-moons, etc. . . . , which they generally do the one to the other (having no razors) by the help of a broken bottle and without soap."

It is hard to imagine a more impressive example of irrepressible cultural vitality than this image of slaves decorating one another's hair in the midst of one of the most dehumanizing experiences in all of history.

We have stressed some of the ways in which the early stages of African-American history fostered the rapid development of local slave cultures. But we believe that this distinctive setting also stamped these cultures with certain general features that strongly influenced their subsequent development and continue to lend to them much of their characteristic shape today. Our speculation runs as follows. While the greatest shock of enslavement was probably the fear of physical violence and of death itself, the psychological accompaniment of this trauma was the relentless assault on personal identity, being stripped of status and rank and treated as nameless ciphers. Yet, by a peculiar irony, this most degrading of all aspects of slavery seems to have had the effect of encouraging the slaves to cultivate an enhanced appreciation for exactly those most personal, most human characteristics which differentiate one individual from another, perhaps the principal qualities which the masters could not take away from them. Early on, then, the slaves were elaborating upon the ways in which they could be individuals—a particular sense of humor, a certain skill or type of knowledge, even a distinctive way of walking or talking, or some sartorial detail, like the cock of a hat or the use of a cane.

At the same time, as we have seen, the initial cultural heterogeneity of the enslaved produced among them a general openness to ideas and usages from other cultural traditions, a special tolerance (within the West African context) of cultural differences. We would suggest that this acceptance of cultural differences combined with the stress on personal style to produce in early African-American cultures a fundamental dynamism, an expectation of cultural change as an integral feature of these systems. Within the strict limits set by the conditions of slavery, African-Americans learned to put a premium on innovation and individual creativity; there was always a place for fads and fashions; "something new" (within certain aesthetic limits, of course) became something to be celebrated, copied, and elaborated; and a stylistic innovation brought by a newly imported African could be quickly assimilated. From the first, then, the commitment to a new culture by African-Americans in a given place included an expectation of continued dynamism, change, elaboration, and creativity.

---

2. Africans in the American World ⁓ John Thornton*

During the eighteenth century, the traffic in slaves across the Atlantic grew explosively. In this selection, historian John Thornton examines the impact of this

---

*From John Thornton, *Africa and Africans in the Making of the Atlantic World, 1400–1800*, 2nd ed. (New York: Cambridge University Press, 1998), 304–5, 318–24. © 1992, 1998 John Thornton. Reprinted with permission of Cambridge University Press.

growth on the development of slave culture in the Americas. Thornton makes the point that, due to the tremendous increase in the number of first-generation Africans living in the Americas, African cultures were not only surviving in the eighteenth century but also, in fact, just arriving. Such a situation amounted to a "re-Africanization" of American slave culture. Thornton explores this phenomenon in the areas of language, nationality, and religion. He finds that enslaved Africans maintained many of their cultural traditions as a way of adapting to the extremely hostile realities of their lives in bondage.

From 1680 to 1800, the Atlantic slave trade grew immensely. From about 36,000 persons per year at the beginning of the century, the trade had more than doubled by the 1760s, and it reached a high point of nearly 80,000 per year in the last two decades of the century. Of the six trading regions identified by David Richardson in his study of the volume of the slave trade (Senegambia, Sierra Leone, Gold Coast, Bight of Benin, Bight of Biafra, and West Central Africa), West Central Africa had consistently the largest volume of exports, running between 30 and 45 percent of the overall trade. The Bight of Benin, mainly from the ports around the Kingdom of Dahomey, was the second most important, with nearly 40 percent of all exports in 1700, which declined to just over 10 percent by century's end. The Bight of Biafra, whose export trade grew rapidly during this time, supplying only 6 percent at the start of the period but peaking at nearly 30 percent in the 1780s, was close behind it. Among them, these three regions supplied nearly three-quarters of all the Africans transported across the Atlantic during the eighteenth century to labor in the Americas. Of the remaining areas, Sierra Leone provided more than one-fifth of the exports for a brief period between 1760 and 1780, at other times less than 10 percent; the Gold Coast never supplied more than 15 percent of the exports; and the exports from Senegal exceeded 10 percent only in the 1720s.

The causes of the prodigious growth of the slave trade are not hard to find. There was certainly a great rise in the demand for slaves in the Americas, especially from the Caribbean islands, settled in the second half of the seventeenth century and transformed economically in the eighteenth, and from Brazil, constantly growing first as a sugar and tobacco producer and then as a mining colony. Sugar in the Caribbean and gold in Brazil paid the increasingly high prices for slaves demanded by those Africans in a position to sell them and, as higher prices brought larger numbers of slaves, promoted continued growth and still higher slave prices in an upward cycle that continued throughout the century.

In the Caribbean and Brazil, the newly arrived Africans were often slated to maintain labor forces on sugar estates and in mines whose owners had been unable to keep up the slave populations by natural increase. In addition to the mortality caused by problems of labor and nutrition, women on sugar-producing estates often had very low fertility rates, and their offspring often suffered very high rates of infant and child mortality. This was true even of the large estates of Peru carefully managed by the Jesuits in the last half of the century.

In addition, the recently arrived were employed to open new enterprises as the economy spread to new land and put larger and larger areas under cultivation. In almost all the colonies, the eighteenth century witnessed increasing density of settlement, as well as colonization of new lands in a relentless movement to take over all the land available for crops that could be profitably grown with slave labor. In these frontier areas, a combination of the newly arrived and creoles* would form the colonizing group. The cultivation of coffee, which allowed the exploitation of new areas in existing colonies, brought largely African labor forces to these frontier areas. In Virginia, where the population of African descent soon became self-sustaining and even growing within a generation of the accelerated arrival of slaves, movement inland and up rivers still brought a mix of the newly imported and a minority of creoles.

The flood of African arrivals often Africanized the areas to which they came. Even areas where there was a preexisting population of African descent were "re-Africanized," as Ira Berlin characterized the early eighteenth-century influx around the Chesapeake. The re-Africanization was dramatic in Cuba. The colony had a well-established, even ancient Afro-creole population, but its subsequent transformation into coffee- and sugar-producing colonies in the 1770s brought thousands of Africans in, raising the population of slaves of African origin from just under 40,000 in 1774 to 212,000 by the early nineteenth century.

The demography of the eighteenth-century Americas points to an important fact—that African-born people, socialized and bearing African culture, were often the majority in American societies among those of African descent in places like North America, where there was a large European or Euro-American population, and in absolute terms in areas like the Caribbean islands and Brazil. In cultural terms the point is vitally significant. Although many scholars discuss the possibility of the survival of African culture into the present day, an important issue to be sure, the fact is that in the eighteenth century African culture was not surviving: It was arriving. Whatever the brutalities of the Middle Passage or slave life, it was not going to cause the African-born to forget their mother language or change their ideas about beauty in design or music; nor would it cause them to abandon the ideological underpinnings of religion or ethics—not on arrival in America, not ever in their lives.

The newly arrived Africans, like those who had come before them, used this African culture to adapt to the Americas. In the New World they were subject to a restrictive regime created by slavery. Slave owners, concerned to the point of paranoia about security, were often hostile to group activities outside of labor, a factor that might restrict many cultural activities, as seen in the formal statements like the French *Code Noir* or the Spanish *Código Carolina*. More importantly, these Africans came to America to work, and the slave regime often made incredibly heavy labor demands, pushing them to, and sometimes beyond, their physical capacity, shortening life spans, and reducing time for cultural life.

---

*Like the Portuguese term *crioulo*, the word "creole" here refers to the people of African descent born in the Americas.

Nevertheless, masters were not always willing or able to restrict cultural life, group meetings, or networks of friendship. Within the space that the slave regime allowed, the Africans re-created an African culture in America, although it was never identical with the one they had left in Africa.

Of course, the Africans retained their native languages, and African languages were widely spoken in eighteenth-century America. There were more first-language speakers of African languages in many parts of America than speakers of English, French, Dutch, Spanish, or Portuguese. Many of these Africans developed a certain necessary proficiency in the colonial language, the European language of their masters and other European or Euro-American settlers, after some years' residence, but it was always a second language, spoken with an accent. They were like the runaway woman, described in a late eighteenth-century Jamaican newspaper advertisement, who "speaks not altogether plain English; but from her talk she may easily be discovered to be a Coramantee." She, like other African-born Americans, probably thought, dreamed, and communicated more often in her native language than in the colonial language.

These African languages formed the basis for the nation*, which along with the estate was one of the two groups that had claims on every new African's time, loyalty, and service. It was in the context of the nation that the African cultures of the Americas reemerged, albeit in a new form. Since the sixteenth century, African religious and aesthetic ideas (music and dance especially) were displayed in gatherings of people from the same nation. The nation was the locus for the maintenance of those elements of African culture that continued on American soil.

Yet, in America these African distinctions were put aside, and linguistic loyalty formed a first order of contact and companionship. Although the linguistically formed nations often united those whose relatives in Africa might have been at war with each other, as the Coromantee nation certainly did, they were real enough entities in America. At Pinkster, a Dutch celebration observed in New York, dancers in 1737 "divided into Companies, I suppose according to their different nations." The distinctions were sufficiently significant for a certain rivalry between groups to be noticeable: One South Carolina observer about 1775 noted how "lbas" and "Gully" often chided each other. A mid-eighteenth-century Virginia preacher urged his flock to "not only pray for your Country-men, who are with you in America but . . . for all the inhabitants of your own Native land."

A nation could also form the locus of a religious community to the degree that it organized funerals. In the seventeenth century, nations were likely to be associated with the cult of ancestors, which was fairly ubiquitous in Africa. In 1765, a planter named Monnereau noted that most assemblies of nations in St. Domingue were to honor the dead. Descendants of a dead person would announce the ceremony, which friends and members of the deceased's nation would attend. Funeral services, conducted according to the "custom of the coast," that is, following national religious norms, were common in the Danish West Indies and elsewhere.

---

*"Nation," here, indicates group identities shared by Africans of similar regional origin.

There were also specific religious ideas particular to each nation that made them distinctive. The Anglican bishop Griffith Hughes noted that the Africans of Barbados in the mid–eighteenth century followed the "Rites, Ceremonies and Superstitions of their own Countries." The Kongolese of St. Jan in the Danish West Indies in the 1750s, as Christians of many generations' standing, took it upon themselves to baptize all newly arrived slaves, serving as godparents of sorts to them. Father Jean Baptiste le Pers, an early Jesuit missionary in St. Domingue, identified three different national religious groups there: the Congos, who were Christians (even if all did not properly know the faith); the Senegalese, who were Muslims; and the Ardas (Fon-speaking peoples), who were "idolatrous" snake worshippers. On the eve of the revolution, [Médéric Louis Elie] Moreau de Saint-Méry grouped these various nations under the general term "Voudou." People from the cultural area around Dahomey (the Jeje nation in Brazil) were indulging in religious practices from their homeland when authorities in Cachoeira, Bahia (Brazil), invaded and seized their goods in 1785.

Many Brazilian slaves, as well as those of Spanish colonies, expressed their national identities in ethnically specific lay brotherhoods. The rules of these brotherhoods, which were intended by the clergy to promote Christian life and charitable works, often specified that members of only one or another nation could be members, and often their charitable works were directed toward the nation at large, presumably even toward those who were not official members of the brotherhood (a minority, and the richest at that). In addition to doing charitable work, brotherhoods proudly paraded on saints' days, performing dances of their nation and singing in their national language.

For the newly arrived, the nation formed a surrogate for the family left behind in Africa. Within that group there were often shipmates who had traveled together to America probably, given shipping patterns, from the same nation—which facilitated communication on board ship. Advertisements in Jamaica often noted that runaways could name "their shipmates and country-men" or might be going to where "shipmates and countrymen" live. National solidarity provided moral support, cultural reinforcement, and familiarity of practices. Often slaves chose their spouses or other domestic partners from their home nation or closely related ones, as they had earlier.

---

3. A Cuban Slave's Testimony ⁓ Esteban Montejo*

Working in the fields was the main activity of most enslaved Africans but not the only one. On Sundays and Catholic holidays, slaves were often allowed to rest and

---

*From Esteban Montejo, *The Autobiography of a Runaway Slave*, ed. Miguel Barnet, trans. Jocasta Innes (New York: Pantheon, 1968), 29–38. © 1968 by The Bodley Head, Ltd. Used by permission of Pantheon Books, an imprint of the Knopf Doubleday Publishing Group, a division of Random House LLC. All rights reserved.

celebrate in their own manner. Such recreational and religious activities were yet another venue for the reworking of African cultural traditions into African American ones. This selection, taken from the testimony of a runaway Cuban slave named Esteban Montejo, takes us inside a barracoon, or living quarters used to house slaves in Cuba, on a typical Sunday on the Flor de Sagua plantation. Montejo's testimony is fascinating for the insight it provides on such Sunday rituals as bathing, music and dance, and religion. Montejo is also a valuable source on the divisions (especially religious) within this nineteenth-century Cuban slave community.

Sunday was the liveliest day in the plantations. I don't know where the slaves found the energy for it. Their biggest fiestas were held on that day. On some plantations the drumming started at mid-day or one o'clock. At Flor de Sagua it began very early. The excitement, the games, and children rushing about started at sunrise. The barracoon came to life in a flash; it was like the end of the world. And in spite of work and everything the people woke up cheerful. The overseer and deputy overseer came into the barracoon and started chatting up the black women. I noticed that the Chinese kept apart; those buggers had no ear for drums and they stayed in their little corners. But they thought a lot; to my mind they spent more time thinking than the blacks. No one took any notice of them, and people went on with their dances.

The one I remember best is the *yuka*. Three drums were played for the yuka: the *caja*, the *mula*, and the *cachimbo*, which was the smallest one. In the background they drummed with two sticks on hollowed-out cedar trunks. The slaves made those themselves, and I think they were called *catá*. The yuka was danced in couples, with wild movements. Sometimes they swooped about like birds, and it almost looked as if they were going to fly, they moved so fast. They gave little hops with their hands on their waists. Everyone sang to excite the dancers.

There was another more complicated dance. I don't know whether it was really a dance or a game, because they punched each other really hard. This dance they called the *mani* or peanut dance. The dancers formed a circle of forty or fifty men, and they started hitting each other. Whoever got hit went in to dance. They wore ordinary work clothes, with colored print scarves round their heads and at their waists. (These scarves were used to bundle up the slaves' clothing and take it to the wash: they were called *vayajá* scarves.) The men used to weight their fists with magic charms to make the mani blows more effective. The women didn't dance but stood round in a chorus, clapping, and they used to scream with fright, for often a Negro fell and failed to get up again. Mani was a cruel game. The dancers did not make bets on the outcome. On some plantations the masters themselves made bets, but I don't remember this happening at Flor de Sagua. What they did was to forbid slaves to hit each other so hard, because sometimes they were too bruised to work. The boys could not take part, but they watched and took it all in. I haven't forgotten a thing myself.

As soon as the drums started on Sunday the Negroes went down to the stream to bathe—there was always a little stream near every plantation. It sometimes happened that a woman lingered behind and met a man just as he was about to go into the water. Then they would go off together and get down to business. If not, they would go to the reservoirs, which were the pools they dug to store water. They also used to play hide-and-seek there, chasing the women and trying to catch them.

The women who were not involved in this little game stayed in the barracoons and washed themselves in a tub. These tubs were very big and there were one or two for the whole settlement.

Shaving and cutting hair was done by the slaves themselves. They took a long knife and, like someone grooming a horse, they sliced off the woolly hair. There was always someone who liked to clip, and he became the expert. They cut hair the way they do now. And it never hurt, because hair is the most peculiar stuff, although you can see it growing and everything, it's dead. The women arranged their hair with curls and little partings. Their heads used to look like melon skins. They liked the excitement of fixing their hair one way one day and another way the next. One day it would have little partings, the next day ringlets, another day it would be combed flat. They cleaned their teeth with strips of soap-tree bark, and this made them very white. All this excitement was reserved for Sundays.

Everyone had a special outfit that day. The Negroes bought themselves rawhide boots, in a style I haven't seen since, from nearby shops where they went with the master's permission. They wore red and green vayajá scarves around their necks, and round their heads and waists too, like in the maní dance. And they decked themselves with rings in their ears and rings on all their fingers, real gold. Some of them wore not gold but fine silver bracelets which came as high as their elbows, and patent leather shoes.

The slaves of French descent danced in pairs, not touching, circling slowly around. If one of them danced outstandingly well they tied silk scarves of all colors to his knees as a prize. They sang in patois and played two big drums with their hands. This was called the French dance.

I remember one instrument called a *marímbula*, which was very small. It was made of wickerwork and sounded as loud as a drum and had a little hole for the voice to come out of. They used this to accompany the Congo drums, and possibly the French too, but I can't be sure. The marímbulas made a very strange noise, and lots of people, particularly the *guajiros**, didn't like them because they said they sounded like voices from another world.

As I recall, their own music at that time was made with the guitar only. Later, in the nineties, they played *danzones* on pianolas, with accordions and gourds. But the white man has always had a very different music from the black man. White man's music is without the drumming and is more insipid.

More or less the same goes for religion. The African gods are different, though they resemble the others, the priests' gods. They are more powerful and less adorned. Right now if you were to go to a Catholic church you would not see

---

*Country people usually not of African descent.

apples, stones, or cock's feathers. But this is the first thing you see in an African house. The African is cruder.

I knew of two African religions in the barracoons: the Lucumí and the Congolese. The Congolese was the more important. It was well known at the Flor de Sagua because their magic-men used to put spells on people and get possession of them, and their practice of soothsaying won them the confidence of all the slaves. I got to know the elders of both religions after Abolition.

I remember the *Chicherekú* at Flor de Sagua. The Chicherekú was a Congolese by birth who did not speak Spanish. He was a little man with a big head who used to run about the barracoons and jump upon you from behind. I often saw him and heard him squealing like a rat. This is true. Until recently in Porfuerza there was a man who ran about in the same way. People used to run away from him because they said he was the Devil himself. You dared not play with the Chicherekú because it could be dangerous. Personally I don't much like talking of him, because I have never laid eyes on him again, and if by some chance. . . . Well, these things are the Devil's own!

The Congolese used the dead and snakes for their religions rites. They called the dead *nkise* and the snakes *emboba*. They prepared big pots called *ngangas* which would walk about and all, and that was where the secret of their spells lay. All the Congolese had these pots. The ngangas had to work with the sun, because the sun has always been the strength and wisdom of men, as the moon is of women. But the sun is more important because it is who gives life to the moon. The Congolese worked magic with the sun almost every day. When they had trouble with a particular person they would follow him along a path, collect up some of the dust he walked upon, and put it in the nganga or in some little secret place. As the sun went down that person's life would begin to ebb away, and at sunset he would be dying. I mention this because it is something I often saw under slavery.

If you think about it, the Congolese were murderers, although they only killed people who were harming them. No one ever tried to put a spell on me because I have always kept apart and not meddled in other people's affairs.

The Congolese were more involved with witchcraft than the Lucumí, who had more to do with the saints and with God. The Lucumí liked rising early with the strength of the morning and looking up into the sky and saying prayers and sprinkling water on the ground. The Lucumí were at it when you least expected it. I have seen old Negroes kneel on the ground for more than three hours at a time, speaking in their own tongue and prophesying. The difference between the Congolese and the Lucumí was that the former solved problems while the latter told the future. This they did with *diloggunes*, which are round, white shells from Africa with mystery inside. The god Elegguá's eyes are made from this shell.

The old Lucumís would shut themselves up in rooms in the barracoon and they could rid you of even the wickedness you were doing. If a Negro lusted after a woman, the Lucumís would calm him. I think they did this with coconut shells, *obi*, which were sacred. They were the same as the coconuts today, which are still sacred and may not be touched. If a man defiled a coconut, a great punishment befell him. I knew when things went well, because the coconut said so. He would command *Alafia* to be said so that people would know that all was well. The saints spoke through the coconuts and the chief of these was Obatalá, who was an old man, they said, and only wore white. They also said it was Obatalá who made you and I don't know what else, but it is from Nature one comes, and this is true of Obatalá too.

The old Lucumís liked to have their wooden figures of the gods with them in the barracoon. All these figures had big heads and were called *oché*. Elegguá was made of cement, but Changó and Yemayá were of wood, made by the carpenters themselves.

They made the saints' marks on the walls of their rooms with charcoal and white chalk, long lines and circles, each one standing for a saint, but they said that they were secrets. These blacks made a secret of everything. They have changed a lot now, but in those days the hardest thing you could do was to try to win the confidence of one of them.

The other religion was the Catholic one. This was introduced by the priests, but nothing in the world would induce them to enter the slaves' quarters. They were fastidious people, with a solemn air which did not fit the barracoons—so solemn that there were Negroes who took everything they said literally. This had a bad effect on them. They read the catechism and read it to the others with all the words and prayers. Those Negroes who were household slaves came as messengers of the priests and got together with the others, the field slaves, in the sugar-mill towns. The fact is I never learned that doctrine because I did not understand a thing about it. I don't think the household slaves did either, although, being so refined and well-treated, they all made out they were Christian. The household slaves were given rewards by the masters, and I never saw one of them badly punished. When they were ordered to go to the fields to cut cane or tend the pigs, they would pretend to be ill so they needn't work. For this reason the field slaves could not stand the sight of them. The household slaves sometimes came to the barracoons to visit relations and used to take back fruit and vegetables for the master's house; I don't know whether the slaves made them presents from their plots of land or whether they just took them. They caused a lot of trouble in the barracoons. The men came and tried to take liberties with the women. That was the source of the worst tensions. I was about twelve then, and I saw the whole rumpus.

There were other tensions. For instance, there was no love lost between the Congolese magic-men and the Congolese Christians, each of whom thought they were good and the others wicked. This still goes on in Cuba. The Lucumí and Congolese did not get on either; it went back to the difference between saints and witchcraft. The only ones who had no problems were the old men born in Africa. They were special people and had to be treated differently because they knew all religious matters.

Many brawls were avoided because the masters changed the slaves around. They kept them divided among themselves to prevent a rash of escapes. That was why the slaves of different plantations never got together with each other.

The Lucumís didn't like cutting cane, and many of them ran away. They were the most rebellious and courageous slaves. Not so the Congolese; they were cowardly as a rule, but strong workers who worked hard without complaining. There is a common rat called Congolese, and very cowardly it is, too.

In the plantations there were Negroes from different countries, all different physically. The Congolese were black-skinned, though there were many of mixed blood with yellowish skins and light hair. They were usually small. The Mandingas were reddish-skinned, tall and very strong. I swear by my mother they were a bunch of crooks, too! They kept apart from the rest. The Gangas were nice people, rather short and freckled. Many of them became runaways. The Carabalís were like the Musungo Congolese, uncivilized brutes. They only killed pigs on Sundays and at Easter and, being good businessmen, they killed them to sell, not to eat themselves. From this comes a saying, "Clever Carabalí, kills pig on Sunday." I got to know all these people better after slavery was abolished.

---

4. A Day on a Coffee Plantation ~ Stanley J. Stein*

Most African slaves brought to the Americas ended up in Brazil, and most Brazilian slaves worked on plantations. In the colonial period, sugar plantations dominated, but by the nineteenth century coffee was on the rise, especially in the south, inland from Rio de Janeiro, the location of Vassouras County. In this passage from his classic study of a nineteenth-century coffee plantation in Brazil, historian Stanley Stein takes us inside the daily routine of plantation slaves. The selection begins with daybreak, follows the slaves through a day in the fields, and ends with nightfall and the return to their quarters. Stein captures not only the rhythm of a typical day but also the way slave culture made the workday more bearable. Students should notice the subtle forms of slave resistance in the passage.

Slave life on the average Vassouras plantation (called a *fazenda*) of approximately eighty to one hundred slaves was regulated by the needs of coffee

*From Stanley J. Stein, *Vassouras: A Brazilian Coffee County, 1850–1900* (Cambridge, MA: Harvard University Press, 1957), 161–69. Reprinted by permission of Harvard University Department of History.

agriculture, the maintenance of work buildings and slave quarters, and the processing of coffee and subsistence foodstuffs. Since the supply of slaves was never adequate for the needs of the plantation either in its period of growth, prosperity, or decline, the slaves' work day was a long one begun before dawn and often ending many hours after the abrupt sunset of the Paraíba plateau.

Cooks arose before sunup to light fires beneath iron cauldrons; soon the smell of coffee, molasses, and boiled corn meal floated from the outdoor shed. The sun had not yet appeared when the overseer or one of his Negro drivers strode to a corner of the *terreiro** and reached for the tongue of a wide-mouthed bell. The tolling of the cast-iron bell, or sometimes a blast from a cow horn or the beat of a drum, reverberated across the terreiro and entered the tiny cubicles of slave couples and the separated, crowded dormitories of unmarried slaves. Awakening from their five- to eight-hour slumber, they dragged themselves from beds of planks softened with woven fiber mats; field hands reached for hoes and bill hooks lying under the eaves. At the large faucet near the slave quarters, they splashed water over their heads and faces, moistening and rubbing arms, legs, and ankles. Tardy slaves might appear at the door of their quarters muttering the slave-composed verse which mocked the overseer ringing the bell:

> That devil of a *bembo* taunted me
> No time to button my shirt, that devil of a bembo.

Now, as the terreiro slowly filled with slaves, some standing in line and others squatting, awaiting the morning prayer, the *senhor* appeared on the veranda of the main house. "One slave recited the prayer which the others repeated," recalled an ex-slave. Hats were removed and there was heard a "Praised-be-Our-Master-Jesus-Christ" to which some slaves repeated a blurred "Our-Master-Jesus-Christ," others an abbreviated "Kist." From the master on the veranda came the reply: "May-He-always-be-praised." The overseer called the roll; if a slave did not respond after two calls, the overseer hustled into the quarters to get him or her. When orders for the day had been given, directing the various gangs to work on certain coffee-covered hills, slaves and drivers shuffled to the nearby slave kitchen for coffee and corn bread.

The first signs of dawn brightened the sky as slaves separated to their work. A few went into the main house; most merely placed the long hoe handles on their shoulders and, old and young, men and women, moved off to the almost year-round job of weeding with drivers following to check stragglers. Mothers bore nursing youngsters in small woven baskets on their backs or carried them astraddle one hip. Those from four to seven trudged with their mothers, those from nine to fifteen close by. If coffee hills to be worked were far from the main buildings, food for the two meals furnished in the field went along—either in a

*A wide patio where the coffee beans were sun-dried.

two-team ox-cart, or in iron kettles swinging on long sticks, or in wicker baskets or two-eared wooden pans on long boards carried on male slaves' shoulders. A few slaves carried their own supplementary articles of food in small cloth bags.

Scattered throughout the field were shelters of four posts and a grass roof. Here, at the foot of the hills where coffee trees marched up steep slopes, the field slaves split into smaller gangs. Old men and women formed a gang working close to the rancho; women formed another; the men or young bucks (*rapaziada nova*), a third. Leaving the little boys and girls to play near the cook and assistants in the rancho, they began the day's work. As the sun grew stronger, men removed their shirts; hoes rose and fell slowly as slaves inched up the steep slopes. Under the gang labor system of *corte e beirada* used in weeding, the best hands were spread out on the flanks, *cortador* and *contra-cortador* on one, *beirador* and *contra-beirador* on the other. These four lead-row men were faster-working pace-setters, serving as examples for slower workers sandwiched between them. When a coffee row ended abruptly due to a fold in the slope, the slave now without a row shouted to his overseer, "Throw another row for the middle" or "We need another row"; another passed on the information to the flanking lead-row man who moved into the next row giving the slave who had first shouted a new row to hoe. Thus lead-row men always boxed-in the weeding gang.

Slave gangs often worked within singing distance of each other and to give rhythm to their hoe strokes and pass comment on the circumscribed world in which they lived and worked—their own foibles, and those of their master, over-seers, and slave drivers—the master-singer of one gang would break into the first "verse" of a song in riddle form, a *jongo*. His gang would chorus the second line of the verse, then weed rhythmically while the master-singer of the nearby gang tried to decipher the riddle presented. An ex-slave, still known for his skill at making jongos, reported that "Mestre tapped the ground with his hoe, others listened while he sang. Then they replied." He added that if the singing was not good the day's work went badly. Jongos sung in African tongues were called *quimzumba*; those in Portuguese, more common as older Africans diminished in the labor force, *visaria*. Stopping here and there to "give a lick" of the lash to slow slaves, two slave drivers usually supervised the gangs by crisscrossing the vertical coffee rows on the slope and shouting, "Come on, come on"; but if surveillance slack-ened, gang laborers seized the chance to slow down while men and women slaves lighted pipes or leaned on their hoes momentarily to wipe sweat away. To rational-ize their desire to resist the slave drivers' whips and shouts, a story developed that an older, slower slave should never be passed in his coffee row. For the aged slave could throw his belt ahead into the younger man's row and the youngster would be bitten by a snake when he reached the belt. The overseer or the master himself, in white clothes and riding boots, might ride through the groves for a quick look. Alert slaves, feigning to peer at the hot sun, "spiced their words" to comment in a loud voice, "Look at that red-hot Sun" or intermixed African words common to slave vocabulary with Portuguese as in *"Ngoma* is on the way" to warn their fellow slaves, who quickly set to work industriously. When the driver noted the approaching planter, he commanded the gang, "Give praise," to which slaves stood erect, eager for the brief respite, removed their hats or touched hands to forehead, and responded, "Vas Christo." Closing the ritual greeting, the master too removed his hat, spoke his "May He always be praised," and rode on. Immediately the industrious pace slackened.

To shouts of "lunch, lunch" or more horn blasts coming from the rancho around 10 a.m., slaves and driver descended. At the shaded rancho they filed past the cook and his assistants, extending their bowls (gourds split in two). On more prosperous fazendas, slaves might have tin plates. Into these food was piled; drivers and a respected or favored slave would eat to one side while the rest sat or sprawled on the ground. Mothers used the rest to nurse their babies. A half hour later the mother was ordered back to the sun-baked hillsides. At 1 p.m. came a short break for coffee, to which slaves often added the second half of the corn meal cake served at lunch. On cold or wet days, small cups of *cachaça* (raw rum) distilled from the plantation's sugarcane replaced coffee. Some ex-slaves reported that masters often ordered drivers to deliver the cachaça to the slaves in a cup while they worked, to eliminate a break. Supper came at 4 p.m. and work was resumed until nightfall when to drivers' shouts of "Let's quit" the slave gangs tramped back to the terreiro. Zaluar, the romantic Portuguese who visited Vassouras, wrote of the return from the fields: "The solemn evening hour. From afar, the fazenda's bell tolls Ave-Maria. (From hilltops fall the gray shadows of night while a few stars begin to flicker in the sky). . . . From the hill descend the taciturn driver and in front, the slaves, as they return home." Once more the slaves lined up for roll call on the terreiro, where the field hands encountered their slave companions who worked at the plantation center rather than in the fields.

---

5. Abolitionism in Brazil ⁓ Joaquim Nabuco*

Joaquim Nabuco was one of the leading figures in the Latin American movement to abolish slavery. The son of an influential liberal senator who had worked unsuccessfully to end slavery in his own day, Nabuco spent several years away from Brazil making connections with the leaders of an international network of antislavery activists and propagandists in Spain, France, and the UK. When he returned to Brazil in 1878, he was elected to congress, where he began his abolitionist work. In 1880, he hosted the founding of the Brazilian Anti-Slavery Society in his home. Three years later, he wrote his most famous book attacking

---

*From Joaquim Nabuco, *Abolitionism: The Brazilian Antislavery Struggle*, ed. and trans. Robert Conrad (Urbana: University of Illinois Press, 1977), 85–91.

slavery in Brazil, Abolitionism, *which is excerpted below. In this passage Nabuco discusses the unavoidable reality of slavery's continued existence in the 1880s, even though some reforms had already been implemented to begin its gradual abolition. He also focuses on the paradox of living under a political constitution that denied slavery's existence.*

It is essential that we outline the condition of the slave today as it appears before the law, before society, before justice, before the master, and before himself, so that it will not someday be said that in 1883, when this book was being written, abolitionists no longer faced the traditional slave system but another kind of slavery, modified for the bondsman by humane, protective, and comparatively just laws. I will sketch this picture of our slavery with strokes perhaps too rapid for a topic so vast.

Whoever arrives in Brazil and opens one of our daily newspapers finds there a photographic image of modern slavery more accurate than any painting. If Brazil were destroyed by a catastrophe, one issue of any of our great newspapers chosen at random would adequately preserve forever the forms and qualities of slavery as it exists in our time. The historian would need no other documents to re-create its entire structure and pursue all its effects.

In any issue of any major Brazilian paper—with the exception, I understand, of those of Bahia, where the press of the capital ceased the publication of slave advertisements—one would find, in effect, the following kinds of information which describe completely the present condition of the slaves: advertisements for purchase, sale, and rental of slaves in which invariably appear the words *mucama, moleque, bonita pega, rapaz, pardinho, rapariga da casa de familia* (free women advertise themselves as *senhoras* in order to differentiate themselves from slaves); official announcements of slave sales, a queer kind of document, of which the latest example from Valença is one of the most thorough; advertisements for runaway slaves accompanied in many papers by the well-known vignette of a barefoot black with a bundle on his shoulder, in which the slaves are often distinguished by the scars of punishment they have suffered and for whom a reward is offered, often as much as a *conto,* to anyone who can catch him and bring him to his master—an encouragement to the bush-captain's profession; rather frequent notices of manumissions; stories of crimes committed by slaves against their masters, but particularly against agents of their masters, and of crimes committed by the latter against the slaves, barbarous and fatal punishments which nevertheless comprise only a very small part of the lordly misuse of power which occurs, since this kind of abuse rarely comes to the attention of authorities or the press, owing to a lack of witnesses and informers willing to testify to this kind of crime.

One finds, finally, repeated declarations that slavery among us is a very mild and pleasant condition for the slave, better for him, in fact, than for the master, according to these descriptions a situation so fortunate that one begins to suspect that, if slaves were asked, they would be found to prefer slavery to freedom; which merely proves that newspapers and articles are not written by slaves or by persons who for one moment have imagined themselves in their condition.

More than one foreign book of travel containing impressions of Brazil reproduces these advertisements as the best way to illustrate local slavery. In reality, no ancient documents are preserved in hieroglyphics on Egyptian papyrus or in Gothic letters on parchment of the Middle Ages which reveal a social order more removed from modern civilization than that which is exposed by these dismal messages of slavery, which seem to us to be only a temporary expedient and which nevertheless continue to form the principal feature of our history. The legal position of the slaves can be summed up in these words: the Constitution does not apply to him. In order to contain some of its more enlightened principles, our Constitution could not sanction slavery in any way. "No citizen can be forced to do or not to do anything except in virtue of the law," [says the Constitution of 1824]. "The home of every citizen is an inviolable asylum. . . . The law will be applied equally to every person. . . . All privileges are abolished. . . . From this time forward whipping, torture, the use of hot branding irons, and all other cruel punishments are abolished. . . . No penalty can be inherited, nor will the infamy of the criminal be passed on to his kinsmen regardless of its degree. . . . *The right to property is entirely guaranteed.*"

For slavery to have been provided for in this code of freedoms, the following restrictions would have had to be included as well: "Aside from the citizen, for whom these rights are guaranteed, and the foreigner, to whom they will be extended, there exist in this country slaves, a class possessing no rights whatsoever. The slave will be forced to do or not to do whatever his master orders, whether in virtue of the law or in violation of the law, which does not grant him the right to disobey. The slave will not possess any inviolable asylum, whether in his mother's arms, under the shadow of the cross, or in his deathbed; in Brazil there are no places of refuge. The slave will be the object of every privilege revoked for all other persons; the law will not be equal in its application to the slave because he is outside the law, and his material and moral well-being will be as much subject to the control of the law as the treatment of animals; for him the punishments of *whipping* and *torture*, abolished for all others, will continue to exist, to be carried out, moreover, with medieval instruments and with the greatest deliberation when used to force confessions or in day-to-day scrutinization of the most intimate secrets. In this class, the punishment of slavery, the worst of all penalties, will be transmitted, along with the infamy which characterizes it, from mother to children, even if they are sons of the master himself."

Thus we have a *free* nation, daughter of the Revolution and the Rights of Man, compelled to employ its judges, its police, and if need be even its army and navy to force men, women, and children to work night and day without compensation.

Any word which would unmask this unfortunate social constitution would reduce the list of Brazilian freedoms and the regimen of the total equality of its democratized monarchy into a transparent fraud. For this reason the Constitution did not speak of slaves or regulate their condition. This in itself was a promise to those unfortunate people that their status was only temporary, if we are to attribute logic to the shameful spectacle created by those who established our nation.

In 1855 the government commissioned one of our most eminent lawyers, Teixeira de Freitas, with the task of consolidating the nation's laws. His work, *Consolidação das leis civis* [Compendium of Civil Laws], now in its third edition, appeared without one reference to slaves. By the terms of the Constitution, slavery *did not exist* in Brazil, and the first general codification of our laws continued this artful fiction. The truth is, to admit that we are—or are not—a nation of slaves offends our national sensibilities, so no attempt is made to regulate their condition.

"It should be observed," wrote the author of *Consolidação das leis civis*, "that slavery is nowhere dealt with in our text. We have slavery among us, of course, but since this evil is an unfortunate exception, condemned to extinction at some more or less remote time, let us also make an exception, placing slavery outside the compendium of our civil laws. Let us not stain those laws with shameful provisions which cannot serve posterity. Let the *condition of freedom* stand without its hateful opposite. The laws concerning slavery (which are not many) will then be classified apart and will form our Black Code."

All of this would be most *patriotic* if it in any way improved the lot of the slaves. But when the slaves are not legislated upon because slavery is repugnant, an affront to patriotism, a sight which a sensitive nation's nerves cannot bear without a crisis, and other equally unreasonable excuses (since in Brazil slavery is practiced night and day and all are accustomed, to the point of complete indifference, to its cruelty and inhumanity, to the moral vivisection which it endlessly imposes upon its victims), this fear of *staining our civil laws with shameful provisions* only serves to keep the slaves in their present barbarous condition.

The provisions of our Black Code are very few. Slavery is not indentured servitude which imposes a certain number of specified responsibilities upon the servant. It is the possession, domination, sequestration of a human being—his body, mind, physical forces, movements, all his activity—and it only ends with death. How can we define in legal terms what the master can do with the slave and what the slave cannot do under the supervision of his owner? As a rule the master can do *anything*. If he wants to shut the slave up inside his house forever, he can do so. If he wants to prevent him from establishing a family, he can do so. If the slave has a wife and children and the master desires that he neither see them nor speak to them, if he decides to order the son to whip the mother, if he wishes to usurp the daughter for immoral purposes, he can do so. Imagine all the most extraordinary injuries which one man can inflict upon another without killing him, without separating him by sale from his wife and children under fifteen, and you will have what slavery is legally among us. The House of Correction, in comparison with this other condition, is a paradise. Excluding thought of the crime of condemning an innocent person to imprisonment as an example to others—which is worse than the fate of the most unfortunate slave—there is no comparison between a system of fixed obligations, of dependence upon law and its administrators, and a system of proprietary subjection to a person who can be a madman or a barbarian.

III

Caudillos

While the Wars of Independence waged in the 1810s and 1820s did not abolish slavery, they did introduce an entirely new conception of political organization to the former American colonies of Spain and Portugal. To justify their separation from European colonial rule, Independence leaders turned, as we saw in chapter 1, to a philosophy that combined elements of liberalism, republicanism, and nationalism. With the notable exceptions of Brazil, which took the form of an independent constitutional monarchy until 1889, and Cuba and Puerto Rico, which remained part of the Spanish empire until 1898, Latin America went solidly republican in the nineteenth century, and even in Brazil evidence of liberalism abounded.

The problem for this first generation of liberal reformers was that it was extremely difficult to change the deeply entrenched realities of colonialism—a colonialism that had roots stretching back over three centuries in many places—in a generation. It proved very difficult, if not impossible, to shake things up below the surface. Whereas liberalism called for legal equality, the reality was that racialized inequality lived on. Whereas republicanism called for the will of the people to rule, the reality was that voting rights applied only to property-owning (or sometimes securely employed), literate, adult males. Whereas nationalism called for the glorification of a common identity, the reality was that the divide between urban and rural society was immense; and the gaps between social classes, enormous. While we must be careful not to fall into the trap of historical inevitability, it is not hard to see why the first wave of liberalism was so terribly unsuccessful and disappointing.

It was the void left by liberalism's failure that was filled by *caudillos*, the interpretive problem to be examined in this chapter. By focusing on *caudillismo*, as the system that produced the caudillo phenomenon was known, students will be exploring a classic problem in the study of Spanish American history. But before we dig into the basic workings of caudillismo, it is worthwhile to pause here for just a moment to discuss briefly the concept of historiography.

The first half of this chapter is composed of three different interpretations of caudillos. Each interpretation represents a different era in the historical study of caudillos. Each has its own approach to the topic, makes assumptions, and contains biases. When one studies the way historical interpretations of caudillos (or any other topic) change over time, one is actually studying what historians call historiography, the history of historical writing. The first three selections in this chapter are thus asking students to develop a historiographical understanding of the problem of caudillos.

What, then, is a caudillo? First of all, he was a type of military/political leader that dominated Spanish America in the middle decades of the nineteenth century, often from a horse's saddle. Instead of caudillos, Brazil had *coronéis*, colonels in the national guard who were often very powerful landowners. The main differences between caudillismo and *coronelismo* are that the central government of the Brazilian empire (1822–1889) was never overthrown, and Brazil's economic growth resumed relatively quickly after independence. In contrast, Spanish Americans experienced civil wars, the militarization of society, and economic decline. Overall, Brazilian coronéis were less important than Spanish American caudillos.

Caudillos were invariably men—men who lived up to the masculine (*macho*) ideals of Spanish American society at that time. They were military men who had experienced the battlefields of Independence and the countless civil wars that broke out between rival political factions in the wake of independence. They were men who made followers of other men who when called upon would go into battle for their leader. Caudillos had charisma. In his teaching and writing on caudillos in nineteenth-century Latin America, historian John Chasteen (the former coeditor of this book) emphasizes the importance of the caudillos' ability to form patron-client networks, broad coalitions of key individuals and groups located at various levels of the social order, to carry out their goals. When such networks were successful, everyone benefitted, though not equally. When they were unsuccessful, all suffered and the network dissolved. The most successful caudillos rose to prominence on the national stage, elevating themselves over regional rivals and seizing control of national governments, sometimes for decades (something that could not be done in Brazil).

Caudillos could be found in almost every corner of Spanish America from the 1840s until the 1860s. After 1870, the liberal reformers rebounded and gradually brought the caudillos to heel. Throughout the twentieth century, however, and even today, powerful leaders arise in Latin America that sometimes win the name "caudillos" because of their political style.

Perhaps the most famous example of a caudillo was the governor of the Argentine province of Buenos Aires, Juan Manuel de Rosas, who used his control of that province to dominate Argentina from 1835 to 1852. During the Rosas era, Argentina gradually became a personal dictatorship, complete (as we will see below) with its own public celebrations and decorations. Rosas was known, by act of the provincial legislature, as "the Restorer of the Laws," a title vehemently disputed by his critics, which included all of the leading liberals of the day. Rosas despised the liberals (who mostly belonged to a political party known as the Unitarians), accusing them of bringing "anarchy" into the country with their strange and foreign ideas.

The key question for students to consider in this chapter is, what made people follow such men? Why, in other words, were caudillos attractive leaders? After all, a leader without followers is no leader at all. By the end of this chapter students should be able to answer these questions.

QUESTIONS FOR ANALYSIS

1. How do the authors of the first three selections explain the pervasive dominance of caudillos in mid-nineteenth-century politics?
2. How do the two primary source excerpts confirm, add to, or raise questions about the secondary sources?
3. What kind of biases can you see in this chapter's selections? Can you relate them to the time in which each author was writing?

1. Caudillos as Scourge ～ Charles E. Chapman*

The following selection comes from a scholarly article written by U.S. historian Charles E. Chapman in a leading academic journal in 1932. It is included here not because it is still so highly regarded for its brilliance or originality but rather because it shows us how much our thinking has changed in the last eighty years, especially with regard to our thinking about race. It will soon become evident to readers that Chapman's interpretation of caudillismo relies heavily on a set of racist assumptions and an unsympathetic view of Catholicism. He views the caudillo phenomenon as a disease or pathology. Nevertheless, we should not totally dismiss these types of interpretations; they are part of the historiographical tradition. Could Chapman's article still be published today?

It is hardly necessary to say that caudillismo grew naturally out of conditions as they existed in Hispanic America. Institutions do not have a habit of springing full-blown and without warning into life. One of the essential antecedents of caudillismo is to be found in the character of the Hispanic races which carried out the conquest of the Americas. Spaniards and Portuguese, then as now, were individualists, at the same time that they were accustomed to absolutism as a leading principle of political life. *"Del rey abajo ninguno"* is a familiar Spanish refrain, which may be rendered freely "No person below the king is any better than I am." It is precisely because of the strength of this feeling that absolutism has become a necessary part of Hispanic practice, because usually only some form of strong dictatorship has been able to hold Hispanic peoples in check. Otherwise, in a truly democratic country of ten million Hispanic persons there would be ten million republics. Furthermore, it was the most adventurous and least conservative elements among the Spaniards and Portuguese who first came to America. Even some of their illustrious leaders were men of comparatively low origin in the mother country. In America, the conquerors were a dominant minority among inferior races, and their individualism was accentuated by the chances now afforded to do as they pleased amidst subjugated peoples. It must be remembered, too, that they did not bring their families, and in consequence not only was there an admixture of blood on a tremendous scale with the native Indians and even the Negroes, but also tendencies developed toward loose and turbulent habits beyond anything which was customary in the homeland.

In other words, Hispanic society deteriorated in the Americas. To make matters worse, there were no compensating advantages in the way of political freedom, for the monarchy was successful in establishing its absolutist system in the colonies, a system which in practice was a corrupt, militaristic control, with scant interest in, or attention to, the needs of the people over whom it ruled. The Anglo-American colonies were settlements of families in search of new homes. They did not decline in quality, as there was no such association with the Indians as there was in Spanish America and Brazil. In Hispanic America, society was constituted on the basis of a union of white soldiery with Indian or Negro elements. It tended to become mestizo or mulatto, with a resulting loss of white culture and the native simplicity of life. Soon the half-castes far surpassed the whites in numbers, and, especially in the case of the mestizos, added to the prevailing turbulence in their quest for the rights of white men. Even in the eighteenth century it was the custom in Buenos Aires for men to go about armed with swords and muskets, for the protection of both life and property depended more upon one's self than upon the law. As for the Indians and Negroes, they were usually submissive, but shared one feeling with castes and native-born whites: abomination for the government. Most persons in colonial days knew no patriotism beyond that of the village or city in which they lived. For this, in keeping with the individualistic traits of their character, they came to have an exaggerated regard.

Without taking too much space for argument, a few words might be added in order to emphasize the existence of the factor of a favorable atmosphere in colonial days for the eventual development of caudillismo. Indeed, the institution really existed throughout the pre-independence era. What were the conquistadores and even the viceroys but absolute military and political bosses? Not infrequently colonial officials continued to wield power despite higher orders to the contrary. It was a natural transition from native chiefs by way of Hispanic officialdom to the caudillos of the early republics. The social keynote was one of individualistic absolutism in all classes, instead of that love of, and subjection to, the law which were such marked characteristics of the Anglo-American colonists. In consequence, with the disappearance of the mother country governments at the time of the revolutions, all authority fell with them, and there was no legal consciousness or political capacity ready at hand to cope with the turbulence which was to facilitate the emergence of the caudillos. When the citizens of Buenos Aires came together on May 25, 1810, to begin the movement for the over-throw of Spanish control, it was the first time that the people of that part of the Americas had exercised civic functions. Only the absolutism of the mother country had existed before, and in the bitter war period after 1810 it became a habit to denounce that dominance in exaggerated fashion as a tyranny of which the last vestige should be destroyed. There was no desire for a continuance of the institutions of the mother country such as there was in Anglo America. There was little in the way of political liberty worth preserving in either Spain or Portugal anyway. So institutions were adopted which were as far removed as possible from those of their former rulers, with the result that they did not fit the peoples of Hispanic America. An attempt was made to pass immediately from colonial absolutism to pure democracy. Naturally, the effort failed. It was possible to tear down the outward forms—one might say the nomenclature—of the old system, but its inner spirit remained, for it was ingrained in the habits of the people.

Ignorance, turbulence, and what proved to be their great ally, universal suffrage, combined to assure the rise and overlordship of the caudillos. The overwhelming majority of the people of Hispanic America were illiterate. Certainly, it would be a generous estimate to assert that 10 percent of the inhabitants could read and write. With this impossible background, democratic institutions were attempted. The meetings of the cabildos became demagogic tumults, with the masses sitting in the galleries and cheering the most radical and violent. It was on this account that new institutions were adopted by law which did not fit actual conditions, a prime cause of the failure of the early independence governments. The turbulence of the new alleged democracy could accept nothing less than universal suffrage, which of course was duly proclaimed. That meant the demagogue in the city.

Much more important, it meant the caudillo in the rural districts, for the "sacred right of voting" became the principal legal basis of the power of the caudillos. Out of this there developed that curious phenomenon, the Hispanic American election. Elections were habitually fraudulent. The question about them was whether the fraud should be tame or violent. If there were no resistance, various devices were employed to obtain the vote desired. But if there were opposition, the caudillo nevertheless won, but to the accompaniment of an orgy of blood. In the beginning the masses supported the demagogue of the city or the country caudillo. In these leaders, with their rhetoric about the "rights of man," they found the vindication of their claims for political recognition. The conservative classes acquiesced. It was better to suffer the mob and grotesque usurpers than to lose one's life and property through any genuine participation in elections. All that remained for the caudillos to do was to conquer the demagogues. Then at last their work was complete.

The different leaders in no respect represented any real political or social conflict, just different leaders. Government reduced itself to dominating and to resisting the efforts of others to dominate. In point of fact this practice of exaggerated expression fitted in with the customs of the people. It was a Hispanic-American habit to conceive of causes in the name of persons. There have been far more "Miguelistas" or "Porfiristas" in Hispanic America than "Progressives" or men of other party names, at least in popular parlance. The leader, which meant the caudillo, was party, flag, principle, and objective, all in his own person. If conditions were bad, it was because another leader was needed, and for that matter each group had its "liberator" or "savior" of the country. Indeed, hyperbole of civic phrase makes its appearance in all the documentation of Hispanic-American history. All prominent men are national heroes or tyrants, according to whatever person happens to be writing. It makes research in this field a matter requiring great discrimination and critical appreciation, for hyperbole, I repeat, was and still is a Hispanic-American disease.

2. Caudillos as Profit Maximizers ⁓
Eric R. Wolf and Edward C. Hansen*

A different approach to caudillos can be found in the following excerpt from another scholarly article published in another academic journal by the anthropologists Eric Wolf and Edward Hansen. But in this case the date of publication is not 1932 but 1967, two very different moments in U.S. history. More important, the historical profession changed a good deal in those thirty-five years. Notice how the interpretation of caudillos explained here has shifted from a focus on race mixture and cultural backwardness to a new concentration on the economic logic of the system. Wolf and Hansen take us inside the "bands" of armed men that constituted the caudillos' patron-client networks to discover what is motivating their action. Such a materialist explanation was typical of that historiographical moment.

*From Eric R. Wolf and Edward C. Hansen, "Caudillo Politics: A Structural Analysis," *Comparative Studies in Society and History* 9 (1967): 168–79. © 1967 Society for the Comparative Study of Society and History. Reprinted by permission of Cambridge University Press.

In spite of the decline of Spanish power in the late colonial period, the New World planter class proved too weak numerically and too lacking in cohesion to oust the Peninsular forces by its own unaided efforts. To gain their own independence they were therefore forced into political alliances with the numerically strong and highly mobile—yet at the same time economically, socially, and politically disadvantaged—social strata of the population which are designated collectively as mestizos. Not without trepidation, criollo leaders armed elements derived from these propertyless strata and sent them to do battle against the Spaniards. Success in maintaining the continuing loyalties of these elements depended largely upon the ability of leaders in building personal ties of loyalty with their following and in leading them in ventures of successful pillage.

Although the alliances of criollos and mestizos was instrumental in winning the Wars of Independence, granting arms to the mestizo elements freed these to create their own armed bands. The mestizos in turn were thus enabled to compete with the criollos for available wealth. The case of Venezuela, while unique in its extreme manifestations, nevertheless demonstrates this new, and continent-wide, ability of the mestizos to act on their own behalf. There the royalists were originally victorious by granting the llanero plainsmen, formerly armed servants of the criollos, pillage rights against their masters. Having eliminated their own masters, the llaneros then turned upon the royalists and massacred them in an effort to obtain additional loot. In granting independent armament to the mestizos, therefore, the criollo gentry also sacrificed any chance it might have had to establish a monopoly of power.

We must not forget that criollo wealth was dependent upon large landholdings, or haciendas. If the hacienda provided a bulwark of defense against the laissez-faire market, the hacienda system itself militated against the development of a cohesive political association of hacienda owners. Geared to a stagnant technology, yet under repeated pressures to expand production, the hacienda tended to "eat up" land, in order to control the population settled upon the land. The aim of each hacienda was ultimately to produce crops through the arithmetic addition of workers, each one of whom—laboring with his traditional tools—would contribute to increase the sum of produce at the disposal of the estate. While in some parts of Latin America, notably in the Andes and in Middle America, the expansionist tendencies of the hacienda could be directed against Indian communities, in areas without Indians a hacienda could expand only at the expense of neighboring haciendas. Not surprisingly, therefore, we find that blood feuds among hacienda owners are a notable feature of this period. Each hacienda owner's bitterest enemy was potentially his closest neighbor. In this competition we must find the economic roots of criollo anarchy.

Such economic determinants of anarchy were reinforced further by social organizational factors. Competition and conflict on the economic plane could, to some extent, be compensated for through the workings of kinship. Arnold

Strickon has noted the growth of regional aristocratic families and their role in national politics. We do not yet possess adequate data on how such alliances were formed, how many people were involved, and how much territory they covered. Theoretical considerations, however, lead us to believe that the organizing power of such alliances must have been relatively weak. If we assume that hacienda owners favored the maintenance of large estates through inheritance by primogeniture; if we assume further that the chances are equal that the chief heir will be either male or female; and if we postulate that each hacienda owner strives to maximize the number of his alliances, then it seems unlikely that the number of strategic alliances based on landed property between a hacienda family of origin and other hacienda families of procreation will exceed three. The marriage of Father with Father's Wife creates one such alliance; the marriage of the first-born son with a woman of another family swells the number to two; and the marriage of the eldest daughter with the first son of a third family brings the number of strategic alliances to three. These considerations are intended to yield a measure of insight into the inability of the criollo gentry to form a wide-ranging network of strategic alliances for political purposes.

In analyzing the caudillo mode of political organization, we are forced to rely on materials dealing with caudillos who made their influence felt on the national level. The available literature deals mainly with these national-level or "maximal" bands, but sheds little light on how the "minimal" bands of local chieftains and followers were first formed. The caudillos who emerged into the light of day are thus all leaders who proved capable of welding a series of structurally similar minimal bands into a maximal coalition, capable of exercising dominance over wide regions. The data dealing with such national caudillos, however, permit some generalizations about the patterns of coalition formation, about the distribution of wealth by the leader to his band, and about the sources of political strength and fragility. We are also enabled to make certain comparisons between the different problems faced by mestizo and criollo chieftains. To describe the model, we shall conjugate verbs in the ethnographic present.

The aim of the caudillo band is to gain wealth; the tactic employed is essentially pillage. For the retainers, correct selection of a leader is paramount. No retainer can guarantee that he will receive recompense from his leader in advance, because the band seeks to obtain wealth which is not yet in its possession. All know that the wealth sought after is finite; only certain resources are "safe game." The band cannot attack with impunity the basic sources of criollo wealth, such as land; and it cannot sequester, without international complications, the property of foreign firms operating in the area. Hence there is not only intense competition for movable resources, but great skill is required in diagnosing which resources are currently "available" and which taboo. The exercise of power therefore gives rise to a code which regulates the mode of access to resources. The code refers to two basic attributes of leadership: first, the interpersonal skills needed to keep the band together; second, the acumen required to cement these relationships through the correct distribution of wealth. Possession of interpersonal skills is the initial prerequisite; it suggests to the retainers that the second attribute will also be fulfilled.

The social idiom in which the first of these attributes is discussed is that of "masculinity": the social assertion of masculinity constitutes what has come to be known as machismo (from *macho*, masculine). According to the idiom, masculinity is demonstrated in two ways: by the capacity to dominate females, and by the readiness to use violence. These two capacities are closely related; both point to antagonistic relations between men. The capacity to dominate women implies the further capacity to best other men in the competition over females.

Assertions of dominance are tested in numerous encounters, in which the potential leader must test himself against other potential claimants. Although Latin American rural communities are frequently isolated by poor communication facilities, the local caudillos are thrown into contact from time to time. Occasionally in activities such as drinking, card playing, carousing, and brawling, a man so stands out that the others automatically accept his authority and extend to him their loyalties. Such situations are charged with potential violence, for in such antagonistic confrontations, the claimants to victory must be prepared to kill their rivals and to demonstrate this willingness publicly. For the loser there is no middle ground; he must submit to the winner, or be killed. Willingness to risk all in such encounters is further proof of masculinity. The drama involved in such tests of leadership is illustrated by the following episode in the rise of the Bolivian caudillo Mariano Melgarejo, an ignorant and drunken murderer given to the wildest sexual orgies, who ran the country from 1864 to 1871. Melgarejo got into power by killing the country's dictator, [Manuel Isidoro] Belzú, in the presidential palace. The shooting took place before a great crowd which had gathered in the plaza to see the meeting of the two rivals. When Belzú fell dead into the arms of one of his escorts, Melgarejo strode to the window and exclaimed: "Belzú is dead. Now who are you shouting for?" The mob, thus prompted, threw off its fear and gave a bestial cry: "Viva Melgarejo!"

Personal leadership may thus create a successful band. By the same token, however, the personal nature of leadership also threatens band maintenance. If the caudillo is killed or dies of natural causes, the band will disintegrate because there can be no institutionalized successor. The qualities of leadership reside in his person, not in the office. To establish a system of offices it would have been necessary to reorganize post-Independence society. Attempts in this direction were continuously thwarted by criollo arms. One has to note the defeat of the "centralists" in all parts of Latin America.

Proof of masculinity does not yet make a man a caudillo. Men will not flock to his banner unless he also proves himself capable of organizing a number of minimal bands into a maximal faction, and demonstrates his ability to hold the faction together. To this end, the caudillo must weld a number of lieutenants into a core of "right-hand men." Important in this creation of a core of devoted followers is not merely assertion of dominance, but also calculated gift-giving to favored individuals who are expected to reciprocate with loyalty. Such gifts may consist of movable goods, money, or perquisites such as the right to pillage a given area or social group. The importance of such gifts is best understood as a presentation of favors defined not merely as objects, but also as attributes of the giver. Where the receiver cannot respond with a counter-gift which would partake equally of his own personal attributes, he is expected to respond with loyalty, that is, he makes a gift of his person for a more or less limited period of time. The existence of such a core of right-hand men produces its own demonstration effect. They are living testimony to the largesse of the caudillo aspirant and to his commitment to grant riches in return for personal support.

To satisfy this desire for riches, the caudillo must exhibit further abilities. We have already discussed some of the limitations under which the caudillo labors in acquiring wealth: there are certain groups he may not attack with impunity. To cast about in quest of riches may stir resistance; resistance may imply defeat. To be successful, therefore, a caudillo needs what we may call "access vision," capabilities closely related to the "business acumen" of the North American entrepreneur. He must be able to diagnose resources which are available for seizure with a minimum of resistance on the part of their present owners. He must estimate how much wealth is needed to satisfy his retainers. He must also control the freelance activities of his followers, such as cattle rustling and robbery, lest they mobilize the resistance of effective veto groups. He must be able to estimate correctly the forces at the disposal of those presently in control of resources. And he must be able to predict the behavior and power of potential competitors in the seizure of wealth. Nor can he rest content with initial success in his endeavors. He must continuously find new sources of wealth which can be distributed to his following, or he must attach resources which replenish themselves. Initial successes are therefore frequently followed by sudden failures. Many caudillo ventures end as "one-shot" undertakings. The caudillo may be successful in seizing the government treasury or the receipts of a custom house, but then no other source of wealth is found, and the faction disintegrates. The more limited the supply of ready wealth, the more rapid the turnover of caudillos. Thus Bolivia, one of the most impoverished countries during this period, averaged more than one violent change of government every year.

Such considerations affected even the most successful caudillos, such as José A. Páez and Juan Manuel Rosas. Páez held sway in Venezuela for thirty-three years (1830–63); Rosas dominated Argentina for twenty years (1829–31, 1835–52). Both owned enormous cattle ranches which furnished large quantities of beef, the staple of the countryside. Both drew their retainers from the ranks of the fierce cowpunchers of the tallgrass prairie, the gauchos in Argentina and the llaneros of Venezuela, whose mode of livelihood provided ideal preparation for caudillo warfare. Time and again, both men defeated the attempts of rivals to set up centralized forms of government. Despite the initial advantages of abundant wealth, their control of "natural" military forces, and their ability to neutralize a large number of competitors, however, both men had to beat off numerous armed uprisings, and both ultimately met defeat. Their cases illustrate the difficulties which beset caudillos operating even under optimal conditions.

3. Caudillos as Culture Heroes ⁓ Ariel de la Fuente*

The final secondary source selection in this chapter comes from a more recent academic book published by a university press in the year 2000. Written by Argentine-born historian Ariel de la Fuente, the book is a close-up historical study of caudillismo in the western Argentine province of La Rioja in the two decades following the downfall of Rosas in 1852. De la Fuente delves into a whole new dimension of caudillismo in this excerpt from the book: the dimension of the oral culture surrounding two famous regional caudillos, Facundo Quiroga and Chacho Peñaloza. In particular, de la Fuente examines the lyrics of popular songs that were associated with these and other caudillos. The shift away from a materialist interpretation toward a more culturalist one is indicative of the more contemporary approach to popular culture that was mentioned in the chapter on slavery and slave culture. De la Fuente also emphasizes the importance of the "fatherly" roles played by caudillos in Argentina's paternalistic, rural society. This is not the only place we will see the notion of political fatherhood in this book.

Politics occupied an important place in the oral culture of the provinces of the Argentine interior in the nineteenth century. This can be seen in many of the songs that remained in the collective memory of the provinces in the early twentieth century. For example, among the thousands of pieces collected in 1921, some 250 songs had a strictly political content, and many of those were principally concerned with nineteenth-century caudillos and their political lives. In terms of the caudillos from the province of La Rioja itself, we find eight songs about Facundo Quiroga and twenty-one about Chacho Peñaloza. The geographic location where the songs were collected reveals the extent of their circulation throughout Argentina. Songs that have as their protagonists Riojan caudillos, for instance,

---

*From Ariel de la Fuente, *Children of Facundo: Caudillo and Gaucho Insurgency during the Argentine State-Formation Process (La Rioja, 1853–1870)* (Durham, NC: Duke University Press, 2000), 115–17, 125–28. © 2000 Duke University Press. All rights reserved. Reprinted by permission of the copyright holder, Duke University Press, www.dukeupress.edu/.

appear not only in the province of La Rioja but also in Córdoba, San Luis, San Juan, Catamarca, Tucumán, Salta, and Jujuy. The collection of 1921 also preserved a good number of stories featuring caudillos as protagonists: twenty-two concerning Facundo and thirteen about Chacho were collected in the provinces of La Rioja, Catamarca, and San Juan.

Testimony from some of the caudillos' contemporaries suggested the importance of such songs and stories in political life. In 1862, an observer noted that after Chacho had successfully resisted the troops from Buenos Aires, the gauchos raised the power and prestige of Peñaloza in the provinces of the interior "by singing the glories of the general." And General José María Paz remembered that in his campaigns in the province of Córdoba toward the end of the 1820s, besides confronting Facundo on the battlefield, he also confronted Facundo's prestige within popular culture:

> I also had a strong enemy to combat in the popular beliefs about Quiroga. When I say popular I am speaking of the countryside, where those beliefs had taken root in various parts and not only in the lower classes of society. Quiroga was thought to be an inspired man, who had well-known spirits that penetrated everywhere and obeyed his mandate . . . and a thousand other absurdities of this type.

The beliefs that circulated in the form of stories and songs, and the resulting perceptions that they generated among the rural population of Córdoba, were key elements of the gauchos' loyalty to the Riojan caudillo.

Oral culture, as Paz recognized, was a political dominion, an arena where the struggle between Unitarians and Federalists (Argentina's two parties of the era) was waged. Humor was also used as a weapon in this conflict, and Unitarian and Federalist leaders became the protagonists (as well as targets) of jokes. In the 1840s, a Unitarian from Santiago del Estero named one of his horses Juan Manuel (a reference to the caudillo Juan Manuel de Rosas) to depict the Federalist caudillo as a beast, belonging in the camp of the barbarians, the enemies of civilization. When Catamarca was occupied by Unitarian troops from Buenos Aires in 1862, a poor black of that locality defiantly called a dog "Bartolo" (short for Bartolomé Mitre, leader of the Unitarian Party) and got 500 lashes for his insolence. And after the death of Chacho, in 1863, a poem of Unitarian origin made fun of his supposed hatred of the emblematic Unitarian color, sky blue:

> Peñaloza died and
> Went straight to heaven,
> But as he saw it was sky blue
> He went back down to hell.
> The Federalist color was red.

Although Unitarians and Federalists competed for primacy in the arena of popular culture, overall Federalism dominated it. Thus, a quick review of the

250 songs collected in 1921 that explicitly referred to the conflict between the two parties shows that two-thirds of them were Federalist. And if we consider the presence of leaders of both parties in those songs, the predominance of Federalism is even more pronounced: of the total number of positive depictions of leaders from both parties, more than four-fifths concerned Federalist caudillos. The names Urquiza, Facundo, Rosas, El Chacho, and Felipe Varela were most often evoked. Among the rarely mentioned Unitarians were the Taboadas, General Lavalle, General Paz, General La Madrid, Mitre, and Sarmiento. While these references do not necessarily reflect the amount of support each party enjoyed, they certainly reveal the predominance of Federalism in the oral culture; and this, in turn, signals the pervasiveness of this partisan identity among the illiterate, the main users of oral culture.

The caudillos, in their day, were perceived as the highest authority. In this respect, popular culture underscored not only their position as political leaders but also distinguished the caudillos as moral authorities and role models in the communities they ruled over. Oral culture integrated well-known motifs from folklore, and invested caudillos with qualities and connotations similar to those that popular classes attributed to kings or patrons in other societies. This association with images of kings stemmed, in part, from the repertoire of preexisting archetypes on which the images of the caudillos were formed, but it could also possibly be the product of three centuries of colonial, monarchical experience, which would have left a model and language through which to define legitimate authority, and the characteristics that holders of that authority should have .

In certain stories, Facundo, hiding his identity, appeared by surprise in various places in La Rioja, although everyone thought he had left the region. These stories attributed to him a special capacity to know what Riojans were doing, and, if necessary, reward or punish them. In one story, after the battle of La Tablada, a group of young Unitarians got together to celebrate the defeat of Facundo. The young men began to sing a song that painted the caudillo negatively, when they realized that among them was "an individual in a poncho, with practically the entire face covered by a big hat." The man in a poncho "asked them in a polite tone to finish the interesting song." When the song came to an end, "Quiroga (for it was none other in the poncho)" called his soldiers and had the singers shot. "Nobody imagined that the disguised figure was the Tiger of Los Llanos," concluded the story, "for he was thought to be thirty leagues away." Here, using the motif that folklorists have classified as "the king in disguise to learn the secrets of his subjects," oral tradition sought to explain a tragic occurrence: the fact that after the battle of La Tablada, Quiroga did have some Unitarians in La Rioja shot "under the pretext that they had been rejoicing in his defeat." The form the story took spoke of the reach of Quiroga's authority and the control that he exercised over the population of La Rioja. Thus, omnipresence was one of the supposed qualities of Facundo, which also suggests an appreciation of his power. But this capacity "to learn the secrets of subjects" may have been a quality attributed to Federalist caudillos more generally. William H. Hudson remembered that a number of stories about Rosas circulated, many of them related to his adventures when he would disguise himself as a person of humble status and prowl about the city [of Buenos Aires] by night, especially in the squalid quarters, where he would make the acquaintance of the very poor in their hovels.

Mediation in the daily conflicts of rural La Rioja was the responsibility of the caudillos. This included interventions in family disputes or conflicts between gauchos and government officials. Sometimes the caudillos proposed solutions, while on other occasions they made sure that the proper authorities intervened. Conflict resolution and justice, then, were some of the caudillos' duties, and to explain them, gauchos used archetypes clearly drawn from the King Solomon legend. Facundo was portrayed as a Solomon-like figure who used his exceptional wisdom or astuteness to resolve disputes and impart justice.

But the caudillo was the highest authority because he was also responsible, ultimately, for the material and moral preservation of the society. The extent of his authority and the nature of this responsibility were expressed in the language of caudillos and gauchos. Chacho reflected on the dimensions of his own authority:

> I have that influence [over the gauchos], that prestige, because as a soldier I fought at their side for forty-three years, sharing with them the fortunes of war, the suffering of the campaigns, the bitterness of banishment. I have been more of a father to them than a leader . . . preferring their necessities to my own. As an Argentine and a Riojan I have always been the protector of the unfortunate, sacrificing the very last that I had to fulfill their needs, making myself responsible for everything and with my influence as a leader forcing the national government to turn its eyes toward these unfortunate people.

Penaloza's authority and status as a caudillo had evolved through the long political experience that he shared with the gauchos since the 1820s, when Chacho had entered into the party struggles as a subaltern of Facundo. His partisan leadership, however, was only one part of his relationship with the gauchos: "I have been more of a father to them than a leader." That is, he had always been "the protector of the unfortunate," putting the needs of the gauchos above his own and sacrificing for them. As a father, then, Peñaloza had made himself "responsible for everything."

The language of kinship emphasized the nature of the obligation and, especially, affective ties that bound caudillos and gauchos. This explains why references to caudillos as fathers were often articulated in an emotive language. Popular songs defined Facundo, for example, as "a dear father." Likewise, it was said of General Octaviano Navarro, from Catamarca, that "he was beloved by his province, he was the father of said province and his heart was tempered by his very warm soldiers, who loved him so much."

The authority of the caudillo as a "father" had moral and ideological dimensions, too, as reflected in a story featuring Facundo as the protagonist. Here, the caudillo was going through a village when he decided to stop and join a crowd assembled for a wedding. During the ceremony, the bride refused to accept the man her father had chosen to be her husband. She pointed out another man in the crowd and said, "He is the one I love, not [indicating her bridegroom] this one." According to oral tradition, "Quiroga sent his officers to take the girl and hang her from the highest Tala tree and to bring the one she loved to judgment, and give him six shots." It was the caudillo who castigated those who would subvert the functioning of matrimony and the authority of the father to choose a daughter's mate. In this episode, however, the "real" father was absent, transforming the tale into an explicit comment on the caudillo's authority. It was Facundo, the father of all Riojans, who exercised patriarchal authority and did what was expected of any father under the same circumstances. The caudillo was "responsible for everything" including the reproduction of patriarchy. And to fulfill that responsibility, oral culture resorted once again to Facundo's omnipresence, which allowed the caudillo to attend an apparently insignificant wedding.

The stories concerning Facundo and Chacho emphasized that these Federalist caudillos appreciated and rewarded the loyalty of the gauchos. Therefore, he who responded when his leader asked for, or needed, help was compensated beyond what a client would hope for from a caudillo. In one of the stories, collected in San Antonio, the home village of Facundo, in Los Llanos, a peon who, without recognizing the caudillo, helped Quiroga to cross a river and escape when the caudillo was pursued by government officials, was later rewarded by Facundo with "ten oxen and ten cows." Any landless worker in Los Llanos understood the significance of this compensation. It allowed the peon to begin raising cattle, thereby distancing him from the periodic specter of hunger that was part and parcel of casual wage labor and subsistence agriculture. In other words, the peon's service to the caudillo was more than amply repaid with an amount of animals that surpassed what the sons of modest ranchers received to start their own ranches. This way of rewarding gauchos appears in stories about Chacho as well. After requisitioning for his troops the "four or five cows" that a couple living in a hut had, "Chacho returned not only the five cows but as many more," doubling the stock of these small landholders.

The poor occupied a privileged and almost exclusive position in the representation of the patron–client relation, which gave the caudillo's following a clear social identity. In a story from Los Llanos about the death of Peñaloza, an elderly woman tried to warn him about the fatal event to come, telling him, "Fly from here, I don't want them to kill you, all us poor folk need you." Her warnings were not enough, and Peñaloza died. His death "was felt by all, since he had been so generous in these villages."

In other tales, elements of Chacho's personal history and his special relationship with the poor made him look almost like a saint. "Chacho was a man who had been a priest, and because he liked to sacrifice for humanity he threw off the priest's habit and took up the dress of the gaucho." With this explanation, one story recounts an episode in which Chacho went to the house of "a woman who had a good amount of livestock but she was very tight-fisted, and she had all her animals hidden." When the caudillo asked her "what she had to offer him, chickens or goats, the woman said nothing." Chacho had her punished, and then the woman admitted that she did have livestock and offered it to the caudillo, who reminded her that "with a man like him, one doesn't tell lies."

---

4. Ribbons and Rituals ⁓ Domingo Faustino Sarmiento*

Domingo F. Sarmiento was one of the staunchest opponents of the Argentine caudillo Juan Manuel de Rosas and a liberal statesman of the first order. After a long period of exile because of Rosas, Sarmiento returned to Argentina in 1855 and went on to serve as a provincial governor and then as president from 1868 to 1874. Through it all he was constantly editing newspapers, writing columns and reviews, and advocating for modernization. It was during a period of exile in Chile that Sarmiento published his most influential book, Facundo, *or Civilization and Barbarism,* which first came out in a Santiago newspaper in 1845. In the book, Facundo Quiroga (one of the regional caudillos discussed by de la Fuente) is representative of the caudillo state headed by Rosas. In this excerpt from the book, Sarmiento discusses the extreme lengths to which the Rosas regime went to control language, behavior, and the environment. What do you make of his use of the word "terror" in the final paragraph?*

Finally, Rosas has the government in his hands. Facundo died a month earlier; the city has placed itself at his discretion; the people have candidly confirmed their surrender of all rights and institutions. The State is a blank slate on which he will write something new and original. He is a poet, a Plato who will now bring into being the ideal republic which he has conceived. He has meditated upon this labor for twenty years, and now he can finally bring it forth unimpeded by stale traditions, current events, imitations of Europe, individual rights, or existing institutions. He is a genius, in short, who has been lamenting the ills of his century

---

*From Domingo Faustino Sarmiento, *Facundo, o civilización y barbarie* (Caracas, Venezuela: Biblioteca Ayacucho, 1977), 123–24, 206–8 (trans. John Charles Chasteen and Leslie Bary).

and preparing himself to destroy them with one blow. All will be new, a work of his creative faculty. Let us observe this prodigy.

Leaving the House of Representatives, where he went to receive his staff of office, he withdraws in a coach painted red expressly for the ceremony. Yoked to the coach by cords of red silk are the men who, with criminal impunity, have kept the city in a state of continual alarm since 1833. They style themselves the People's Society, and they wear knives at the waist, red vests, and red ribbons with the slogan: "Death to the Unitarians."* At the door of his house, these same men form an honor guard. Next he gives audience to citizens, and then to generals. Everyone must show his limitless personal loyalty to him, "the Restorer [of the Laws]."

The next day, a proclamation appears with a list of proscriptions. This proc- lamation, one of Rosas's few writings, is a wonderful document that I am sorry not to have on hand. It was his program of government, undisguised and unam- biguous: whoever is not with me is my enemy. That is the axiom of the policy enshrined in the document, which announces that blood will flow, and promises only that property will be respected. Woe to those who provoke his fury!

Four days later, the parish of San Francisco announces its intention to celebrate a Mass to give thanks to the Almighty for the rule of Rosas, inviting the people of the neighborhood to solemnize the event with their presence. The surrounding streets are dressed with banners, bunting, and carpets. The place becomes an Oriental bazaar displaying tapestries of damask, purple, gold, and jewels in whimsical array. People throng the streets: young people who are at- tracted by the novelty, ladies who have chosen the parish for their afternoon stroll. The ceremony of thanksgiving is postponed for a day, and the city's excite- ment—the agitated coming and going, the interruption of all work—lasts for four or five days in a row. The government's *Gazette* supplies the most insignificant details of the splendid event. And eight days later, another parish announces its own ceremony of thanksgiving. The people of that neighborhood are determined to surpass the enthusiasm of the first parish, to outdo the first celebration. What excess of decoration! What ostentation of wealth and adornment! The portrait of Rosas "the Restorer" is placed on a dais in the street, swathed in red velvet, with golden cords and braid. The hubbub returns, for as many more days. In the privileged parish, people seem to live in the street. And, a few days later, there is another celebration, in another parish in another neighborhood. But how long can this go on? Do these people never tire of spectacles? What sort of enthusiasm is this, which does not subside in a month? Why do not all the parishes have their celebrations at the same time? No, it is a systematic, organized enthusiasm, ad- ministered a little at a time. A year later the parishes still have not concluded their

---

*The Unitarians were a political faction of Argentine liberals who favored a strong central govern- ment over the federalist arrangement favored by Rosas and his supporters.

celebrations. The official giddiness has passed from the city to the countryside. It appears endless. The government's *Gazette* is occupied for a year and a half with descriptions of Federalist celebrations. The famous portrait of Rosas appears unfailingly, pulled along by generals, by ladies, by the purest of Federalists, in a carriage made especially for the purpose.

After a year and a half of celebrations, the color red emerges as the insignia of loyalty to "the cause." The portrait of Rosas first graces church altars and then becomes part of the personal effects of each and every man, who must wear it on his chest as a sign of "intense personal attachment" to the Restorer. Last, out of these celebrations comes the terrible Mazorca, the corps of amateur Federalist police, whose designated function is, first, to administer enemas of pepper and turpentine to dissenters, and then, should this phlogistic treatment prove insufficient, to slit the throat of whomever they are told.

All America has scoffed at these famous celebrations of Buenos Aires and looked at them as the maximum degradation of a people. But I see in them nothing but a political strategy, and an extremely effective one. How does one teach the idea of personalist government to a republic which has never had a king? The red ribbon is a token of the terror which goes with you everywhere, in the street, in the bosom of the family; you must think of it when dressing and undressing. We remember things always by association; the sight of a tree in a field reminds us of what we were talking about as we walked under it ten years ago. Imagine what ideas the red ribbon brings with it by association, the indelible impressions it must have joined to the image of Rosas. . . . The story of the red ribbon is, indeed, curious. At first, it was an emblem adopted by enthusiasts. Then they ordered everyone to wear it in order "to prove the unanimity" of public opinion. People meant to obey, but frequently forgot when they changed clothes. The police helped jog people's memories. The Mazorca patrolled the streets. They stood with whips at the church door when ladies were leaving Mass and applied the lash without pity. But there was still much which needed fixing. Did someone wear his ribbon carelessly tied?—The lash! A Unitarian!—Was someone's ribbon too short?—The lash! A Unitarian!—Someone did not wear one at all?—Cut his throat! The reprobate!

The government's solicitude for public education did not stop there. It was not sufficient to be a Federalist, nor to wear the ribbon. It was obligatory also to wear a picture of the illustrious Restorer over one's heart, with the slogan "Death to the Savage, Filthy Unitarians." Enough, you think, to conclude the job of debasing a civilized people, robbing them of all personal dignity? Ah! They were not yet well enough disciplined. One morning, on a street corner in Buenos Aires, there appeared a figure drawn on paper, with a ribbon half a yard long floating in the breeze. As soon as someone saw it, that person backed away in fright and spread the alarm. People ducked into the nearest store and came out with ribbons half a yard long floating in the breeze. Ten minutes later, the entire population was out in the street wearing ribbons half a yard long. Another day the figure reappeared with a slight alteration in the ribbon. The maneuver repeated itself. If some young lady forgot to wear a red bow in her hair, the police supplied one free—and attached it with melted tar! That is how they have created uniformity of public opinion! Search the Argentine Republic for someone who does not firmly believe and maintain that he is a Federalist!

It has happened a thousand times: a citizen steps out his door and finds that the other side of the street has been swept. A moment later, he has had his own side swept. The man next door copies him, and in half an hour the whole street has been swept, everyone thinking it was an order from the police. A shopkeeper puts out a flag to attract people's attention. His neighbor sees him and, fearing he will be accused of tardiness by the governor, he puts out his own. The people across the street put out a flag; everyone else on the street puts one out. Other streets follow suit; and suddenly all Buenos Aires is bedecked with flags. The police become alarmed and inquire what happy news has been received by everyone but them. And these people of Buenos Aires are the same ones who trounced eleven thousand Englishmen in the streets and then sent five armies across the American continent to hunt Spaniards!

Terror, you see, is a disease of the spirit which can become an epidemic like cholera, measles, or scarlet fever. No one is safe, in the end, from the contagion. Though you may work ten years at inoculating, not even those already vaccinated can resist in the end. Do not laugh, nations of Spanish America, when you witness such degradation! Look well, for you, too, are Spanish, and so the Inquisition taught Spain to be! This sickness we carry in our blood.

5. Protagonist on a National Stage ~ Antonio López de Santa Anna*

Antonio López de Santa Anna is another famous example of a caudillo, in this case a Mexican caudillo who is primarily known in the United States for commanding the Mexican Army in the 1836 Battle of the Alamo in Texas. Santa Anna started his career in the military during the War for Independence (he was a royalist opposed to Hidalgo and Morelos). He fought the French Navy in the 1838 Pastry War (in which he lost the foot he refers to below) and the U.S. Army in the Mexican-American War of 1846–1848. He served numerous times (often for only a few months) as President of Mexico between 1833 and 1847. In the following excerpt from The Eagle, *his autobiography written in exile, Santa Anna tells the story of his political and military involvements in the early 1840s, a time of great turmoil in Mexico. What is most interesting to consider in this selection*

*From Antonio López de Santa Anna, *The Eagle: The Autobiography of Santa Anna*, ed. and trans. Ann Fears Crawford (Austin, TX: Pemberton, 1967), 65–69.

is the self-dramatizing way Santa Anna presents himself as a man who needed to be called to service by his people, rather than a typical military strongman. Does Santa Anna appear to have a political philosophy? Did caudillos?

Sixty-two days after my foot had been amputated, Gen. Guadalupe Victoria called on me at the instigation of the government. He informed me that a revolution was threatening, and that the government desired me to take [Anastasio] Bustamante's place as temporary president in this time of trial. How well the people knew me! They knew I would never desert my principles and would always be on hand when my country needed me!

I was carried to the capital on a litter. Although my trip was made with extreme care, the hardships of the journey and the change of climate weakened me. However, despite my poor health, I assumed the office of president immediately. The tasks involved completely overwhelmed me, but I pulled through. The government forces triumphed throughout the country. Gen. Gabriel Valencia captured and executed the hope of the revolution, José A. Mejia, in the vicinity of the town of Acajeta. The dreaded threat of revolution died, and peace was restored.

Bustamante once again took up the reins of government, and I retired to [my estate] to complete my recovery. However, Bustamante's loss of prestige with the people caused his government to fail. In the town of Guadalajara, in the early months of 1841, arrangements were made for Bustamante to abdicate and for the reform of the Constitution of 1824. In Tacubaya, a council of generals agreed upon basic ground rules to help bring about these reforms, and once again I assumed the office of provisional president.

In order to conform to public opinion, I called together a group of prominent citizens from all states in the nation to instigate needed reforms. This group drew up *The Principles of Political Organization* on June 12, 1844. This constitution was circulated by the government, and each of the states accepted and ratified it without dissension.

In September 1844, my beloved wife died. Greater sorrow I had never known! General of Division Valentín Canalizo substituted for me while I devoted myself to family matters.

During the first session under our new Constitution, I was duly elected president and called to the capital to administer the customary oath. The election saddened me even more. My deep melancholy drove me to abhor the glamorous life of the capital and to prefer a life of solitude. I resigned the noble office to which I had been called, but the public intruded upon my privacy, pleading that I return. My friends, with the greatest of good faith, also begged me to resume my office. Their pleas led me to sacrifice myself to the public good. I withdrew my resignation.

Near the end of October, General [Mariano] Paredes rebelled against the government in Guadalajara. When the news was communicated to me by the government, they ordered me to take the troops quartered in Jalapa and march to the capital. I instantly obeyed the orders. Paredes had been relieved of his command of the Capital District due to excesses of intoxication while he was commanding his troops. He bore a grudge and was determined to take revenge. In our country one spark was sufficient to set aflame a revolution.

I was marching toward Guadalajara under orders, when I received the news of an upheaval in the capital. The situation seemed serious, and I halted my advance. Details of the revolt in the capital arrived soon after my halt. The messenger read me the following infamous words:

> The majority of Congress openly favor the Paredes revolution. The government, in self-defense or wishing to avoid revolution, has issued a decree by which the sessions of Congress have been suspended. This decree has served as a pretext for General José J. Herrera to join the revolt. Rioters have torn down the bronze bust of President Santa Anna that stood in the Plaza del Mercado. They have also taken his amputated foot from the cemetery of Santa Paula and proceeded to drag it through the streets to the sounds of savage laughter.

I interrupted the narrator, exclaiming "Stop! I don't wish to hear any more! Almighty God! A member of my body, lost in the service of my country, dragged from the funeral urn, broken into bits to be made sport of in such a barbaric manner!" In that moment of grief and frenzy, I decided to leave my native country, object of my dreams and of my illusions, for all time.

At the head of eleven thousand well-trained and well-armed men and with partisans in the capital, I could have taken it easily. However, I was drained of all vengeance and was determined merely to leave my country forever. I countermarched toward Puebla, avoiding everyone.

IV

Liberalism and the Catholic Church

While the Catholic clergy supplied the movement for independence with some of its most important early leaders, in general the relationship between the Church and the independent states has been troubled. Liberals of the Independence generation and after decried the power of the Church over political life, railed against its monopoly over education, and despised its vast real estate and landholdings, its stultifying influence on banking and commerce, and the exploitative fees that its priests sometimes charged even the poorest peasant for its sacramental services. In sum, Latin American liberals, like their Anglo-American counterparts of the previous half century, wanted to reform completely the relationship between church and state.

In this chapter, students will explore the nineteenth-century clash between Latin America's liberals and the Church, a problem that continues to resonate in the region to this day. Indeed, in the view of many contemporary observers, Latin America is the most devoutly Catholic part of the world today, the global home of the faith's most intensely held feelings. And yet it is also a region that has embraced the ideas and values of nineteenth-century liberalism, an ideology incompatible with (or at least antagonistic toward) the worldview of the Roman Catholic Church. With this conflict in mind, let us take a step back to analyze the intellectual content of the term "liberalism."

Nineteenth-century liberalism—or classical liberalism, as it is sometimes called—is based on the belief that human progress is best achieved by unleashing the energies of the individual human being. Nineteenth-century liberals sought freedom from constraints that impede each individual's innate creativity. Such a belief first arose in the European context as a consequence of the rising power of the bourgeoisie, the capitalist middle class that wanted liberation from medieval traditions and, to get it, carried forward such major historical movements as the Renaissance, the Reformation, and the French Revolution. In their belief that individual liberty was the key to human progress, European liberals called for the abolition of class privileges that had been inherited from the Middle Ages. To destroy the vestiges of Europe's unjust and unproductive old order, liberals attempted to wipe away intermediaries such as artisan guilds or religious orders that stood between the state and the individual. Human beings were to be freely constituted, rational actors who would act on their own behalf. In this clash of free and competing interests, affirmed liberal thinkers, societies would find the proper means of governing themselves.

What did classical liberalism mean in practice? In political terms, liberalism became associated with ideas of citizenship, the social contract, constitutional government, and the will of the majority. In economic terms, the liberal promotion of individual initiative matched the capitalist spirit of entrepreneurship. Governments, in the view of liberal theorists, were to keep out of economic matters, permitting free enterprise (laissez-faire) and allowing the "invisible hand" of markets to determine the allocation of resources. In social terms, nineteenth-century liberals thought of themselves as revolutionaries out to change the world. Active intervention was needed to dismantle the old ways and establish a new order based on the legal equality of all individuals. In practice, however, when nineteenth-century liberals discussed the "equality of individuals," for the most part they assumed that the discussion was limited to literate, property-owning white men. In cultural terms, liberals strongly distrusted the traditional sources of authority, particularly the Roman Catholic Church, which they thought infested by superstition, ignorance, and empty ritual. The famous French liberal Voltaire summed up their attitude in his phrase against superstition: "écrasez l'infâme," which loosely translated means "crush the infamous thing!"

The writings of Voltaire, Jean-Jacques Rousseau, and other influential French liberals were banned from colonial Latin America. Nonetheless, Latin American liberals read them, took them to heart, and after the break with Spain and Portugal, attempted to implement them. Civil wars between political parties or factions that called themselves Liberals and Conservatives became commonplace. Invariably, the Church allied itself with the Conservatives, who made defense of the Church their rallying cry. Versions of this conflict played out in every Latin American country as the age of the caudillo faded away in the 1850s and 1860s. In most places, the Liberals were triumphant by the 1870s, ushering in a wave of modernization across the region.

In Mexico, where the tensions created by the Liberal-Conservative split were unrivalled in their intensity, this period of liberal activism is known simply as La Reforma. It was a period dominated by the great liberal leader (and Zapotec lawyer) Benito Juárez. Juárez, who served as President of Mexico for multiple terms in this period, established tough new laws curbing the power of the Church. In the 1860s, Juárez also led the opposition to the French invasion force that, with the assistance of Mexican conservatives, created a short-lived Mexican empire under the authority of an Austrian prince named Maximilian.

As students will see in this chapter, Mexico was not alone in experiencing the struggle between Latin American liberals and the Catholic Church (and their conservative supporters). By the end of this chapter, students should be able to describe the liberal diagnosis of the problems they saw in society, as well as the prescriptions they advocated for fixing those problems.

QUESTIONS FOR ANALYSIS

1. What were the goals of nineteenth-century Latin American liberals? What did they want to accomplish?
2. How did liberalism threaten the Church's interests, both material and spiritual, in Latin America?
3. What were the long-term effects of the conflict between liberalism and the Church? How might the conflict have affected the region's subsequent development?

1. A New Generation of Liberals ~ Frank Safford*

The first generation of Latin American liberals failed in their attempts to uproot three centuries of colonialism in a single decade. But beginning around the 1840s, a new generation of liberals, newly born in the independent republics of Spanish America, arrived on the scene. This generation, many of whom were extremely militant in their opposition to the colonial past, was more successful. In this selection, historian Frank Safford explains some of the chief characteristics of this new generation of liberals, focusing on their class and geographical origins, their precarious electoral alliance with urban artisans, and their connection to political and intellectual currents emanating from mid-nineteenth-century Europe. In Safford's view, this generation was consciously completing the mission begun by the previous one.

In the 1840s, a new generation of politicians emerged, challenging the persons and policies of those who had held power since the end of the 1820s. Most Spanish American countries had been ruled by the same generation that had made independence. In Mexico, Peru, Venezuela, and New Granada presidential power seemed to be the monopoly of the military heroes of Independence, with civilian elites of the same generation collaborating in the organization of politics and the management of government. Men born at the eve of independence, particularly civilians, had cause to wonder when their time might come. Tulio Halperín Donghi has suggested that the fiscal penury endured by almost all Spanish

*From Frank Safford, "Politics, Ideology, and Society," in *Spanish America after Independence, c. 1820–c. 1870,* ed. Leslie Bethell, 91–97 (New York: Cambridge University Press, 1987). © 1987 Cambridge University Press. Reprinted by permission of Cambridge University Press.

American governments limited their capacity to absorb the younger generations into public posts. Whatever the reason, the fact is that in the 1840s the younger generation began, in many places quite consciously, to challenge the existing political establishment which in some places, it should be said, had lost its will or ability to dominate. In Venezuela, by 1844, General Carlos Soublette, who currently governed for the Venezuelan oligarchy, calmly tolerated the mobilization of university students (including two of his sons) in opposition, making little effort to generate support for the established system. In Mexico, disastrous defeat in war with the United States (1846–48) undermined the authority of established politicians in all the major factions and filled the new generation with a sense of the urgency of taking radical measures in order to form a strong, modern state. In New Granada in 1848–49, the government party split, thus opening the way for challenge by a new generation. In Chile, the political system also began to show signs of wear as elements in the governing party began to break away in opposition to President Manuel Montt, thus encouraging a series of liberal rebellions in the 1850s.

Although the political dynamic of the period may be seen as a challenge from a new age group within the upper social sectors, the struggle also had a class aspect in some places. Historians of the *Reforma* period in Mexico (1855–76) consider many of the liberal protagonists of this struggle to have been a "new" generation not merely in the sense of age but also in that of social origin. The new liberal generation that emerged in the 1840s is described as typically composed of mostly ambitious provincials whose social mobility was made possible by the expansion of secondary education during the early Independence period. A similar generalization might be made about New Granada and, to a lesser degree, Peru and Chile. Young men of such social origins had particular reason to challenge the monopoly of power by established groups and to wish to destroy those remnants of colonial institutions that tended to block social mobility.

The emerging generation of upper-sector politicians, seeking to develop its own sense of political identity as against the older generation, was receptive to new European influences that had little appeal to the already formed, established politicians. The impact of these new external influences, along with the dynamic of intergenerational tensions, helped to polarize politics from the middle of the 1840s until 1870, by which time the new generation was thoroughly dominant.

The European political events and ideological currents influencing the new generation varied depending upon local political conditions. In much of Spanish America the powers and privileges of the Church remained a central, and unresolved, problem. Consequently, agitation in France over ecclesiastical issues in the 1830s and 1840s influenced some of these countries after 1845, most particularly Mexico, New Granada, Chile, and Peru. The attacks of [Jules] Michelet and [Edgar] Quinet on the role of the Church in higher education in the 1840s and their book assailing the Jesuits had an impact upon young democrats like Francisco Bilbao (1823–65) in Chile and also served to inflame antagonism toward the Jesuits among the younger generation in New Granada.

In Buenos Aires and Montevideo, where many of the Church's powers and privileges had already been stripped away before 1835, religio-political controversies in Europe were of relatively little concern to young intellectuals. [Giuseppe] Mazzini's Young Italy, however, had a notable influence among the dissident youth of the Rio de la Plata region; one of their intellectual leaders, Esteban Echeverría, for example, proclaimed a Young Argentina. Echeverría and his associates also found some interest in French Socialism, particularly in Saint-Simonian currents. This was much less true in other parts of Spanish America, at least until the European Revolution of 1848.

The inflammation of Church–State issues between 1845 and 1870 in some Spanish American republics, and the new, more fervent spirit with which civilian politicians approached these issues, derived in part from the influence of [Félicité de] Lamennais. His criticism of the Church as a political establishment concerned primarily with money, power, and dignities, and his advocacy of a primitive, popular, extra-ecclesiastical Christianity, inspired many in the new generation. He provided them with a rhetoric with which to attack the established Church as part of the old, oppressive order while claiming adherence to a purer democratic Christianity. His insistence upon the separation of religion and politics, and therefore upon the separation of Church and State, found echo in Mexico, New Granada, Peru, and Chile. His strongly democratic spirit, with his support of a wide extension of the suffrage, also encouraged the democratic enthusiasms of the new generation, just as his call for administrative decentralization reinforced the federalist political currents in Spanish America. Lamennais's influence, perhaps more than any other, demarcates the generation of the 1840s from its predecessors, who for the most part ignored him. Undoubtedly, Lamennais, like Mazzini, had a special appeal for the younger generation in symbolizing rebellion against established authority.

The European Revolution of 1848 both drew attention to, and crystallized the influence of, utopian Socialist ideas in Spanish America. Shortly after the European revolutions began, aspiring young politicians, influenced by European example, began to reach out to elements in the urban underclasses—and principally to the artisan class, not the very poorest—in an effort to mobilize them politically.

The Revolution of 1848 was greeted enthusiastically in New Granada, Peru, and Chile, where the new generation had to contend with established government groups that could be viewed as essentially elitist and where, consequently, democratic revolution appealed as a means of political change. In the Rio de la Plata, however, the dictatorship of Juan Manuel de Rosas in Buenos Aires, like the regimes of lesser caudillos in the provinces, had enjoyed widespread support from the popular classes. In the Plata, therefore, younger intellectual politicians tended to take a more negative view of democratic revolution. In exile in Chile in the 1840s, Domingo Faustino Sarmiento and Juan Bautista Alberdi, even before the European revolutions, expressed the belief that popular sovereignty, in the hands of an ignorant mass, would inevitably lead to dictatorship. While Francisco Bilbao and others in the new generation of Chileans attacked their government as elitist, their Argentine contemporaries resident in Chile defended the existing regime as the rule of an enlightened minority, far preferable to the tyranny produced in Argentina by a barbarous majority. The Revolution of 1848, with the subsequent election of Louis Napoleon, served to confirm Sarmiento and Alberdi in their distrust of democracy, at least in countries where the large majority was illiterate. Thus, whereas in parts of Spanish America the new generations tended to a democratic rhetoric (not necessarily democratic practice) even after they became ascendant between 1850 and 1870, in Argentina after the overthrow of Rosas in 1852 the newly dominant intellectual elite tended to have a more conservative view of political democracy.

The new generation of liberal politicians that emerged in the 1840s in many respects pursued the same tendencies as their political progenitors, the liberal reformers of the 1820s. But they did so with a new spirit and intensity, in the belief that the earlier generation had failed in its mission to liberalize Spanish American society. Like the liberals of the 1820s, the reformers of 1845–70 affirmed essentially individualist conceptions of state, society, and economy. Like their predecessors, they were libertarian constitutionalists, in belief if not in behavior. But they tended to be more absolute in their individualism, more fervent in their libertarian rhetoric. The called not merely for individual freedoms but for an absolute freedom of conscience, of the press, of education, and of commerce—in New Granada even to the extent of sanctioning an absolute freedom of commerce in arms. They called not merely for trial by jury and the abolition of the death penalty but also for constitutional recognition of the right to insurrection. To safeguard these individual freedoms liberals in Mexico, New Granada, and Venezuela recommitted themselves to the ideal of federalism looking to the United States as a model, and they resurrected plans of 1825–35 to limit the size of the army and to establish citizens' national guards.

In economic and social policy also the mid-century reformers rededicated themselves to liberal individualism and the ideal of legal equality, both of which they felt had been compromised by their predecessors. They sought to rationalize their countries' economies in accord with nineteenth-century liberal conceptions. This meant abolishing enterprise-constricting taxes that had been allowed to hang on from the colonial period, such as the *alcabala* (sales tax), the tithe, and government monopolies. At least during the 1850s they rather dogmatically opposed government intervention in the economy, whether in the form of public enterprise, the extension of monopoly privileges to private enterprise, or protectionist tariffs. Their affirmation of the ideal of legal equality meant the elimination of the juridical privileges of the Church and the military. They also sought the fulfillment of legal equality, as well as of individualist social conceptions, through the abolition of slavery and the incorporation of Indian communities into the dominant, capitalistic, European society. The new generation of reformists recognized that these were themes pursued by the earlier liberals of the 1820s. But they believed that the earlier generation had taken only the first tentative steps toward a necessary elimination of colonial structures. They saw themselves as carrying out a political, economic, and social revolution that would bring to completion the movement that had begun in 1810, but had been betrayed during the 1830s.

2. Liberalism as Anticlericalism ⁓ Helen Delpar*

In nineteenth-century Latin America, as in most places, liberalism was strongly associated with anticlericalism. Anticlericalism was based on the idea that the clergy (especially prelates who ran the administrative offices of the church) were preventing social progress in areas such as public education and economic development. In this selection, historian Helen Delpar views Colombian liberals and conservatives largely in terms of clericalism and anticlericalism. She provides details on the types of laws and policies that liberals adopted when they took office and the reactions that such laws and policies drew from conservatives. She is also careful to point out the divisions within the Liberal Party on just how far anticlericalism could be pushed.

To ensure the proper functioning of republican institutions, most Liberals thought that three conditions were necessary. The first of these was cessation of the political disorders that had ravaged the nation since independence. Although they continued to be concerned about this problem, Liberals were optimistic about an eventual reign of peace once the two other conditions had been realized: an enlightened citizenry and economic prosperity. An editorial entitled "Needs of the Country" in 1866, for example, stressed the importance of improving primary education and hoped that at least two schools could be established in each district. "Free education for the masses—this is the motto of the true patriot and the sincere republican. Only an ignorant people can be deceived; only a brutish people can be made the victim of despotism." President [Eustaquio] Salgar expressed a similar opinion while congratulating the Chamber of Representatives for appropriating $100,000 for the establishment of normal schools in 1870. Emphasizing the relationship between democracy and education, he declared that the former did not exist in Latin America. Instead, more or less well-educated minorities managed

*From Helen Delpar, *Red against Blue: The Liberal Party in Colombian Politics, 1863–1899* (Tuscaloosa: University of Alabama Press, 1981), 68–70, 78–80. © 1981 the University of Alabama Press. Reprinted with permission of the University of Alabama Press.

affairs as they saw fit while the great majority of workers and taxpayers, who lived in rural areas, bore all the burdens of the republic but received none of its benefits. What was the point, he asked, of guaranteeing freedom and individual rights if the citizens were too ignorant to be aware of their existence?

In the opinion of Liberals, the expansion of public education was but one aspect of the struggle against ignorance. If it was to be truly successful, the hold of the clergy on the masses also had to be reduced. Liberals invariably emphasized, however, that they were not antagonistic to religion itself but to the political activity of some members of the Roman Catholic clergy and to their efforts to hinder the intellectual and spiritual enlightenment of the Colombian people. An apologist for the anticlerical policies of the mid-1870s explained: "Colombian Liberalism, far from being hostile to the true religious spirit, draws inspiration from it and seeks its protection, for it knows that freedom is in essence of divine origin and that it appears, grows, and produces its fruits only among people in whom conscience—that is, moral sense—is allowed to develop fully and with complete guarantees."

Liberal leaders varied greatly in their personal religious convictions. Eustaquio Salgar and Santiago Pérez, for example, were said to be practicing Catholics. When the latter was nominated for the presidency in 1873, Medardo Rivas declared that his only blemish was the fact that he attended Mass; Rivas conceded, however, that this was a purely private act that in no way rendered Pérez unfit for the presidency. Miguel Samper has been described as a convinced Christian who became a practicing Catholic toward the end of his life. Many other Liberal leaders, however, were probably free-thinkers who, like Teodoro Valenzuela, believed that the universe is governed by a supreme intelligence; organized religion had a social value, he felt, but was otherwise meaningless.

Regardless of their personal beliefs, Liberal leaders could generally be divided into two camps with respect to religious issues. On the one hand were those who thought that the government should take an active role in extirpating clerical influence, both temporal and spiritual, and that in order to do so it should be invested with powers similar to those enjoyed by the Spanish crown in the colonial era. On the other were those who might deplore the power of the clergy but believed that extreme anticlericalism was not only futile but violated Liberal principles as well. Liberals of this school were likely to regard separation of church and state as the best solution for the religious question. This was the position of Salvador Camacho Roldán, who wrote in 1878: "What we seek in this country is not the repression of the Catholic idea but the complete emancipation of human thought, and this requires liberty for Catholics and non-Catholics, for those who believe and those who do not."

Liberal attitudes toward the Church were shaped not only by ideological considerations but also by Conservative exploitation of clerical grievances for political ends and by Liberal suspicions about the subversive designs of the clergy, which were strengthened by the condemnation of liberalism by Pope Pius IX in 1864 and by the proclamation of the dogma of papal infallibility six years later. As a result, even Liberals who favored separation of church and state at times became alarmed by the possibility of a clerical-Conservative alliance to drive them from power. In 1874 an editorialist in the *Diario de Cundinamarca* warned that if the Conservatives attempted to use religion for partisan purposes, the Liberal party would react energetically "to annihilate completely" the political power of the clergy.

The differences between these various points of view were never fully resolved while the Liberals were in power. Although separation of church and state had been decreed in 1853, the Liberal constitution empowered the federal and state governments to exercise the right of inspection over religious cults, and the law of 23 April 1863 required of all clergymen, on pain of banishment from Colombia, that they swear to obey the constitutions, laws, and authorities of the nation and the states. By 1864, however, the belief that this law was unduly harsh and vindictive had become sufficiently widespread among Liberals to permit its substitution by a milder measure (17 May 1864), which required the oath of obedience only from prelates. In addition, Manuel Murillo, who took office as president on 10 April 1864, made a conciliatory gesture by lifting the sentence of banishment decreed in 1861 against the archbishop of Bogotá, Antonio Herrán, provided he took the required oath.

Relations between the federal government and the Church again deteriorated during the presidential term of Tomás Mosquera (1866–67), but after his deposition the 1864 law was repealed. This meant that in the future, relations between church and state would be governed only by the general dispositions in the constitution. In the following years tension between the Church and the federal government was at a relatively low ebb, but became increasingly severe after 1870, mainly because of clerical opposition to the educational program launched by the Salgar administration in that year. After the Conservative revolution of 1876–77, which was openly supported by some clergymen, the "hard line" temporarily gained ascendancy, winning adherents even among Liberals who had previously eschewed extreme anti-clericalism.

Colombian Conservatives were no more uniform or consistent in their thinking than Liberals, but there were several principles basic to Conservative ideology that set them apart from Liberals. The first of these principles was a belief in the universality and infallibility of the precepts of Christianity. Secondly, Conservatives regarded the Catholic Church as the sole depository and interpreter of the divine truths of Christianity. Thirdly, they considered the Conservative party as the political agency by which the teachings of Christ and the interests of the Church might best be protected and advanced in Colombia. For both clergymen and Conservatives, this last proposition occasionally raised dilemmas that could not always be satisfactorily resolved: for the clergy, the extent to which party leaders should be encouraged to act as spokesmen for the interests of the Church, and for the Conservatives, the extent to which the interests of the party were identical with those of the Church.

Conservatives also tended to feel that Catholicism and by extension the entire fabric of society were gravely menaced by Liberalism, which, by asserting that the mind is shaped only by sensory experiences, repudiated the concept of divine will as the source of human nature and institutions. The Conservative newspaper *La América* declared in 1874 that Catholic morality was the basis of its doctrine. The editorial continued:

> Today Liberalism aims to establish a school of negation [and] seeks utility or sensationalism as [the basis of] morality, and this is where the true division between the parties lies. It is natural that we who raise as a moral banner the one left to us in the Gospel by the Son of God should form ranks around the Church which received it. Those who seek in pleasure or pain the norm for their actions are the enemies of this Church, and therefore in every political question a religious question is involved.

Convictions such as these frequently led Conservatives to assert that a Catholic could not be a Liberal. Thus a Medellín newspaper stated in 1875: "the doctrinaire Liberal party is anti-Catholic, and . . . no Catholic can vote for any of its members without betraying his conscience."

The association between Catholicism and Conservatism remained close. In fact, on occasion Conservatives did not hesitate to censure publicly clerics whom they considered lukewarm in the struggle against Liberalism. One such incident in 1873—involving the archbishop of Bogotá—led to a decision of the Second Provincial Council of Colombian bishops that Catholic writers should not anticipate the judgment of the hierarchy on any issue related to the Church and that they were to submit to the authority of the prelates should they disagree with them. To Miguel Antonio Caro, this ruling meant the imposition of "shackles" on Catholic writers.

Conservatives had no difficulty in accepting republican government, though they assigned a much higher priority than the Liberals to the maintenance of order and were uncomfortable with the extensive liberties enshrined in the 1863 constitution. While they affirmed the right of all citizens to equality of treatment before the law, they were likely to express hostility to those who condemned economic inequality. On 9 July 1848, for example, *El Nacional* of Bogotá declared that the achievement of de facto equality (as opposed to legal equality) would be the equivalent of robbery, for it meant elevating the lazy to the rank of the worker. Later, in the aftermath of the Paris Commune, *La Sociedad* of Medellín condemned "socialist equality," which it said was engendered by envy and based on injustice. "Its purpose is to level the human race, reducing all that is outstanding until it descends to the lowest, meanest, and most brutish level in society." This kind of equality, the newspaper asserted, was totally incompatible with Christian equality, which rested on the oneness of the "human race and the universality of God's moral law."

---

3. The Postcolonial Church ~ John Lynch*

In this survey of the postcolonial church in Latin America, historian John Lynch examines the problem of liberalism from the Church's point of view. He finds that the Church's chief concern was not the devotion of the poor masses but rather the faithfulness of the new states' ruling elites. Lynch also describes how the principal nineteenth-century leader of the Roman Catholic Church, Pope Pius IX, reacted to the challenge of liberalism with his famous Syllabus of Errors *(1864), a document that provided conservatives in Latin America and elsewhere with guidelines for dealing with the liberal challenge.*

The Church in Latin America after independence bore the marks of its Iberian and colonial past. From Spain, Catholics inherited a tradition of strong faith, a basic doctrinal knowledge, and an enduring piety. Observance itself was a medium of knowledge, for in the Mass, the Litanies, and the Rosary the people learned the doctrines, the Scriptures, and the mysteries of the Catholic faith. Portugal too transmitted an orthodox Catholicism, but with less doctrinal knowledge and a lower degree of observance. Everywhere, religion in Latin America was a religion of the people, and the Church continued to receive the adherence and the respect of the Indians, *mestizos*, and other popular sectors. Ruling groups were less committed, and the great fear of the Church in the nineteenth century was the apostasy of the elites, not the desertion of the masses. The Iberian tradition in religion favored a privileged and a state-controlled Church. After independence, however, the wealth, influence, and privileges of the Church were viewed by the new states as a rival focus of allegiance, an alternative power, and a source of revenue. The threat of state control appeared in a new form. The Church had to look to its own resources—and these in the early nineteenth century were diminishing.

Independence administered a great shock to the Church. To many it was the end of an epoch, the collapse of an entire world, the triumph of reason over faith. If Iberian power was broken, could the Catholic Church survive? Independence exposed the colonial roots of the Church and revealed its foreign origins. Independence also divided the Church. While some of the clergy were royalists, many were republicans, a few were insurgents, and most were influential in encouraging mass

---

*From John Lynch, "The Catholic Church," in *Latin America: Economy and Society, 1870–1930*, ed. Leslie Bethell, 301–70 (New York: Cambridge University Press, 1989), 301–5, 315–17. © 1989 Cambridge University Press. Reprinted by permission of Cambridge University Press.

support for the new order once the last battle had been won. The hierarchy was less divided by independence, but its unity was hardly a source of strength. A few bishops accepted the revolution. The majority rejected it and remained loyal to the crown. They might justify themselves in religious terms but they could not disguise the fact that they were Spaniards, identified themselves with Spain, and had, in effect, abandoned the American Church. From Rome they received little guidance. The papacy, pressed by Spain and the Holy Alliance, refused to recognize Latin American independence. This was a political error, the fruit of human judgment and not of Church doctrine. But it was a costly error, and when the irrevocability of independence and the need to fill vacant sees forced the papacy, from 1835, to recognize the new governments, great damage had been done.

The Church moved from Spain and Portugal to Rome in the nineteenth century, from Iberian religion to universal religion. While this avoided the emergence of national churches, it did not remove the threat of state control of the Church. The *patronato* (*padroado* in Brazil), the royal right to appoint Church officials, was now claimed by the national governments and placed in the hands of liberal and agnostic politicians.

Yet the Church survived, its mission defended if inert, its assets real if diminished, its offices intact if often unfilled. This was not a Church in decline, and, if it was temporarily weak, the state was weaker. Here was a paradox and a problem. In the aftermath of independence the Church was more stable, more popular, and apparently more wealthy than the state. The state reacted by seeking to control and to tax the Church and to restore the balance in its own favor. After a period of relatively conservative government in Spanish America, from 1830 to 1850, the advent of the liberal state heralded a more basic rupture with the past and with the Church. The principle behind liberal policy was individualism, a belief that the new states of Latin America could only make progress if the individual were freed from the prejudice of the past, from corporate constraints and privilege, privilege which in the case of the Church was accompanied by wealth in real estate and income from annuities. These gave the Church political power, retarded the economy, and stood in the way of social change. The Church was thus seen as a rival to the state, a focus of sovereignty which should belong to the nation alone. These assertions were not necessarily true, but they were the liberal perceptions of the time. And liberalism represented interests as well as principles. In Mexico, for example, where typical mid-century liberals were young upwardly mobile professionals, these considered the Church as a major obstacle not only to nation-building but also to their own economic and social ambitions.

The post-colonial Church, therefore, encountered from specific social groups a hostility which it had never experienced before. For the first time in its history, in the period 1850–80, the Latin American Church acquired enemies who hated it with an intensity born of frustrated conviction. It is true that not all liberals shared these convictions. Some were simply seeking to reform the state, to constitute the rule of law for all, and to modernize the economy. None of these objects were necessarily a threat to religion. But more radical liberals went beyond an attempt to establish the appropriate autonomy of the state: they favored an all-out attack on the Church's wealth, privileges, and institutions, for they believed that without the destruction of ecclesiastical power and the death of its accompanying dogma no real change could be made. So secularization in the nineteenth century took various forms and drew various responses, some of them violent. The battle was fought over the right to appoint bishops, over ownership of property, over the legal and political sanctions of religion, and over education. And secularism had a social base, among the elite or those aspiring to the elite. The masses, it seemed, preferred their ancient beliefs.

In reaction the Church sought allies where it could. Throughout Latin America Catholic political thought became more conservative in the mid–nineteenth century. Churchmen aligned themselves with civilian conservatives in the belief that religion needed a political defense. In turn the dominant ideology of conservatism was Catholicism, and a belief that the alleged irrationality of man created a need for strong government supported by the Church and the sanctions of religion. The conservative political philosophy was not essentially religious but an interest and an ideology. Conservatives believed that without the restraint of religion, people would be turbulent and anarchic, a defense of religion on the grounds not of its truth but of its social utility. The alliance was harmful to the Church, for it placed it among a complex of interests identified as obstacles to change by liberals and Progressives, and it shared in the reverses of its associates.

The doctrinal heritage of Latin American Catholicism was not different from that of the rest of the Church. Bishops and priests received and transmitted traditional Catholic theology and scholastic philosophy. Whatever its past service to religion in reconciling faith and reason, scholasticism had become inert and repetitive. It failed to respond to the ideas of the Enlightenment, and in the nineteenth century Latin American Catholicism did not have the intellectual tools to confront the utilitarians, liberals, and positivists, with the result that the Christian argument went by default. The Bolivian priest Martín Castro complained of the education given in the seminaries and of the dominance of scholasticism "which is rightly banned by modern civilization." The Church relied not on new philosophical expression of religious dogma but on dogmatic restatement of ancient beliefs.

The doctrinal inspiration of the Latin American Church in the nineteenth century came from Rome and standards were set by Pope Pius IX (1846–78), who, in December 1864, published the Encyclical *Quanta Cura*, with its annex, the *Syllabus of Errors*. The Syllabus condemned liberalism, secularism, freedom of thought, and toleration. It specifically condemned lay education and the idea that state schools should be freed from ecclesiastical authority. It condemned the proposition that "in our age it is no longer expedient that the Catholic religion should be regarded as the sole religion of the State to the exclusion of all others," and it condemned, too, the proposition that "the Roman Pontiff can and should reconcile and harmonize himself with progress, liberalism, and recent civilization." The attitude of the papacy, of course, had a philosophical and historical context. The liberalism of the time was seen as an assertion of man's emancipation in relation to God and a deliberate rejection of the primacy of the supernatural. As Rome was bound to deny a rationalist and purely humanist conception of man, so it opposed the political conclusions which liberals drew from this. The papacy, moreover, was itself beleaguered by the Piedmontese government which, as it annexed the papal states, systematically applied a secular regime and imprisoned priests and bishops who opposed it. The *Syllabus* was a defense reflex. Even so, it was a crude and uncompromising compendium.

The *Syllabus* was a weight round religion's neck, a burden which damaged its prospects of peaceful growth in Latin America. Catholic moderates seeking a middle way were embarrassed by its intransigence. Conservative Catholics could appeal to it against moderates. And liberals could cite it as proof of the danger from the Catholic Church. As applied to Latin America the policy of Pius IX can be seen in his reaction to the Peruvian liberal priest, González Vigil, who attacked papal power and advocated a new national and liberal organization for the Church. Pius IX banned his book and excommunicated the author for denying that the Roman Catholic faith was the only true belief, for proclaiming religious toleration, and for preferring clerical marriage to celibacy. Some of these views would have been regarded as heterodox in any age of the Church and were probably unrepresentative of Catholic opinion. The policy of Pius IX, therefore, did not introduce a new or "romanized" faith and morals to Latin America but, after a period of regalism and laxity, defined more clearly doctrines and discipline as they were and asserted the primacy of Rome. It was papal definitions which were new, not papal authority.

What were the instruments of papal influence in Latin America? Ultimately it depended upon the respect of Catholics for the successor of Saint Peter. But it also had a number of more worldly agents. First, Rome sought to retain the nomination or confirmation of bishops, and only those who looked to Rome for authority were considered. In this context it has been remarked that Rome did not always get the bishop it preferred, but it never permitted a bishop it disapproved. A second means of influence was the Catholic media in Latin America; the papal position was propagated in the Catholic press and by individual writers and clerics. A third power base were the seminaries, bastions of orthodoxy, where the faith and morals of future leaders of the Church were formed. In 1858, Pius IX established the Latin American College in Rome, and future graduates of the Gregorian University would return to Latin America as an ecclesiastical elite. Fourthly, the new religious orders, many emanating from Europe, were key agents of Rome and took modern Catholicism to the length and breadth of the subcontinent. Finally, the Holy See had its own representatives in Latin America, though its diplomatic presence was not consistently strong.

---

4. Generational Warrior ⁓ Francisco Bilbao*

This selection is composed of three related primary source documents from mid-nineteenth-century Chile. The first is an abridgment of an essay published in the Santiago magazine The Dawn *on June 1, 1844. Its author, twenty-one-year-old Francisco Bilbao, was a university student and a member of one of the country's most prominent liberal families. His essay "Chilean Sociability," which aimed at inspiring his fellow students to become agents of revolutionary change, was deeply critical of the Church's influence on Chilean social development. It also owed a great intellectual debt to the French Catholic socialist Félicité de Lamennais. The next document is the government prosecutor's indictment of Bilbao's essay on the charges of blasphemy, immorality, and sedition. It reveals the Church's power to drive state action as well as the Chilean Church's rigid religious orthodoxy of the 1840s (notice especially the government's reaction to Bilbao's "immoral" views on marriage). The final document is Bilbao's defense of his essay, which he presented at the jury trial that was convened to hear the case. His defense argued passionately on behalf of "innovation" and the need to push Chile into the modernity of the nineteenth century. Bilbao was found guilty of blasphemy and immorality (but not sedition) and forced to leave the country or face imprisonment. Within a month he was on his way to Paris, where he witnessed the Revolution of 1848. He returned to Chile in 1850 and tried to start a revolution of his own.*

"Chilean Sociability" by Francisco Bilbao

S pain is our past.
     Spain is the Middle Ages. The soul and body of the Middle Ages are composed of Catholicism and feudalism.

We look to the peculiar characteristics of Spain to see our own character.

The Middle Ages were completed in Spain, that is to say, they achieved their full development in the Catholic domination of Spain.

America came from Spain and carries her stamp; the Spanish past on American soil brings us to Chile.

Let us quickly review the relations that the Catholic Church sanctions with regard to the state, the customs, and the philosophy of the time in which we live.

---

*Adapted from Pedro Pablo Figueroa, ed., *Obras completes de Francisco Bilbao*, 2 vols. (Santiago, Chile: El Correo, 1897), 1:11–19, 28–31, 51–55, 59–61, 81 (trans. James A. Wood).

There is no doubt that Christianity was a major advance in the religious rehabilitation of men; but Catholicism, which is oriental and reactionary with regard to symbolism and formula, reacted with hostility to the primitive purity of the doctrine of Jesus.

Under Catholicism, women are subordinated to their husbands. The result is the slavery of women. Paul, the primary founder of Catholicism, did not follow the moral religion of Jesus Christ. Jesus emancipated women. Paul subordinated them. Jesus was Western in his spirit, that is to say, liberal. Paul was oriental and authoritarian. Jesus founded a democratic religion, Paul an ecclesiastical aristocracy. From there originates the logical consequence of the slavery of women. Jesus introduced matrimonial democracy, that is to say, the equality of spouses. Paul put *authority* and the inequality of privilege in its place, in favor of the strongest, in favor of men.

Matrimonial inequality is one of the most outdated aspects of the elaboration of our customs and laws. Incessant adultery, the sentinel that announces the imperfection of our laws, is a protest against the poor organization of marriage. France is at the head of this protest, George Sand* at the head of France. She is the priestess who sacrifices herself, but her prophetic visions signal the dawn of the regeneration of matrimony.

When children are irremediably subordinated to fathers, the result is the slavery of children. This principle is of great importance in Catholic logic. In the family, the father, the elder, the old man is the authority; the power he possesses is absolute. Political laws can limit this power. Because we recognize the authority of individual reason in *every* individual, despotism is illegitimate; the child is his own person, whose liberty is sacred.

When individuals are subordinated to authority, the result is the slavery of citizens. "Obey the authorities," says Saint Paul. A diplomatic principle in origin, it began so as to avoid the persecution of pagan authorities and was converted later into an active instrument of subjugation. This also explains the union that has almost always existed between the clergy and the Catholic monarchies. Monarchy is a government of divine or heroic *tradition*, of privilege or authority; of course it needs the aid of religion. The clergy dominate individual citizens and obstruct free analysis and free thought, which are the enemies of tradition. The clergy, for its part, needs the aid of earthly power for the creation and maintenance of its private interests, for the persecution of heresy. How clearly the logic of the French Revolution appears now. The people, free individuals, free analysis, the present cut loose from the past. Bury the monarchy, the clergy, and the nobility; bury the Catholic synthesis of the past.

---

*George Sand was the pen name of a female novelist in nineteenth-century France known for her criticism of traditional social institutions such as marriage.

When thought is chained to the text and intelligence molded by beliefs the result is slavery of the mind. Education, logically, was entrusted to the convents. This also explains the predominance of Aristotle in the Middle Ages. Aristotle was logic then. One could only deduce from given principles.

What was the culmination of the eighteenth-century revolution and of the American* revolution? The liberty of men, the equality of citizens, individuals vindicated in all their rights, and the applications of those rights. The recognition of the equality of man's origins, both in means and ends. The individual, as a man, asks for the freedom of thought, where the freedom of religion is born. The individual, as a free spirit, exposed to both good and evil, needs *education* in order to recognize good. The individual, as a *human being*, body and soul, needs *property* in order to fulfill his purpose in life. He needs property to develop his intellectual life, his physical life, and the lives of his children. Thus he needs the necessary conditions to acquire property, and to acquire it in a complete manner, as it is owed to him. Here the destruction of privilege and feudalism is born, as well as the raising of wages to a measure that raises human dignity.

The inescapable point of departure, the foundation of all human systems, is *the equality of liberty.*

It is the Paradise from which we were dispossessed, the infiniteness of human greatness, the kingdom of heaven on earth.

The equality of liberty is a universal religion; it is the government of humanity; it is the future unity.

Indictment of Bilbao's "Chilean Sociability"

The interim prosecutor of the Court of Appeals, having seen issue number two of the periodical titled *The Dawn*, states: everything written under the title "Chilean Sociability" suffers from the odious stain of blasphemy, immorality, and sedition in the third degree in the view of this Ministry.

As the present indictment deals principally with this printed work, this Ministry feels it is necessary to enter into a meticulous analysis and a listing of the particulars of the passages that contain the crimes mentioned above.

In talking about the depredations of the feudal lords and the ferocity with which they took the lives of other men, the author refers to those who suffered punishment under that system, as expressed in this manner: "Desperation grows, but the Catholic priest says there is nothing but misery in this world. All power comes from God [say the priests], submit yourselves to his power. This is the glorification of slavery."

---

*"American" is used here in the hemispheric sense of the word.

Next the author analyzes the symbol of the Catholic faith in a manner that attacks and ridicules all aspects of the religious dogma of the State.

He goes further, and in manifesting his audacity in combating the most sacred institutions, he questions the principles of the Christian religion, the doctrines of the wise apostle of the people, Saint Paul:

> Under Catholicism, women are subordinated to their husbands. The result is the slavery of women. Paul, the primary founder of Catholicism, did not follow the moral religion of Jesus Christ. Jesus emancipated women. Paul subordinated them. Jesus was Western in his spirit, that is to say, liberal. Paul was oriental and authoritarian. Jesus founded a democratic religion, Paul an ecclesiastical aristocracy. From there originates the logical consequence of the slavery of women. Jesus introduced matrimonial democracy, that is to say, the equality of spouses. Paul put *authority* and the inequality of privilege in its place, in favor of the strongest, in favor of men.

Of the principles cited in the paragraph above, Bilbao infers vices in the marriages celebrated under the Catholic rite, and from that point in the article he becomes immoral, as well as blasphemous.

Speaking of marriage he says: "Matrimonial inequality is one of the most outdated aspects of the elaboration of our customs and laws. Incessant adultery, the sentinel that announces the imperfection of our laws, is a protest against the poor organization of marriage."

After reproaching the system of marital indissolubility he says that the Catholic rites affirming arranged marriages impede the spontaneity and liberty of the heart. These rites are maintained to give protection to the privileged classes and so that authority and tradition are not weakened.

From the tradition of arranged marriages, he says, are born misanthropic isolation, and the system of life that he explains in these terms:

> The passion of youth is silenced. Such exalted passion is an instrument of instinctive revolution. It is taken to church, dressed in black, its face hidden from the street, not allowed to say hello, to look to its side. It is kept on its knees, told to mortify its flesh, and, what is more, the confessor examines its conscience, and imposes an authority on it that cannot be appealed. The chorus of old men carries on with the litany of the dangers of fashion, of contact with visitors, of dress, of glances and words. One ponders the monastic life, the stupid mysticism of God's acceptance of physical suffering. This is youth. What of the young man who comes home late, who listens to amorous words? Pity on him who is caught reading a banned book; in sum, on he who goes out, dances, falls in love! The father's whip and eternal condemnation are anathema. There is no rationality between fathers and sons. After work the son will go to pray the rosary, pass along the sacred path, go to the school of Christ, to hear stories about witches, spirits, and purgatories. Imagine a young man of robust constitution, of good health, of ardent imagination, under the weight of that mountain of worries.

Not content at having committed the crimes of blasphemy and immorality, the author concludes his work with sedition.

He complains that the Executive Power will not change the State religion by allowing religious pluralism, thus destroying a fundamental law:

> The Constitution, which organized the Republic in this despotic, unitary mode, is what rules us. The code that legally organized despotism, destroying all the guarantees that republicanism had conquered, still exists. Ecclesiastical organization exercises an influential power that is separate from its political influence. The Catholic system reigns without limits. The priest still collects the tithe, the priest still sells marriages and baptisms. Ecclesiastical power has an imposing pension fund that the government tolerates. The government is hypocritical.

It is under the authority of Your Honors to proceed with the arrangements to affect a judgment on the present indictment.

Bilbao's Defense of "Chilean Sociability"

Society has been shaken to its core. From its profound disturbance we have come today to the surface: you, Mr. Prosecutor, the accuser; I, the accused.

The place in which we find ourselves and the accusation made against me reveal the state in which we find our institutions and ideas.

The prosecutor is trying to cover himself with the dust of Spanish laws. The jury can remove that dust with its breath.

A hand appears trying to uphold fourteen collapsing centuries, in order to destroy a face baptized in the rising dawn.

The hand belongs to you, Mr. Prosecutor; the face is mine.

Yours is the mouth through which fading subterranean echoes denounce me; I am the conscience that faces its anathema.

We have two names, accuser and accused, two names brought together by historic fate that will live on in the history of my country.

Some day we will see, Mr. Prosecutor, which of the two will have the blessings of posterity. Now then, which one of us is right to rejoice before our fellow men? History will tell us.

History always shows innovators as idols; reactionaries it paints as the snake that bites the traveler's shoe along the side of the road.

Which one of us is right to rejoice before the divinity? History, which teaches us the laws that God has imposed on humanity, will also tell us. These are the laws of innovation and disintegration.

To oppose the development of these laws I find difficult to understand. Now then, Mr. Prosecutor, you call me a blasphemer: I, who obey and try to follow the laws. But those who call on authority for help in slowing the march of innovation, I do not call them blasphemous—I call them ignorant!

I have always felt the activity of my conscience, and the reasoned application of that activity has always tormented my human existence.

Study and observation have showed me the law of duty. With my thoughts submerged in the investigation of the human mission, I found myself awakening in the nineteenth century, and in Chile, my homeland.

In my beliefs I wanted (call me foolish if you want) to take this country I love so much in my weak hands, and give it the push that the present century dictates to me—I wanted, in the audacity of my journey, to thrust the Chilean flag into the vanguard of humanity—but a hand subdued me; with its touch, it reminded me of the reality that I wanted to remove, and tried to crush me, accumulating anathema after anathema. That hand is yours, Mr. Prosecutor. Here you have me, then, before the jury, soon to be sentenced as a dangerous innovator.

I have acquired a great reputation for protecting liberty and I have sought to broaden the minds of my fellow men by giving them that understanding with its social consequences. I have cried with the tears of the people for their present state and their gloomy future: I have tried to show them the happy regions of equality. I have obeyed the sacrosanct voice of fraternity, which extinguishes pride and brings humanity together. Your Honors of the Jury, I am not a blasphemer because I love God; I am not immoral because I love and search for the obligation to perfect it; I am not seditious because I want to prevent the exasperation of my oppressed fellow men.

Your Honors of the Jury, I have looked into the grave that opens before me. I have measured the gravestone that rises in front of me and I have come with a peaceful conscience to reflect on a verdict of not guilty or resign myself to the crime of which I am condemned. But I also say, Your Honors of the Jury, that I can already envision the dawning of the day in which my country, motivated by human activity, will look upon me again, its presently lost son, and that illuminating look will imprint my name radiantly on the civilized memory of my country.

5. The Triumph of Reform ~ Justo Sierra*

Justo Sierra was one of the leading intellectuals of Mexican liberalism in the closing decades of the nineteenth century and the beginning decade of the twentieth, by which time the Liberal Parties had taken firm control of the region. A contemporary of the Brazilian abolitionist Joaquim Nabuco, Sierra's mission was not to abolish slavery but to modernize Mexican society, particularly through

---

*From Justo Sierra, *The Political Evolution of the Mexican People*, with notes and a new introduction by Edmundo O'Gorman, prologue by Alfonso Reyes, trans. Charles Ramsdell (Austin: University of Texas Press, 1969), 248–49, 265–66, 272–73, 275–77. © 1969 the University of Texas Press. Reprinted by permission of the University of Texas Press.

the means of public education. Sierra's government service began in the Reform Era of Juárez and ended with the lengthy dictatorship of Porfirio Díaz known as the Porfiriato *(1876–1911). While Sierra was undoubtedly a liberal, his liberalism differed from Bilbao's in its embrace of positivism, a European philosophy of science that emphasized the existence of natural laws of social development. The positivists were also influenced by the English scientists Charles Darwin and Herbert Spencer, who gave them the idea that societies were like social organisms that evolved from simpler to more complex forms of life. In the following selection taken from his classic work,* The Political Evolution of the Mexican People, *published in 1900–1902, Sierra interprets the history of La Reforma. Where do you see evolution at work?*

Mexico has had only two revolutions, that is, two violent accelerations of its evolution. They were results of that forward drive, propelled by the interaction of environment, race, and history, which continually moves a human society to realize an ideal, to improve its condition. This drive, when it collides with external forces, nearly always speeds up, at the risk of provoking formidable reactions; this, then, is a revolution. The first was Independence, emancipation from the motherland, which grew out of the Creoles' conviction that Spain was not able to govern them and that they were well able to govern themselves. This first revolution was triggered by Napoleon's attempt to conquer the Iberian Peninsula. The second revolution was the Reform, which sprang from the profound need for a stable political constitution—that is, a guarantee of liberty, which would be based on a transformation of the social order, on the suppression of the privileged classes, on the equitable distribution of the public wealth (stagnant, for the most part), on the regeneration of labor, and on the creation of a national conscience by means of popular education. This second revolution was triggered by the American invasion,* which exposed the impotence of the privileged classes to save the country and the amorphousness of an organism that could hardly be called a nation. In the perspective of history, the two revolutions are successive phases of a single social movement: the first being emancipation from Spain, the second, emancipation from the colonial system. They were two stages in the creation of a national personality fully aware of itself.

The Reform took its first steps gradually. The reformists went about their task with good sense and determination. They abolished the immunity of the clergy under civil law and barred them from voting in elections. The bishops protested, but too late. They themselves were responsible for their plight. They had not only stood adamantly against all attempts at reform, resisting even the timid efforts of the moderates; they had openly made themselves parcel of a political party and had used every weapon at hand, including money, to serve that

---

*A reference to the U.S. invasion of Mexican territory at the beginning of the Mexican-American War in 1846.

party. During the dictatorship, which the more thoughtful of the clergy did not applaud, the most arrogant of the Church's heads had done everything possible to bring back the supremacy of their class in colonial times, setting themselves athwart the path of intellectual progress, a path whose signposts are freedom of belief and of thought. The liberties that are essential to civilization—and these are the very same ideals that the finest human minds strive eternally to achieve—cannot exist without freedom of conscience, any more than the planetary system can exist without the sun.

There could, therefore, be no truce. The battle was on. The reactionaries put their final trust in civil war, preparing for it openly. If only they could contrive to involve some great Latin nation in their crusade! Spain? A hope. France? A dream.

The debate on the new constitution had barely ended before the infallible voice of the Pope thundered in the ears of Mexican Catholicism, denouncing the entire Reform program and the constitution about to be promulgated.* Raising his pontifical voice with apostolic license in the open Consistory, he condemned as an insult to religion and declared null and void the laws and the constitution and hurled anathemas at those who had obeyed their government. Not a glimmer of hope, not a word of peace, not a hint of compromise with the inevitable. Only the Church's inalienable right to its property and its privileges. And what of God's right to harmony, to love? Never, not even when the Church denied us the right to be independent, had its voice been heard in such harsh accents, so pregnant with death and disaster.

The Constitution [of 1857] was promulgated in the midst of political uproar and was solemnly sworn to by Goméz Farías, patriarch of the Reform, and by all the deputies, and by the President of the Republic, and by the administrative and political chiefs. The bishops, faithful to the commands of Pius IX, lashed out right and left with excommunications, demanding that the oaths be retracted. The result was complete anarchy in the public conscience. The new Constitution was furiously assailed from all sides. As everybody knew, the President himself was averse to it. The Reform party was painfully aware of impending civil war and terrified at the prospect that the President himself might start the conflict.

Liberty and democracy and equality—the abolition of privileges and the establishment of equal suffrage in elections—have nothing to do with nature but are conquests of mankind, of human civilization. They are not natural rights but ideals which the noblest of men strive to attain by changing the structure of the social body, which is the joint creation of nature and of history. No people, however high their culture, have fully succeeded in attaining them. But all peoples, though on different levels of development, are gradually moving upward in the direction of these ideals. An ideal is a force which can change and shape reality. There is an art in making a people aware of the necessity for a change, an art

---

*Sierra refers here to the Mexican Constitution of 1857, which reflected the anticlerical values of the liberals.

which consists in recognizing the ideal that their progress has made them readiest for and in holding it constantly before their eyes.

Now, a new religion, new dogmas, a new faith confronted the old. To the soul's yearning for Heaven, with the Church as guiding light, there was opposed man's longing to conquer the future. Never before, as in this Constitution, had the rights of man been penned so precisely or with such breadth, even though it was taken from other constitutions, including the American (which was poorly understood) and from our own, which, whether federalist or centralist, invariably tried to avert despotism by erecting a fragile barrier of constitutional guarantees. Here, however, each right had its condition, which was tantamount to a guarantee: that is, to the equation between social duty and individual right. The right to life was conditioned by the social duty of justice (for the Constitution recognized that society is a living being capable of rights and duties); and the rights of the accused and of the convicted were minutely defined, man being essentially free, according to theory. Declared unconditionally free was the slave who took refuge in our territory, and this declaration, in the purest tradition of our history, stemming from our own emancipation, amounted to a serenely heroic defiance of the slave-holding United States and Cuba. "All men are free"—this was the theme. Nobody may force a man to do anything without his consent; his liberty is so absolute, he may not even sell himself into slavery; only society itself may oblige him to respect the individual or social rights of others. The Constitution set out, after this general thesis, a bill of rights: freedom to teach, to work, to express opinions and to publish them, to petition, to hold meetings, and so on, together with society's limitations on these rights.

"Equality," so the authors of the Constitution solemnly proclaimed, "is the prevailing law in the Republic." Whereupon all social classes in the Republic became legally extinct. And yet, the exigencies of a revolution required that one class be made—legally—political pariahs: the clergy, who were not allowed to vote. The same exigencies obliged the Congress to forbid the acquisition of landed properties by religious corporations. And these contradictions between stated principles and the ineluctable ends of the revolution afforded the enemies of the Constitution a vantage point from which to attack its works. But the very dispositions that were most severely censured, those relating to the clergy, turned out to be, because of their vital place in the country's evolution, the most significant, the most lasting of all.

V

Race and Nation Building

Beginning in the 1870s and continuing until the Second World War, world history was dominated by a new age of European empire building in Africa and Asia. The expanding core of industrialized societies (mainly in Europe) needed raw materials and markets for their products. What followed was the "Scramble for Africa," the British raj in India, and a wave of imperialism around the world. Unlike most African and Asian countries, Latin America was able to avoid direct European recolonization in the nineteenth century (though there were some exceptions to this rule). Latin Americans, instead, had to deal with the rising power of the United States of America, especially after the Spanish-American War of 1898 confirmed the United States as the most powerful country in the Western hemisphere. While the U.S. armed forces did on many occasions invade and occupy Caribbean and Central American countries in the thirty years following 1898, U.S. government officials and business leaders generally preferred to control their emerging sphere of influence through trade and investment. The British got in on the action, too, greatly expanding their economic power in Latin America in the second half of the 1800s. Thus, while Latin American countries generally held on to their formal sovereignty in this period, that sovereignty was now being undermined by a new set of economic and cultural arrangements. The term historians use to describe the new forms of domination that emerged in this new era of industrial capitalism is neocolonialism.

This chapter explores the cultural dimensions of neocolonialism in Latin American history. As we will see below, the neocolonial system that arose in the late nineteenth century drove Latin American elites (those with the power to shape the states and societies in which they lived) toward the cultural values of modernizing Europe. On one level, this was nothing new; Latin American elites had always been attracted to European culture. Many traveled there as students, touring the great cities of Paris, London, and Rome. This was certainly the case with the young liberator Simón Bolívar and the young Chilean rebel Francisco Bilbao, each of whom was deeply impressed by the European world of ideas. Latin Americans avidly read European literature, followed European fashion, and listened to European music. So when the European scientific establishment claimed to have found scientifically based justifications for racism and white supremacy, Latin Americans heartily embraced that idea, too.

Given their ability to dominate huge areas of the world, European cultural models claimed a privileged place in the minds of elite Latin Americans. One of those models was the form of political and social organization known as the nation-state. The nation-state was just what its name suggests: a single, unified nation of people living within the borders of a sovereign state. While numerous independent Latin American states had been in existence since the 1820s, Latin Americans found it difficult to say that they were part of unified nations. The Latin American desire to emulate Europe thus produced a related aspiration to forge single nations out of the diverse and divided societies that surrounded them. Progress, they believed, depended on it.

Remember that Latin America in the 1800s was a region of extreme racial diversity. In some places, like Cuba, the majority of the population was Afro-Latin. In other places, like Bolivia, the majority was indigenous. Everywhere the mixed-race population (known in the colonial period as the *castas*) was growing. The selections in this chapter will show how the obsession with race made the project of building new Latin American nations extremely complicated, if not impossible.

The culture of neocolonialism was heavily influenced by the teachings of the European social and natural sciences. Who were these new influences? In the natural sciences, the English biologists Charles Darwin and Herbert Spencer stand out. Their explanations of the theory of evolution forever changed the intellectual environment of the modern world. It did not take long for Darwin's dubious successors (known as social Darwinists) to redirect his theory of natural selection of the species to justify the separation of the races. French social psychologist Gustave Le Bon contributed to neocolonial culture by propagating the idea that the character of human societies was the product of the racial traits of those societies. French sociologist Auguste Comte's positivist philosophy added to the mix the notion that human societies evolved through progressive stages of development. Taken together, the new thinking about race posed a dilemma for Latin Americans seeking to unify their own multiracial societies.

Latin American intellectuals, statesmen, and artists found different ways of working out the tensions between race and nation within the overall cultural context established by neocolonialism. One extreme solution to this problem, proposed on more than one occasion, was genocide, the deliberate extermination of people who stood in the way of progress. Another less extreme but no less racist solution was the "whitening" of Latin American societies through a policy of increased European immigration. The most surprising solution to the problem of race and nation to be surveyed in this chapter comes from the unlikely island of Cuba, which continued to live under Spanish colonial rule until 1898. In 1868, Cuban patriots followed the example of the patriot movements of the 1810s and

declared independence, igniting a war against the royalists. During the three decades of war that followed, Cubans of all races rejected the doctrine of scientific
racism and, instead, embraced their Cubanness. One Cuban exile living in the
United States, José Martí, went so far as to deny the very existence of race. By the
end of this chapter, students will have a much greater understanding of the ways
elite Latin Americans attempted to reconcile the teachings of "scientific" racism
with their desire to build nations.

QUESTIONS FOR ANALYSIS

1. Why did Latin American intellectuals allow themselves to be
influenced by European doctrines of scientific racism?
2. Race and nation were important themes in many nineteenth-
century works of fiction. How can novels like the one excerpted in this
chapter be used as sources of historical analysis?
3. Is Cuba an exceptional case in the broader thinking about race
and nation building that characterized this period of Latin American
history?

1. Neocolonial Ideologies ⁓ E. Bradford Burns*

*Ideologies are complex sets of ideas about the way the world works and how it is
supposed to work. They offer a diagnosis of problems and also prescriptions for
solving them. In his highly influential book,* The Poverty of Progress *(1980), U.S.
historian E. Bradford Burns focused attention on the way Latin American elites in
the neocolonial era thought about the progress of civilizations. In his view, progress was the "link" that connected all of the new thinking in the European social
and natural sciences. According to Burns, this new thinking about progress led
Latin American intellectuals and government officials to implement some shocking solutions to what they viewed as the "Indian problem." Notice the reference
to Justo Sierra, the* científico *liberal from the previous chapter.*

The Latin American elites of the nineteenth century boasted of their European
heritage and even those with Indian or African ancestors dwelt more on their
European ties than otherwise. England and France, in particular, were their models enhanced by distance, some misconceptions, and the elites' fears of their own

*From E. Bradford Burns, *The Poverty of Progress: Latin America in the Nineteenth Century* (Berke-
ley: University of California Press, 1980), 18–20, 29–30. © 1980 The Regents of the University of
California. Reprinted by permission.

provinciality or inferiority. They readily understood what was happening in Europe and ably discussed the latest ideas radiating from the Old World, which they welcomed to the New. But European thought was no intellectual spring: it proved to be an ideological flood, which swept before it most American originality. Generally speaking, three major European philosophies shaped the ideology of the elites during the nineteenth century: the Enlightenment, the ideas of evolution put forth by Charles Darwin and Herbert Spencer, and Positivism. The concept of "progress," perhaps the key word for understanding nineteenth-century Latin American history, linked the three.

Stressing the vincibility of ignorance, the Enlightenment philosophers concluded that if people had the opportunity to know the truth, they would select "civilization" over "barbarism." Those influenced by Enlightenment ideas believed in a universally valid standard to judge civilization, and the criteria for such a judgment rested on European concepts of progress. Civilization and the progress that led to it became identified with Europe, or more specifically with England, France, and Germany. Moreover, a burgeoning faith in science directed judgments on progress itself away from philosophical and moral matters toward material change. The popularized idea of Darwin that organic forms developed over the course of time and represented successive states in a single evolutionary process toward perfection further heightened the interest in progress, giving it a scientific veneer. Very propitiously, Spencer, who enjoyed tremendous circulation in nineteenth-century Latin America, applied the same principle of evolution to society. To Spencer, progress signified a march toward the establishment of the greatest perfection and the most complete happiness. However, that march subsumed a great many economic changes and adaptations. As one example, Spencer advocated railroads as a vital part of the organic system of a modern society. As another, he regarded industrialization as a certain manifestation of progress. Many Latin Americans drew from Spencer the interrelationship of science, industry, and progress, a combination pointing to future glory through societal evolution. Like most European thinkers, Spencer said much that damned Latin America: his racism, for example.

Many of the ideas on progress pulled from the Enlightenment, Darwin, and Spencer, as well as other sources, seemed to converge in the form that Auguste Comte's Positivism assumed in Latin America during the last decades of the century. To Comte that progress was attainable through the acceptance of scientific laws codified by Positivism. Outward manifestations of progress—again, railroads and industrialization—assumed great importance in Positivism and emphatically so among the Latin Americans, whether they acknowledged Comte or not.

A part of the elites had initiated a serious and escalating questioning of some of the Iberian values during the last decades of the eighteenth century. It goes without saying that they were even more critical of Indian and African contributions to Latin American life if, in fact, they ever considered them. Increased contacts with Northern Europeans, an expanding book trade, and more opportunities for foreign travel facilitated the elite's introduction to the ideas of the Enlightenment. A selective reading of those ideas buttressed the disenchantment with Iberian rule and provided ready formulae for alternatives. The intellectuals flirted with a political ideology complementary to independence, in most cases republicanism, and economic ideas harmonious with free trade specifically and with emerging capitalism generally. Latin American elites continued the search for, as well as exploitation and export of, raw materials, the continuation of a well-established pattern of thought and practice of the colonial period which augured poorly for economic independence.

Many of the intellectuals who questioned their Iberian experience while embracing various, varying, and sometimes contradictory Northern European examples held important governmental posts after political independence had been won from Spain and Portugal while others occupied secondary, but still influential, positions in the nascent governments. They found ample opportunity to put their ideas and preferences into practice.

Intensified contacts with Europe throughout the nineteenth century reaffirmed the conclusion reached by many of the elites familiar with the philosophies of the Enlightenment that the Europeans, particularly the English and the French, had confected a desirable civilization worthy of emulation. The opinion of a Bolivian visitor to the continent in 1877, José Avelino Aramayo, that Europe not only represented progress but was needed to foment a similar progress in the New World, typified the thought of most of the elites. Aramayo did not hesitate to praise those Latin American nations that most nearly seemed to duplicate Europe. In truth, Europe's rapid industrialization and technological change awed most of the impressionable Latin American cosmopolites who clamored to replicate the process in their own localities, to graft the novelties on the quite different political, social, and economic institutions and realities of the New World. The effort to acquire the outward or material manifestations of the progress they acknowledged as civilization meant that for these Latin Americans in the nineteenth century progress could be measured quantitatively by the amount of exports, the number of steam engines, railroad mileage, or gas lights. The more the capital city architecturally resembled Paris, then ipso facto the greater degree of progress that particular country could proclaim. Many a Latin American aristocrat echoed the sigh of the Brazilian Eduardo Prado in the last decade of the century, "Without a doubt, the world is Paris."

Most Latin American elites subscribed to the European racial doctrines of the day, which ranked European whites at the pinnacle of civilization while regarding the Africans and Indians as real obstacles to progress. A mixture of the European with either the Indian or black was regarded—as European social doctrine prescribed—as a sure condemnation to an inferior status. A leading cultural review published in Rio de Janeiro in 1895, *Dom Quixote*, castigated the Brazilian "race" composed of the "backward" African, the "decadent" Portuguese, and the "primitive" Indian. The authors' recommendation was standard for the times: "What we need are new forces, originating in the strong and vigorous races that on arrival here will work by absorption to improve our race." Rather than a novelty, the article simply recapitulated and reemphasized an idea current for at least half a century among urban elites. The Brazilian intellectuals put great faith in the "whitening" process, the eradication of the "weak" Indian and African genes by the "stronger," meaning "more dominant," European ones. The theory might not have squared with European anthropological thought, but it provided a necessary solution for the distraught Brazilian elite and according to its proponents offered the surest method to reproduce European civilization in their vast nation. Paralleling similar hopes in Argentina and elsewhere, the Brazilian intellectual despaired of remolding the local populations and so planned to replace them. By mid-century, the Indians had withdrawn into the Amazonian hinterlands, and the prohibition of the slave trade had stopped the African inflow. The government threw open the doors to European immigration, which in fact did change the racial characteristics of the Brazilian population.

The intellectuals of Indo-America demonstrated no greater understanding or tolerance of the Indians than their Brazilian counterparts did of the Africans. The huge Indian populations of Mexico, Guatemala, Ecuador, Peru, Bolivia, and Paraguay embarrassed the intellectuals, who regarded them as barbaric at worst and childlike creatures at best. The Indians' disdain of European civilization only intensified the suspicions of the elites. Governments and landowners felt perfectly correct in forcing the Indians to labor for them under the rationalization that it fostered contact with the elites and thus exposed the Indians to the indubitable benefits of European civilization. Whatever their professed political persuasion, the Latin American elites seldom shied away from exploiting the Indians.

Mexican intellectuals vigorously debated the "Indian problem" in the nineteenth century, a debate that accelerated during the long government of Porfirio Díaz (1876–1911), whose policies divested the Indian communities of several million acres and literally enslaved entire Indian groups. The intellectuals divided over the intelligence and ability of the Indians as well as the feasibility of integrating them into national life—that is, making Europeanized Mexicans of the indigenous inhabitants. One side emphasized the potential of the Indians and urged the government to improve their conditions. Intellectuals like Justo Sierra believed education and greater exposure to Westernization while rescuing the Indians would transform them into mestizo Mexicans. To others, however, the Indians constituted an insuperable obstacle to national progress. They particularly decried their communal spirit and lack of individualism. Writing in the 1860s Antonio García Cubas identified Indians as the "enemies" of other Mexicans and predicted that their "decadence and degeneration" could not be reversed. Decades later, Francisco Bulnes, the quintessential Social Darwinist, published his blunt and influential *The Future of Spanish American Nations* (1899), which concluded that the racial inferiority of the Indians prohibited national development. The almost universal solution to the "Indian problem" advocated the encouragement of European immigration with the hope that the new blood would dilute the Indian. The debates focused exclusively on whether or not the Indians could be Europeanized. The intellectuals entertained no other alternatives. None recognized that the Indians might want to draw on their own past rather than Europe's or perceived any attributes in the Indian community worthy of incorporation into the national ethos.

A somewhat different debate on the Indians took place in Guatemala City in 1893 at the Central American Pedagogical Congress, whose first topic for discussion was: "What would be the most efficient method of civilizing the Indian race in order to imbue it with the ideas of progress and the habits of cultured peoples?" In a preliminary study for the congress, the Guatemalan Juan Fernández Ferraz rejected the idea that the Indians were condemned to backwardness and eventual extinction. As one Honduran delegate, Professor Alberto Membreno, noted, the Organization Committee of the Congress left no doubt that the Indians possessed the aptitude for "civilization." The question before the congress revolved around how to civilize them. The delegates roundly condemned the racism prevalent in the hemisphere which hastened the extinction of the native population and castigated both the United States and Argentina for genocide. In a very perceptive speech, Ferraz denounced the alienation of the Indians from their own environment and advised that the first step toward helping them would be the return of their lands. Although the Central American intellectuals showed a far greater understanding of the problems and a more perceptive insight into the Indian mentality than their Mexican counterparts at a similar time, they, too, saw Europeanization as the ultimate fate of the Indians. Unlike many of their Mexican colleagues, however, the Central Americans judged the native population intellectually capable of adopting European ways.

While the Mexican and Central American intellectuals debated national Indian policies, the Argentine government aggressively pursued its own policy of genocide. In Argentina's so-called Conquest of the Desert, 1879–80, the army under the command of General Julio A. Roca, who later served twice as president, fanned out across the pampas to clear the land of Indians once and for all. In an Order of the Day to his troops dated April 26, 1879, General Roca left no doubt in the minds of the soldiers of their exalted duty to the fatherland, a fatherland that seemed to have no place for the original inhabitants. These few sentences from the Order revealed the full intentions of the government in Buenos Aires:

> When the wave of humanity invades these desolate fields that were yesterday the state of sanguinary and devastating raids to turn them into markets of wealth and flourishing towns, in which millions of men may live rich and happy—then and

not till then the true worth of your efforts will be perceived. Destroying these nests of land pirates and taking possession of the vast region that shelters them, you have opened and widened the horizons of your country toward the South-land, tracing as it were with your bayonets an immense field for the development of future greatness.

2. Civilization versus Barbarism ⁓ Domingo Faustino Sarmiento*

This is the second excerpt included from Domingo F. Sarmiento's classic Fac-undo, or Civilization and Barbarism, *published while the future Liberal president of Argentina was living in exile in Chile in 1845. It is thus an early expression of the problem of race and nation, and one that was indicative of the approach that Sarmiento would bring with him to the presidency from 1868 to 1874. In this famous passage, Sarmiento lays out an elaborate dichotomy of Argentine soci-ety that reveals his disdain for the barbaric country man and his praise for the civilized city man. While he does not refer directly to race in this passage, there is no doubting the racial dimension of his thinking. What are the characteristics (racial and otherwise) that Sarmiento associates with both types of men? Notice also his solution to the problem.*

The question is to be or not to be savage.

One illness which afflicts the Argentine Republic is its vast expanse. The desert surrounds it. Solitude and wilderness without human habitation isolate its provinces from one another. There is immensity everywhere: immense plains, woods, and rivers, the horizon always uncertain, always blended with the earth among varicolored clouds and tenuous vapors which prevent us from determining that distant point at which the world ends and the sky begins.

The agglomeration of navigable rivers is a notable trait of the country. But these immense canals excavated by Nature's solicitous hand have left no mark on the customs of the Argentine people. An Argentine countryman considers him-self imprisoned in the narrow confines of a boat. When a great river cuts off his passage, he calmly undresses, prepares his horse, and guides it swimming to an islet made out from afar. There the horse and rider rest, and from islet to islet the crossing is finished at last. Thus, the Argentine countryman disdains to navigate these river roads, the greatest favor Providence has supplied to the country, seeing them only as an obstacle to his movements.

As for the city man of Argentina, he wears a European suit and lives a civilized life. In the cities there are laws, ideas of progress, means of instruction,

*From Domingo Faustino Sarmiento, *Facundo, o civilización y barbarie* (Caracas, Venezuela: Biblio-teca Ayacucho, 1977), 123–24, 206–8 (trans. John Charles Chasteen and Leslie Bary).

municipal organization, and regular government. Outside the cities, the look of everything changes. The countryman wears different clothing, not European but American. His way of life is different, his necessities peculiar and limited. Argentina is therefore composed of two entirely different societies, two peoples unconnected with each other. What is more, the countryman, far from aspiring to resemble his urban counterpart, disdainfully rejects urban luxuries and cultivated manners. All aspects of urban civilization are banned in the countryside. Anyone who dared appear in a frock coat, mounted on an English saddle, would bring upon himself the jeers and brutal aggression of the barbarous country people.

The triumph of European civilization encounters practically insuperable barriers in the Argentine countryside. It cannot, on the other hand, be denied that this situation has its poetic side, worthy of a novelist's pen. If a sparkle of national literature can shine momentarily in the new American societies, it will arise from the description of grand natural scenes, and, above all, from the struggle between European civilization and indigenous barbarity.

Great difficulties for any political organization are born from the conditions of country life. Would England like to find consumers for its products in Argentina, irrespective of its government? Fine, but what can six hundred thousand poor Argentine country people, without industry, almost without necessities, consume, under a government which, by extinguishing European customs and tastes, necessarily diminishes the consumption of European products? When there is a cultured government that cares about the national interest, then what business, what industrial movement there will be!

The principal element of order, and the main hope for the future that Argentina possesses today is European immigration, which by itself, and in spite of the lack of security offered it, rushes in daily to the Plate region. If there were a government capable of directing this immigration, it would by itself be enough to cure in no more than ten years all the wounds which the bandits who have dominated the country—from Facundo to Rosas—have inflicted upon Argentina.

---

3. The Specter of Degeneration ~ Martin S. Stabb*

Neocolonial ideologies caused many Latin American intellectuals to take a dim view of their countries' prospects. Scientific racism told them that the nonwhite populations in their home countries were an obstacle to progress. The following selection, taken from an essay written by Martin Stabb, a U.S. professor of Spanish, in 1967, provides a review of the writings of two Latin American intellectuals

*From Martin S. Stabb, *In Quest of Identity: Patterns in the Spanish American Essay of Ideas, 1890–1960* (Chapel Hill: University of North Carolina Press, 1967), 12–22. © 1968 by the University of North Carolina Press. Used by permission of the publisher.

*from the neocolonial era, Carlos Octavio Bunge of Argentina and Alcides Argue-
das of Bolivia. Stabb emphasizes the writers' strong disapproval of race mixing
(what was often called pejoratively miscegenation). What do you make of Stabb's
reference at the very end of this excerpt to Adolf Hitler?*

An important expression of positivism's scientific approach to man and his society was a strong interest in race and racial theories. The biological thought
of the nineteenth century—diffused through such popularizing movements as
Darwinism, social organicism, and the relatively new discipline of physical an-
thropology—provided abundant material upon which the racial theorizer could
draw. Moreover, the fact that Spanish America had a population of great ethnic
complexity naturally led her thinkers to consider race in assessing the continent's
problems. The effect of the U.S.–Spanish War of 1898 must also be taken into
account in this connection. Although it was Spain rather than Spanish America
who had suffered the defeat, the weakness of the mother country at the hands of
the vigorous and ambitious Anglo-Saxon certainly disturbed the Hispanic world.
The popular mind undoubtedly saw in the defeat of a swarthy southern "race" by
a blue-eyed northern "race" a good example of the triumph of a "more fit" people
over an "inferior" group.

One of the most complete raciological analyses of Hispanic America to
appear in this century was *Nuestra América* (1903) by the Argentine, Carlos
Octavio Bunge (1875–1918). The route which Bunge's thinking will follow is
indicated early in his book: "What I would call the practical objective in this book
is to describe, with all its vices and all its forms, the politics of Spanish America.
In order to understand this, I must first investigate the collective psychology
which produces it."

When Bunge turns his attention to the nonwhite elements in Spanish
America's racial composition, his deeply engrained racism is very apparent.
The Indian, he feels, is characterized by "passivity" and "oriental fatalism,"
and these traits account for the Spaniards' easy conquest of Peru and Mexico.
The Negro receives similar treatment. After a brief moment's consideration
of the validity of the concept of superior versus inferior races, he proceeds to
analyze the "positive facts" regarding the Negro's attainments. These he finds
to be utterly lacking: the Negro has not invented anything, he is not capable of
intellectual leadership or of artistic creativity. His typical traits are "servility"
and "vanity." Similarly, his characterization of the mulatto plainly reveals his
utter disdain for this group: "Impulsive, perfidious, petulant, the mulatto is a
complex amalgam of the Spanish and African spirit. . . . He is as touchy and
as fickle as a woman, and, like a degenerate, like a devil himself, he aspires to
be strong but is necessarily weak. . . . He lacks personal valor. In dangerous
situations he has difficulty in overcoming his fear. But by means of trickery
and fraud, he can escape his enemy with reptilian undulations." The mestizo

hardly fares better. He is accused of "rapacity," of intensifying and aggravating the Spaniard's arrogance, and of having a love for brutality inherited from his Indian ancestors. In short, both the mulatto and the mestizo reflect the worst of their parent stocks: "Both impure, both atavistically anti-Christian, they are like the two heads of a mythical Hydra which encircles, constricts, and strangles in its gigantic coils a beautiful and pale virgin: Hispanic America!"

A book such as *Nuestra América* would have little appeal to present-day Spanish Americans. The author's racism is only the outward manifestation of attitudes which run counter to contemporary thought and sensibility. The most striking feature of Bunge's view of the New World (at least the Hispanic portion of it) is that it cannot measure up to what he considers the only culture worthy of emulation, the European. The complete falseness of his "objective" positivistic pose is frequently revealed by violent, impassioned outbursts against specific groups, particularly mulattoes and mestizos.

Like Bunge, Alcides Arguedas (1879–1946) of Bolivia undertakes the investigation of his region's problems with a desire for a realistic, "surgical," hardheaded approach. In keeping with this spirit, he urges his compatriots to face the facts of national backwardness and political chaos directly: "we must agree frankly, vigorously, and directly that we are sick and that our total collapse may be certain." The causes of this sickness are then sketched out in broad terms: "Heredity, lack of culture, laziness, and poverty; here you have in summation the real underlying causes of the sickness of the Andean countries." Arguedas traces the ills of the Andean countries to both "inheritance" and environmental forces.

Arguedas's characterization of the Indian occupies an important place in his analysis. The native American, he asserts, "carries in his blood" a marked lack of foresight. He possesses an "atrophied" aesthetic sense. And the Indian's willingness to die in battle "comes to the poor unfortunates by heredity." Although these traits are apparently considered innate in the native American, a few other characteristics are ascribed to environmental conditioning. In an early chapter of Arguedas's best known book, *Pueblo Enfermo* (*Sick People*, 1909), for example, Arguedas maintains that the "hypocrisy and deceit" of the Indian were developed as defense mechanisms against the brutality of the conqueror. In a similar manner, according to Arguedas, twentieth-century Indians find that feigned stupidity affords an escape from distasteful work.

Arguedas discusses the Bolivian mestizo, or *cholo*, at great length. Significantly, this group fares considerably worse in his view than does the pure Indian. Speaking of alcoholism and laziness, he asserts that while there is some justification in the Indian's being a sluggard and a drinker, these vices are found in the cholo simply "by inclination." Arguedas's overall characterization of the cholo stresses his "atavistic" traits, though the Bolivian writer does concede him a degree of intelligence and an "enviable" ability to adapt to his environment. Moreover, he is "generous and considerate." Having taken brief note of the few good cholo characteristics, Arguedas goes on to present the catalog of his faults. These include a lack of sense of duty, a lack of discipline, bellicosity, egocentrism, vanity, hypocrisy, servility, and lack of loyalty.

Given this view of mestizo character, it is not difficult to predict how Arguedas will "explain" his region's social and political shortcomings. In language reminiscent of Bunge, he states that "mestizo blood" has molded Bolivian society to the point that "we are burdened with imprudence, cheating, falseness, and other evils which unavoidably turn man aside from the pursuit of moral perfection, the highest goal of life." It is to miscegenation that Bolivia owes its slow development of democratic institutions. It is because of "a certain uniqueness of the Indo-Hispanic character" that the people lean too heavily upon the state for all their needs. And, had Indian blood not predominated in his country's racial composition, Bolivia would have adopted "all kinds of moral and material advances and would today be at the same level as many of the more favored nations." Again, Bunge may be recalled when Arguedas states that "with mestizos and cholos one cannot utilize institutions made for pure-blooded and thoroughly educated peoples."

The theory that miscegenation produces degeneracy and the complementary notion that racial purity leads to superior culture occupies a central place in Arguedas's thought. As late as 1937, in the third edition of *Pueblo Enfermo*, Arguedas is unequivocal in his view that racial mixing is the explanation of Bolivia's backwardness: "In short, I repeat that miscegenation is the most obvious and the most enslaving phenomenon in Bolivia, and it is the only thing that explains reasonably and satisfactorily our present backwardness." As in the 1909 edition, he seeks support for his position in the literature of European raciology. By the 1930s, however, such support could no longer be found within the ranks of scientific anthropologists and social psychologists. As the critic Zum Felde notes, Arguedas's thesis was never corrected in the light of modern race concepts. His racism, in fact, became so entrenched that he could only find substantiation for his views in the writings of that distinguished raciological "expert" of recent history, Adolf Hitler.

---

4. Brazilianization ～ Aluísio Azevedo*

Neocolonial ideologies found their way into the arts as well. Many of the great novels of nineteenth-century Latin America dealt with the intertwined themes of race, nation, and romance. In such works of fiction the nation was often personified as a young woman forced to choose between two different men, who repre-

---

*From Aluísio Azevedo, *A Brazilian Tenement*, trans. Harry W. Brown (New York: R. M. McBride, 1926), 97–99, 120.

sented different paths to the future. In this excerpt from famed Brazilian novelist Aluísio Azevedo's novel, A Brazilian Tenement *(1890), a hardworking immigrant from Portugal, Jeronymo, falls for Rita, a dark-skinned beauty who lives in his building. Notice the changes that occur in Jeronymo. Notice also the ambiguity in Azevedo's condemnation of Jeronymo's Brazilianization. While this may be his downfall, it is not without its joys and pleasures.*

Suddenly Porfirio's mandolin, aided by Firmo's guitar, broke forth in a *chorado* of Bahia, and at the first vibrant note of the exhilarating Negro music, the pulses of the tenement quickened and gloom disappeared. As it continued it became, not merely the sound of a mandolin accompanied by a guitar, but the expression of a people—moans and sighs freed in a torrent, gliding and writhing like serpents in a burning forest—the music increased in intensity, music made up of caresses, of kisses and of happy sobs, of brutal caresses of agony.

Filled with the fire of madness was this strange music, like the sharp and smarting aroma of certain poisonous plants deep in the Brazilian forest, and astonishing was its effect on its hearers. Their bodies swayed with the sensual rhythm of the melodies, their senses intoxicated with exhilaration. Dispelled was Portugal's gloom by the quick pulsing joyousness of Bahia—the clouds and shadows of old Europe routed by young America's brilliant sunshine.

Jeronymo laid aside his guitar and with rapt attention listened to the weird music, which was carrying on a strange revolution within him—a revolution that had begun the day he felt in his face, like a challenging blow, the dazzling sunshine of this new world; a revolution that revived the first time he heard the chirp of a tropical cricket and the song of a Brazilian bird, that progressed with the taste of the first juicy fruit he had sampled in this new, young land, and that was to be completed by the first woman here who attracted him—a half-white, whose sinuous movements fascinated him as a helpless bird is transfixed by the deadly eyes of a serpent.

"What's the matter with you, Jeronymo?" asked his [Portuguese] wife Piedade, marveling at his tense expression.

"Wait," he replied; "I want to listen." For Firmo had started singing the chorado, accompanied by the rhythmical hand claps of the others. Jeronymo arose, almost mechanically, and approached the group surrounding the two musicians, Piedade following him. With his elbows on the fence surrounding Rita's little patch of flowers and his chin resting on his clasped hands, he stood, neither moving nor speaking, giving body and soul to the seduction of the voluptuous music, as a giant tree allows itself to be encircled and bound by the caressing tentacles of a treacherous vine.

And then came Rita Bahiana, who had shed her ruffles and appeared with arms and neck bared to dance. The moon burst through the clouds at this moment, bathing the scene with a soft, silver glow and lending to the rich, warm skin of the mulata a pallor that made her really beautiful. With infinite grace she danced, simple, primitive, seemingly formed solely to delight the senses, a creature from Eden's garden, much of the woman and much of the serpent.

She danced within the circle, her hands at her waist and her entire body in movement. Now her arms were outstretched and raised, and then lowered till her finger tips touched her neck. At times she sank till she appeared to be almost sitting on the ground, while the movement of her arms and hips never ceased. Then she leaped into the air and danced, faster and faster, her arms twisting and writhing, and her blood boiling with a passion that communicated itself to the onlookers.

As she flung herself into a chair, the enthusiasm of her admirers knew no bounds. An explosion of applause rent the air and cries of delight burst from every throat. She must dance more; they would not be refused. Seizing Firmo, she dragged him into the center and made him dance. Agile and supple, seemingly made of rubber, he performed astonishing feats. He doubled his legs beneath him and danced with his body almost on the ground, then leaped aloft and cut the most fantastic capers, his arms and legs appearing about to be shaken from his trunk. The dance spirit proved to be contagious; Florinda started dancing and so did even slim Albino.

The spell of the chorado enchained them all despotically, those who did not dance as well as those who did. But none was so affected as Rita. She only, with the sinuous grace of the cursed snake, could truly interpret and express the spirit of her native Bahia—a combination of movement, of the strange perfume of the mulata, and of the seduction of her voice—low and sweet, with no spoken words, but startling little cries and a crooning murmur, as she danced.

Jeronymo gazed and listened, spellbound, feeling his soul pour out of his eyes, which he could not turn from the mulata. She was a mystery to him, and he was dimly conscious of a confusion of impressions as he stood and stared. She was the brilliant glare at mid-day, the red heat of the plantation field; she was the aroma of the vanilla tree, filling the Brazilian forest; she was the virgin palm which lifts its head aloft and scorns contact with another living thing; she was poisonous—and marvelously sweet; she was the sapoti fruit with its juice like honey, and she was the caju nut, whose fiery oil causes running ulcers; she was the treacherous green snake, a reptile of rare beauty, which had entwined itself about him and filled him with desires beside which his longing for his old home was a sentiment poor, indeed, and its fangs had penetrated his arteries and poisoned him with a venom that he knew would make him burn with fever—a fever of passion for the mulata, for the half-white Rita, who danced to the music of Bahia.

All this Jeronymo felt but only half understood, so giddy was he with the change that had come over his spirit. The subsequent impressions of that Sunday ever remained a hazy recollection of events, of the experiences attendant upon unaccustomed drunkenness—an intoxication, not of wine, but of the bitter honey from the calyx of the baneful tropic lily. So he remained, looking on. Other girls danced, but the tall Portuguese had eyes only for the mulatta, even as she fell exhausted into the arms of her lover. Piedade, her head nodding with drowsiness, called to him to come along several times, receiving in reply only an unintelligible mutter, after which she departed alone. Hours passed by, but still he could not leave.

The circle had increased. Izaura and Leonor, on cordial terms with the tenement dwellers, were in the front row. João Romão and Bertoleza, the day's labors finally over, had come out for a moment to enjoy the scene before wearily falling into their bed. Miranda's family were at their high, next-door windows, highly diverted with the merry-making. Many passersby could not resist coming in for the frolic. But of all this Jeronymo had no consciousness; there was but one object before his eyes—the panting mulata twisting voluptuously in the arms of Firmo.

Several weeks passed, Jeronymo now taking every morning a cup of strong coffee "like Rita makes," and accompanying it with two fingers of the local liquor, paraty. A slow but relentless transformation was in progress within him, hour by hour, and day by day, silently but surely remolding him, body and soul. For his energy, even, was weakening. He became contemplative and romantic. This New World atmosphere and his Brazilian surroundings presented to him now unexpected and seductive aspects that moved him. He forgot his early ambitions and gave himself over to the idealizing of new pleasures, sharper and more violent. He became liberal and improvident, more given to spending than to saving. He lost his old-time austerity and became pleasure-loving and, to a certain extent, indolent, no longer defying the blazing sun, the barricade of heat which the quarry wall threw back as a desperate last defense against the conquering invader.

Thus were slowly modified in him the old habits of the Portuguese villager. Jeronymo's house lost its former air of severity, and friends occasionally dropped in for a little glass of paraty after work hours, while on Sundays there was now and then a dinner there. Eventually, the revolution was complete: Portuguese wine gave way to the Brazilian rum made from the cane juice. Stewed dried beef with black beans and mandioca succeeded codfish with potatoes and boiled onions, and, one by one, the other viands of old Portugal were crowded aside by dishes peculiar to Bahia, or Minas, or the shores of Guanabara. Once coffee had firmly established its welcome at No. 35, it began dragging in its twin sister, tobacco, and soon Jeronymo was contentedly puffing with the rest.

The more he dropped into the life and habits of Brazil, the finer his sensibilities became, even though his physical force weakened. He began to enjoy music and even comprehended to some extent the wilderness poets who sang of blighted love, their songs accompanied on the violin, or native guitar—indeed, Jeronymo himself had discarded the old instrument for the Brazilian. Formerly his one dream had been an eventual return to Portugal, but now, like the sailor on the high seas, his eyes became accustomed to the broad sweeps, and the turbulent Brazilian atmosphere, with its savage gaiety, no longer disconcerted him. Jeronymo had become Brazilianized.

---

5. A Raceless Nation ⁓ Ada Ferrer*

This chapter's final selection, which comes from historian Ada Ferrer, presents a stark alternative to the scientific racism and white supremacist thinking that flourished in Latin America under neocolonialism. It focuses on the Cuban movement that formed in the 1860s to overthrow Spanish rule once and for all. Historians generally explain Cuba and Puerto Rico's lack of participation in the independence struggle of the 1810s as a result of the Haitian Revolution, which terrified the islands' slave-owning planters. Slavery was not abolished on these islands until 1873 (Puerto Rico) and 1886 (Cuba). Hundreds of thousands of newly enslaved Africans came to the islands in the 1800s. Despite this horrendous backdrop, Ferrer argues that the Cuban independence struggle produced a movement that defined itself as neither black nor white but "raceless." Its adherents were Cuban, nothing more and nothing less. But was this really a raceless movement or a multiracial one?

Cuba's nineteenth-century revolution emerged from a society that seemed highly unrevolutionary—a society that in the political ferment of the Age of Revolution earned the designation "the ever-faithful isle." Between 1776 and 1825, as most of the colonies of North and South America acquired their independence, Cuba remained a loyalist stronghold. The story of Cuba's deviance from the Latin American norm is, by now, a familiar one: in the face of potential social revolution, criollo (Cuban-born) elites opted to maintain the colonial bond with Spain. With that bond, they preserved as well a prosperous and expanding sugar industry built on the labor of enslaved Africans. After the Haitian Revolution of 1791, Cuba replaced colonial St. Domingue as the world's largest producer of sugar. Content with their new position in the world market, Cuban planters did not want to emulate Haiti again by becoming the hemisphere's second black republic. Thus, colonialism survived in Cuba even as it was defeated to the north and south; and peace and slavery prevailed over insurrection and emancipation.

The colony that outlived those Atlantic revolutions was, however, a fractured and fearful one. In 1846, 36 percent of the population lived enslaved. Even well into the nineteenth century, a thriving (and illegal) slave trade continued

---

*From Ada Ferrer, *Insurgent Cuba: Race, Nation, and Revolution, 1868–1898* (Chapel Hill: University of North Carolina Press, 1999), 1–5, 7–10. © 1999 by the University of North Carolina Press. Used by permission of the publisher.

to replenish the supply of enslaved Africans. More than 595,000 arrived on the island's shores in the last fifty years of the trade, between 1816 and 1867—about as many as ever arrived in the United States over the whole period of the trade (523,000). About half those slaves labored on sugar plantations. Under brutal work regimes, many continued to speak African languages and to have only minimal contact with the criollo world outside the plantation. Free persons of color constituted another 17 percent of the population. Though legally free, they faced numerous constraints on the exercise of that freedom: prohibitions on the consumption of alcohol, bans against marriage to white men and women, and restrictions on the use of public space, to name but a few.

At mid-century, then, enslaved and free people of color together constituted a majority of the population, outnumbering those identified as white. That white population, educated in the fear of black and slave rebellion, looked to Haiti and clung to Spain in fear. Haiti's slave revolution served as a perpetual example of what might happen to whites in the midst of armed rebellion, but there were smaller local examples as well. The most famous, perhaps, was the alleged conspiracy of 1843—said to involve a massive number of slaves, free people of color, and abolitionist statesmen from England. Even as late as 1864, only four years before the outbreak of nationalist insurgency, authorities uncovered a conspiracy in El Cobre in which slaves from seven area farms were allegedly to join forces to "kill all the whites and make war in order to be free." When the would-be rebels were captured and tried in a Spanish military court, translators had to be hired, for the enslaved suspects spoke no Spanish. In this context of slavery and division, the colonial state and many influential white creoles asserted that to risk expelling Spain was to invite a more horrible fate. Cuba, they said, would either be Spanish or it would be African. It would be Spanish or it would be another Haiti. For those with the power to decide, the answer came without hesitation: Cuba would remain a Spanish colony. There did exist a handful of prominent intellectuals willing to consider, if hypothetically, the founding of a Cuban nation independent from Spain. But, always, they were careful to specify that the Cuban nationality they desired—"the only one that any sensible man would concern himself with—[was] a nationality formed by the white race."

It was onto this world that revolution erupted on October 10, 1868. And when it did, it seemed to defy the fear and division that formed the society from which it emerged. Led initially by a handful of prosperous white men, the revolution placed free men of color in local positions of authority. It also freed slaves, made them soldiers, and called them citizens. And that was just the beginning. The movement formally inaugurated on that day went on to produce three full-fledged anticolonial rebellions over the thirty years that followed: the Ten Years' War (1868–78), the Guerra Chiquita, or Little War (1879–80), and the final War of Independence (1895–98), which ended with the Spanish-American War. All three rebellions were waged by an army unique in the history of the Atlantic world—the Liberation Army, a multiracial fighting force that was integrated at all ranks. Historians estimate that at least 60 percent of that army was composed of men of color. But this was not just an army in which masses of black soldiers served under a much smaller number of white officers, for many black soldiers ascended through the ranks to hold positions as captains, colonels, and generals and to exercise authority over men identified as white. By the end of the thirty-year period, estimates one historian, about 40 percent of the commissioned officers were men of color.

If this integrated army was one pillar of the revolution, the other was significantly less tangible. It was a powerful rhetoric of antiracism that began to flourish during the first rebellion and became much more dominant in the years between the legal end of slavery in 1886 and the outbreak of the third and final war in 1895. This new rhetoric made racial equality a foundation of the Cuban nation. Espoused by white, mulatto, and black members of the movement's civilian and military branches, it asserted that the very struggle against Spain had transformed Cuba into a land where there were "no whites nor blacks, but only Cubans." It thus condemned racism not as an infraction against individual citizens but as a sin against the life of the would-be nation. Revolutionary rhetoric made racial slavery and racial division concomitant with Spanish colonialism, just as it made the revolution a mythic project that armed black and white men together to form the world's first raceless nation.

That this revolution emerged from that slave society makes the story of Cuban independence a remarkable and compelling one. That it emerged from the late-nineteenth-century world makes it seem even more so—for the Cuban revolution unfolded as European and North American thinkers linked biology to progress and divided the world into superior and inferior races.

Those ideas, espoused or encouraged by the work of thinkers as diverse as Charles Darwin, Herbert Spencer, and Joseph-Arthur de Gobineau, had a profound influence on Latin America. Yet in that world "under Darwin's sway," the Cuban movement's principal intellectual leader, José Martí, professed the equality of all races. Indeed, he went further, boldly asserting that there was no such thing as race. Race, he and other nationalists insisted, was merely a tool used locally to divide the anticolonial effort and globally by men who invented "textbook races" in order to justify expansion and empire. Here, then, were voices raised not only in opposition to Spanish rule but also in opposition to the prevailing common sense of their time.

Furthermore, what Cuba's nationalist leaders preached and (less perfectly) practiced stood in stark and concrete contrast to the emerging racial order of its neighbor to the north. Cuban rebels spoke of a raceless nation in the period that represented the nadir in American racial politics. Thus the escalation of racial violence, the spread of spatial segregation by race, and the dismantling of political gains made during the Reconstruction of the South occurred in the United

States precisely as black and mulatto leaders gained increasing popularity and power in Cuba. Arguably the most popular leader of the nationalist movement was Antonio Maceo, a mulatto who had joined the movement in 1868 as a common foot soldier and rose to the rank of general. By 1895, he led the insurgent army across the entire territory of the island and won the allegiance of white and non-white men and women—a national, multiracial following that in the United States would have been rare in local contexts and unthinkable at the national level. Thus, as the color line in the United States grew more and more rigid, and as the consequences of crossing that line became more and more brutal, a revolutionary movement in Cuba appeared willing, sometimes eager, to eradicate those lines in Cuba. And it was the victory of this revolution that American intervention helped block after 1898.

The nationalist movement thus gave rise to one of the most powerful ideas in Cuban history—the conception, dominant to this day, of a raceless nationality. In rebel camps and battlefields, as well as in memoirs, essays, and speeches, patriot intellectuals (white and non-white) made the bold claim that the struggle against Spain had produced a new kind of individual and a new kind of collectivity. They argued that the experience of war had forever united black and white; and they imagined a new kind of nation in which equality was so ingrained that there existed no need to identify and speak of races, a nation in which (to borrow the phrase of the mulatto general Antonio Maceo) there were no whites nor blacks, but only Cubans. Thus the rebel republic declined to record racial categories of identification on army rosters, and a great many citizens repeatedly asserted (and today continue to assert) the non-existence of discrimination and the irrelevance of race. This study of anticolonial revolution, then, is also a story of the emergence of a particularly powerful racial ideology. It is the story of the tensions and transformations that produced that ideology and of those that it, in turn, produced.

As that ideology of raceless nationality emerged, it clashed with longstanding colonial arguments about the impossibility of Cuban nationhood. Since the end of the eighteenth century, advocates of colonial rule in Cuba had argued that the preponderance of people of color and the social and economic importance of slavery meant that Cuba could not be a nation. Confronted by threats to political order, they invoked images of racial warfare and represented the nationalists' desired republic as Haiti's successor. Such arguments worked well in the Age of Revolution, when Cuban elites decided to forgo independence and to maintain a prosperity built largely on the forced labor of Africans in sugar. These arguments continued to work, in modified form, even after the start of anticolonial insurgency in 1868, when nationalist leaders of the first rebellion (the Ten Years' War) began to challenge traditional formulations about the impossibility of Cuban nationhood. They established a rebel republic and placed free people of color in public office at the local level. They mobilized enslaved workers and declared (falteringly and ambivalently) the (gradual and indemnified) end of slavery.

Spanish authorities and their allies responded to these challenges by deploying familiar arguments about the racial dangers of rebellion. As usual, the references to Haiti became ubiquitous. But they were almost always brief and nebulous—as if merely to speak the name sufficed to call up concrete images of black supremacy: of black men who raped white women and killed their husbands and fathers, of political authority exercised by self-anointed black emperors, of wealth and property annihilated, of God and civilization spurned.

The movement's detractors utilized the same images and arguments again—to even better effect—during the second separatist uprising known as the Little War of 1879–80. Colonial officials, however, did more than merely label the independence movement black. They also consciously and skillfully manipulated features of the rebellion to make them more closely correspond to their interpretation. They tampered with lists of captured insurgents, omitting the names of white rebels. They made surrendering white insurgents sign public declarations repudiating the allegedly racial goals of black co-leaders. And the blacker colonial officials made the rebellion appear, the more white insurgents surrendered, and the blacker the rebellion became, and so on. Race, and its manipulation by colonial authorities, are therefore absolutely central to understanding the limits of multiracial insurgency in the first half of the nationalist period.

Thus, as independence activists prepared to launch a final and, they hoped, successful rebellion against Spain, they faced not only the challenge of uniting different separatist camps and of amassing men, arms, and money for the struggle. They faced as well the imperative of combating colonial representations of the independence movement. To succeed at anticolonial insurgency, separatists had to invalidate traditional claims about the racial risks of rebellion. They had to construct an effective counterclaim to arguments that for almost a century had maintained that Cuba was unsuited to nationhood. "The power to represent oneself," they had come to realize, was "nothing other than political power itself." The struggle for that power of representation required that patriot-intellectuals reconceptualize nationality, blackness, and the place of people of color in the would-be nation. In the process, black, mulatto, and white intellectuals constructed powerful and eloquent expressions of raceless nationality, of a nationality that had antiracism as a solid foundation. Among these intellectuals were José Martí, white son of a Spaniard and a Cuban, who in 1892 founded the Cuban Revolutionary Party in New York; Juan Gualberto Gómez, a mulatto journalist born to enslaved parents, educated in Paris and Havana; and Rafael Serra y Montalvo, a prominent journalist who began his career as a cigar worker. All wrote of the union of blacks and whites in anticolonial war, and in that physical and spiritual embrace between black and white men in battle they located the symbolic and material birth of the nation. In their vision, black and mulatto men could never threaten that nation with aspirations to a black republic. Such portrayals thus explicitly countered colonialist claims about race war and the impossibility of Cuban nationhood. To powerful notions of racial fear and unrest they juxtaposed equally powerful images of racial harmony and racial transcendence.

But if this complex process of reconceptualizing race and nationality occurred in dialogue with the racialist claims of the colonial state, it also emerged from—and produced new—tensions within the nationalist community itself. By declaring that there were no races and by asserting that racism was an infraction against the nation as a whole, nationalist rhetoric helped defeat Spanish claims about the impossibility of Cuban nationhood. That same rhetoric, however, also provided a conceptual framework that black soldiers could use to condemn the racism not only of their Spanish enemies but also of their fellow insurgents and leaders. Thus the ideology of a raceless nationality, even as it suggested that race had been transcended, gave black insurgents and citizens a powerful language with which to speak about race and racism within the rebel polity—a language with which to show that that transcendence was yet to occur. And, in fact, throughout the period of insurrection, especially during and after the final War of Independence in 1895, black soldiers and officers used the language of nationalism to expose and condemn what they perceived as racism within the nationalist movement. Thus the language of raceless nationality, a language of harmony and integration, became also a "language of contention."

Just as nationalist rhetoric shaped black political behavior, so too did black participation profoundly affect both the discourse and practice of nationalism. The mobilization of free and enslaved Cubans of color helped radicalize Cuban nationalism and made the rebellion militarily viable. Black participation was even celebrated in the nationalist prose of the period. But black mobilization—in the beginning because its only precedent lay in slave rebellion and later because it was accompanied by significant black leadership—also created anxieties among insurgents and fed the forces of counterinsurgency. Black political activity and power led some white leaders to impugn the motives of black co-leaders. And it led others to abandon the movement altogether and ally with Spain to secure its defeat. Black participation in insurgency—and representations of that participation—thus had the power on the one hand to compromise the success of nationalist efforts and, on the other, to strengthen the appeal of the movement.

VI

Nationalism

The Cuban war for independence from Spain that was waged from 1868 to 1898 clearly demonstrated that there were alternatives to the cultural values of neocolonialism. The Cuban patriot movement that was discussed by Ada Ferrer in the previous chapter showed that it was possible to reject the teachings of the European social and natural sciences when there was a strong desire to achieve a lofty goal. This chapter digs further into the reaction against the racist thinking of the neocolonial era by examining the rise of Latin American nationalism. It focuses on the writings of a diverse group of Latin American nationalists. As we will see below, while the backgrounds of the writers examined in this chapter are indeed diverse, the common theme sounded in their writings was the assertion of a common national identity.

Nationalism, meaning the identification of a large group of individuals with a nation, is one of the most widespread and influential ideologies in modern world history. Nations can be defined in terms of language, religion, or a shared historical experience, as long as that experience creates a strong common bond of identification between the individuals in the group. The writers surveyed in this chapter developed their ideas about nationalism systematically in response to the world around them. They were deeply critical of the power that outsiders wielded in their societies, but they often saved their most virulent criticism for the previous generation of Latin American liberals who had embraced foreign ideologies such as positivism and scientific racism.

During the Wars of Independence some early expressions of Latin American nationalism surfaced. Rooted in the idea that *Americanos*, or natives of Spain's American colonies, were being persecuted by an unjust king, these expressions of Latin American proto-nationalism are sometimes referred to as nativism because of their emphasis on the place of one's birth. Generally speaking, the nativist calls for unity did not fully grapple with the deep legacies of conquest and slavery that defined the region's colonial experience.

One leader of the Independence era who did address the question of the nation in an innovative way was Simón Bolívar, whose "War to the Death" decree of 1813 was excerpted in chapter 1. In addition to being known as El Libertador (the

Liberator) of Venezuela and several other present-day Spanish American countries, Bolívar is considered by many to be the founder of the movement to form some sort of regional federation of Spanish American countries. During the war, Bolívar made numerous references to Spanish American unity, most famously in the "Jamaica Letter" of 1815. In 1826, Bolívar held an American congress in Panama that was attended by delegates from several Spanish American republics (Brazil was excluded because of its status as a monarchy). Unfortunately for the Liberator, nothing of substance was achieved at the congress. But Bolívar's "supreme dream" of Spanish American unity has proven to be resilient, as we will see below in the selection from Nicaraguan nationalist Augusto Sandino.

This chapter features historical inversions, role reversals, and armed resistance. The dominant idea of scientific racism explored in the previous chapter was reversed by the nationalists. Race mixing was for them not something to be abhorred or hidden away. It was now proudly seen as a defining characteristic of the Latin American nations. An inverted set of cultural values was asserted, too. The strong gravitational pull of European science and North American industry that we saw in the neocolonial era was now reversed; foreign thinking and solutions offered by nonnative models were rejected. In some cases, Latin American nationalists did more than write and speak about their opposition to the old, racist ways of thinking about their nations. Some of the writers excerpted below took up arms and risked their lives for the cause of the nation. This was true of the Cuban José Martí, who fought Spain, and of the Nicaraguan Sandino, who fought the United States. Resisting the increasingly imperialist ambitions of the United States was a major factor in the development of Latin American nationalism, one that can come as a shock to U.S. citizens who have never studied the interventionist history of their government in the Caribbean and Central America.

To properly understand the selections that follow, it is also important to understand that nationalism achieved a significant advantage in Latin America after 1930. Around that time Latin American governments were compelled to respond to the global economic crisis known as the Great Depression. The Depression crisis destabilized the neocolonial system that had dominated Latin America since the late 1800s, opening the door for new political forces to seize control of national governments. These new political coalitions were much more supportive of nationalist thinking than were their predecessors. New opportunities were created for nationalistic expressions of all sorts, from music—think of Dominican merengue, Brazilian samba, or Argentine tango—to educational reform. Never before had the culture of the Latin American masses received the endorsement of state elites.

By the end of this chapter, students will have a much better grasp of the problem of Latin American nationalism. They will have to consider whether the region is composed of many nationalisms or just one. They will also have to consider the role of the United States in the development of Latin American nationalism.

QUESTIONS FOR ANALYSIS

1. What did the nationalists think about the previous generation of liberals who obeyed the logic of neocolonialism? Do the selections offer any insights into this question?

2. Obviously Bolívar's goal of Spanish American federation was important to Sandino, but do you think it mattered to the other authors in this chapter?

3. How does it feel to have a Latin American intellectual like Arévalo explain U.S. history to you?

1. Our America ~ José Martí*

José Martí is known as the apostle of Cuban independence, a title earned through many years of tireless campaigning on behalf of his cause. He dedicated a good part of his life to writing and speaking about the Cuban people's aspiration for self-government and died on a battlefield in Cuba fighting for independence in 1895. As a result of his belief in Cuban separatism, Martí was imprisoned in Cuba at a young age and subsequently sent into exile. He would live in Mexico, Guatemala, and the United States, mostly in Florida, where the Cuban émigré community was the strongest, and New York, where he continued his political work and also wrote poetry and fiction. In the following excerpt from his most famous essay, "Our America," published in newspapers in New York and Mexico City in January 1891, Martí ridicules the blindness of all previous Latin American governments to the realities of life in the region. Notice how he invokes Sarmiento's classic dichotomy in his argument. How does Martí's view of "natural men" differ from Sarmiento's?

For in what lands can men take more pride than in our long-suffering American republics, raised up from among the silent Indian masses by the bleeding arms of a hundred apostles, to the sounds of battle between the book and the processional candle? Never in history have such advanced and united nations been forged in so short a time from such disorganized elements.

The presumptuous man feels that the earth was made to serve as his pedestal because he happens to have a facile pen or colorful speech, and he accuses his

---

*From José Martí, *Our America by José Martí: Writings on Latin America and the Struggle for Cuban Independence*, ed. Philip S. Foner, trans. Elinor Randall, with additional translations by Juan de Onís and Roslyn Held Foner (New York: Monthly Review Press, 1977), 86–88. © 1977 Philip S. Foner. Reprinted with permission.

native land of being worthless and beyond redemption because its virgin jungles fail to provide him with a constant means of traveling over the world, driving Persian ponies and lavishing champagne like a tycoon. The incapacity does not lie with the emerging country in quest of suitable forms and a utilitarian greatness; it lies rather with those who attempt to rule nations of a unique and violent character by means of laws inherited from four centuries of freedom in the United States and nineteen centuries of monarchy in France. A decree by [Alexander] Hamilton does not halt the charge of the plainsman's horse. A phrase by [the Abbé] Sieyès does nothing to quicken the stagnant blood of the Indian race. To govern well, one must see things as they are. And the able governor in America is not the one who knows how to govern the Germans or the French; he must know the elements that compose his own country, and how to bring them together, using methods and institutions originating within the country, to reach that desirable state where each man can attain self-realization and all may enjoy the abundance that Nature has bestowed on everyone in the nation to enrich with their toil and defend with their lives. The government must originate in the country. The spirit of the government must be that of the country. Its structure must conform to rules appropriate to the country. Good government is nothing more than the balance of the country's natural elements.

That is why the imported book has been conquered in America by the natural man. Natural men have conquered learned and artificial men. The native half-breed has conquered the exotic Creole. The struggle is not between civilization and barbarity, but between false erudition and Nature. The natural man is good, and he respects and rewards superior intelligence as long as his humility is not turned against him, or he is not offended by being disregarded—a thing the natural man never forgives, prepared as he is to forcibly regain the respect of whoever has wounded his pride or threatened his interests. It is by conforming with these disdained native elements that the tyrants of America have climbed to power, and have fallen as soon as they betrayed them. Republics have paid with oppression for their inability to recognize the true elements of their countries, to derive from them the right kind of government, and to govern accordingly. In a new nation a governor means a creator.

In nations composed of both cultured and uncultured elements, the uncultured will govern because it is their habit to attack and resolve doubts with their fists in cases where the cultured have failed in the art of governing. The uncultured masses are lazy and timid in the realm of intelligence, and they want to be governed well. But if the government hurts them, they shake it off and govern themselves. How can the universities produce governors if not a single university in America teaches the rudiments of the art of government, the analysis of elements peculiar to the peoples of America? The young go out into the world wearing Yankee or French spectacles, hoping to govern a people they do not know. In the political race entrance should be denied to those who are ignorant of the rudiments of politics. The prize in literary contests should not go for the best ode, but for the best study of the political factors of one's country. Newspapers, universities, and schools should encourage the study of the country's pertinent components. To know them is sufficient, without mincing words; for whoever brushes aside even a part of the truth, whether through intention or oversight, is doomed to fall. The truth he lacks thrives on negligence, and brings down whatever is built without it. It is easier to resolve our problem knowing its components than to resolve it without knowing them. Along comes the natural man, strong and indignant, and he topples all the justice accumulated from books because he has not been governed in accordance with the obvious needs of the country. Knowing is what counts. To know one's country and govern it with that knowledge is the only way to free it from tyranny. The European university must bow to the American university. The history of America, from the Incas to the present, must be taught in clear detail and to the letter, even if the archons [lords] of Greece are overlooked. Our Greece must take priority over the Greece which is not ours. We need it more. Nationalist statesmen must replace foreign statesmen. Let the world be grafted onto our republics, but the trunk must be our own. And let the vanquished pedant hold his tongue, for there are no lands in which a man may take greater pride than in our long-suffering American republics.

2. Education and the Mexican Revolution ~ Octavio Paz*

The Mexican Revolution of 1910 posed a revolutionary challenge to the neocolonial system. In that year Francisco Madero led a campaign to overthrow the long-running, positivist dictatorship of Porforio Díaz. For a decade Mexico was thrown into a bloody civil war (1910–1920). While the revolution had many twists and turns, it gradually became institutionalized in the 1920s, which then created space for a rich variety of nationalistic expressions to appear. Mexican mural painting, for example, achieved world acclaim. The following selection comes from Mexican writer and diplomat Octavio Paz's classic collection of essays, The Labyrinth of Solitude, *published in 1950. In this excerpt from his essay on the "Mexican Intelligentsia," Paz focuses on the great educational reformer and philosopher of the Mexican Revolution, José Vasconcelos, whose efforts to formulate a Mexican national identity, Paz argued, were representative of the true goals of the Revolution. Vasconcelos was the author of the 1925 book* The Cosmic Race, *which turned the teachings of scientific racism on their head. Notice the reference to Justo Sierra, and consider the differences between him and Vasconcelos.*

*From Octavio Paz, *The Labyrinth of Solitude and Other Writings*, trans. Lysander Kemp, Yara Milos, and Rachel Phillips Belash (New York: Grove Press, 1985), 152–55. © 1961 by Grove Press, Inc. Used by permission of Grove/Atlantic, Inc.

If the Revolution was a search and an immersion of ourselves in our own origins and being, no one embodied this fertile, desperate desire better than José Vasconcelos, the founder of modern education in Mexico. His work was brief but fecund, and the essence of it is still alive. In part he carried on the task begun by Justo Sierra, which was to extend elementary education and to improve the quality of instruction on the higher levels, but he also tried to base education on certain principles that were implicit in our tradition but had been forgotten or ignored by the positivists. Vasconcelos believed that the Revolution was going to rediscover the meaning of our history, which Sierra had sought in vain. The new education was to be founded on "our blood, our language and our people."

The character of the educational movement was organic. It was not the isolated work of one extraordinary man—though Vasconcelos was certainly that, in several ways—but rather an accomplishment of the Revolution, and its realization expressed the finest and most secret element of the revolutionary movement. Poets, painters, prose writers, teachers, architects and musicians all collaborated in the project. All, that is, of the Mexican intelligentsia, or almost all. It was a social effort, but one that required the presence of a man who could catch fire and then transmit his enthusiasm to others. Vasconcelos, as a philosopher and a man of action, possessed that unity of vision which brings coherence to diverse plans, and although he sometimes overlooked details, he never lost himself in them. His work, subject to a number of necessary and not always happy corrections, was the work of a founder, not of a mere technician.

Vasconcelos conceived of instruction as active participation. Schools were established, readers and the classics were published, institutes were created, and cultural missions were sent to the remotest parts of the country. At the same time, the intelligentsia turned toward the people, discovering their true nature and eventually making them the center of its activities. The popular arts emerged again, after centuries of having been ignored; the old songs were sung once more in schools and concert halls; the regional dances with their pure and timid movements, combining flight and immobility, fire and reserve, were danced for a wider audience. Contemporary Mexican painting was born. Some of our writers turned their eyes to the colonial past, and others used Indian themes; but the most courageous faced up to the present, and created the novel of the Revolution. After the lies and pretences of the dictatorship, Mexico suddenly discovered herself, with astonished and loving eyes: "We are the prodigal sons of a homeland which we cannot even define but which we are beginning at last to observe. She is Castilian and Moorish, with Aztec markings."

As a member of the Ateneo group* and as a participant in the battle against positivism, Vasconcelos knew that all education entails an image of the world and

---

*A group of young Mexican artists and intellectuals that rebelled against the positivist philosophy of the previous generation.

a program for living. Hence his efforts to base the Mexican schools on something more concrete than Article 3 of the Constitution [of 1857], which stated that education was to be secular. Of course, secularism had never been neutral, and its pretended indifference toward ultimate questions was an artifice that deceived nobody. Vasconcelos, who was neither a Catholic nor a Jacobin, was not a neutral either. He wanted to base our school system on tradition, in the same way that the Revolution attempted to create a new economy on the basis of the *ejido*.* To do so meant to formulate the impulses behind the Revolution in an explicit way, since up till then they had only expressed themselves in a kind of instinctive stammering. Our tradition, if it was really still alive, would link us to a universal tradition that would enlarge and justify our own.

Every time we return to tradition we are reminded that we are part of the universal tradition of Spain, the only one that Spanish Americans can accept and carry on. There are two Spains: the Spain that is closed to the outside world, and the open, heterodox Spain that breaks out of its prison to breathe the free air of the spirit. Ours is the latter. The former—pure-blooded and medieval—never accepted us, never discovered us, and our whole history, like a part of the history of the Spaniards themselves, has been a struggle against it. Now the universal tradition of Spain in America, as we have already noted, consists above all in conceiving of the continent as a unit superior to national divisions. A return to the Spanish tradition, therefore, can have no other meaning than a return to the unity of Spanish America. The philosophy of the "cosmic race" (that is, of the new American man who would resolve all racial conflicts and the great opposition between East and West) was the natural and ultimate consequence of Spanish universality. The ideas expounded by Vasconcelos had little or no relation to the caste-conscious traditionalism of the Mexican conservatives: he saw our continent, as did the founders of America, as futurity and newness. "Spanish America is magnificently new, not only as a geographical region but also as a realm for the spirit." His traditionalism did not look to the past for support: it was to be justified in and by the future.

This Ibero-American philosophy was the first attempt to resolve the conflict that had been latent in the Revolution from the beginning. The revolutionary movement was an instinctive explosion, a longing for communion, a revelation of our being; it was a search for, and discovery of, the ties that had been broken by liberalism. But that rediscovered tradition was not enough to feed the hunger of a newborn country; it lacked the universal elements necessary for the building of a new society now that Catholicism and liberalism, the two great universal forces which had shaped our culture, could no longer serve us. In fact, the Revolution was unable to justify itself even to itself, because it had scarcely any ideas. The

---

Ejido refers to a parcel of communally held land in Mexico, a form of agricultural production with roots in the country's pre-Columbian past that was reinvigorated during the Mexican Revolution.

only choice left, then, was between feeding on itself and inventing a new system. Vasconcelos tried to resolve the question by offering his philosophy of the Ibero-American race. The motto of positivism, "Love, Order and Progress," was replaced by a proud boast: "The Spirit Shall Speak through My Race."

---

3. Mestizo Pride ~ Gilberto Freyre*

When the Great Depression hit Latin America in the 1930s, it devastated the neocolonial system. The culture of scientific racism was dethroned, creating an opportunity for Latin American artists, intellectuals, and politicians to redefine the region's culture along nationalist lines. In Brazilian politics, this redefinition process was led by Getúlio Vargas, who headed the 1930 Revolution that overthrew the Old Republic and implemented a kind of Brazilian New Deal. Vargas, who we will learn more about in chapter 8, went on to rule Brazil until 1945. Brazilian anthropologist Gilberto Freyre became one of the leading spokesmen for a new vision of the Brazilian nation during the Vargas era. In the following excerpt from his most famous book, The Masters and the Slaves, *published in 1933, Freyre addresses the role of sex and sexuality in the making of Brazil's mixed, multiracial nation. Freyre's analysis follows Vasconcelos in the sense that he sees the Portuguese "disposition to mix" with tropical racial groups as a positive not a negative in terms of the development of the nation.*

When Brazilian society was first organized socially and economically in 1532, the Portuguese colonizers had already had an entire century of contact with the tropics. Their aptitude for tropical life had already been demonstrated in Africa and India. The colonization of Brazil would put that aptitude to the test by shifting from the easier path of trade, characteristic of Portuguese activities in Africa and India, to the more substantial and arduous practice of tropical agriculture. Cultivation of the land required stable, patriarchal families and a system of slavery to regulate agricultural labor. The sexual union of Portuguese males with indigenous women incorporated local populations into the culture, economy, and society of the invaders.

Portuguese colonies in tropical America became, in their demographic composition, hybrids of European, Indian, and later, African [*sic*]. The societies that developed there were carved out not so much by state action as by the swords of private individuals. They were societies regulated not so much by ra-

---

*From Gilberto Freyre, *Casa grande e senzala: Formação da família brasileira sob o regime da economia patriarcal*, 28th ed. (Rio de Janeiro: Editora Record, 1992), 4–10, 283–84 (trans. John Charles Chasteen).

cial consciousness (of which the flexible, cosmopolitan Portuguese had little) as by religious exclusivity, all subordinated to economic imperatives. . . . Those in charge in Brazil were always the great landowners with their sugar mills, their private chapels and chaplains, their Indian followers armed with bow and arrow or their slaves armed with blunderbusses. These lords of land and labor always spoke with a loud voice when addressing the king's representatives in Brazil or protesting the actions of mother country or mother church.

The singular Portuguese predisposition for this sort of slave-based, demographically hybrid colonization of the tropics can be explained by the historical experience of Portugal—the experience of a people culturally intermediate between Africa and Europe. African influence bubbled beneath the European, giving a special pungency to Portuguese diet, religion, and sexual life. The blood of Moors or black Africans was widespread in the light-skinned Portuguese population when not the dominant strain, as it is to this day in certain regions of Portugal. African winds mitigated the Germanic harshness of the country's law and institutions, the doctrinal and moral rigidity of the medieval church, softening the Portuguese versions of feudalism, Gothic architecture, even its Latin tongue. European culture reigned, but African culture governed.

The tense and often conflictive human relations between Europe and Africa somewhat offset the softening effect of climate. Constant war stiffened the Portuguese character and victory provided labor for agriculture and industry in the form of enslaved war captives. But these conflictive relations did not exclude the possibility of miscegenation and cultural intercourse between Portuguese and Africans. . . . "One looks in vain for a unified physical type," Count Hermann Keyserling recently observed in speaking of Portugal. Instead, he noted diverse and even opposing elements, people with a Scandinavian air and blacks living together in what seemed to him "a state of profound unity." An earlier history of Portugal described "an indeterminate population in the midst of two contending groups, half-Christian, half-Muslim, with relatives and friends in both groups. . . ."

Within this bi-continentalism or dualism of culture and race, there are other, subordinate factors that call for attention. One is the presence of individuals of Semitic origin or stock, people of a mobility and adaptability that one easily detects in the Portuguese navigators and cosmopolitans of the fifteenth century. Hereditarily predisposed to life in the tropics by long experience there, the Semitic element conferred upon the Portuguese colonizers of Brazil some of the principal physical and psychological attributes required for endurance and success. Among these was the economic realism that tended from an early date to correct the excesses of military and religious zeal in the formation of Brazilian society.

Mobility and a disposition to mix with other peoples were the particular secrets of Portuguese success in the colonization of Brazil. Otherwise, how could an under-populated country like Portugal have managed to spread its blood and culture through areas of the world so diverse and so distant from each other—in Asia, Africa, America, and numerous archipelagos? Wherever they settled, the Portuguese took wives and engendered offspring with a fervor due as much to the instincts of individuals as to policies adopted by the state for obvious economic and political reasons.

No other colonizing people in modern times has equaled the Portuguese in their readiness to mix with others. "Mixibility," in a word, was the quality that allowed the Portuguese to compensate for their small population. From their first contact with women of color, the Portuguese mingled with them and procreated children of mixed race. The result was that a few thousand daring males took firm control of vast territories, vying successfully with much more numerous peoples in the extension of their colonial domain and the efficiency of their colonizing activity. Their history of living intimately with darker races in and near their peninsular homeland had prepared the Portuguese for this colonial undertaking.

Significantly, one of these darker races, the Moors of Islamic faith, was more highly skilled technically and possessed an intellectual and artistic culture superior to that of the Christians. Long contact with the Moors had led the Portuguese to idealize the figure of the Moorish enchantress—brown-skinned and black-eyed, enveloped in a sexual mystique, always dressed in red, always combing her tresses or bathing in the river or in the water of an enchanted spring—that the colonizers found almost perfectly reproduced in the indigenous women of Brazil. The indigenous women had dark, flowing hair they were fond of combing, and they adored bathing their ardent, red-painted bodies in the river. The indigenous women were heavy-set like the Moorish women, too. But they were much less aloof and freely gave themselves to the woman-starved colonizers in return for trinkets like small pieces of mirror.

Today, all Brazilians (even the light-skinned, blond ones) carry in their souls (when not in both soul and body) the mark of Africa or indigenous America. Up and down the coast of Brazil, from Maranhão in the far north to Rio Grande do Sul in the far south, as well as inland in Minas Gerais, the predominant of these influences, whether direct or remote, is that of Africa. We reveal it in our tenderness, in the way we illustrate our words with abundant gestures, in our form of Catholic worship that delights the senses, also in our music, our speech, our gait, and our way of singing lullabies. The mark of Africa is on our sincerest forms of self-expression. It is the influence of the slave "mammy" who rocked us to sleep, who breast-fed and then spoon-fed us, after mashing the food to a pulp in her hand. It is the influence of the old woman who told us ghost stories, of the young boy who was our first playmate, of the mulata who groomed us and, in the creaking cot where we felt for the first time the sensation of complete manhood, initiated us in the ways of physical love.

4. Plan for the Realization of Bolívar's Supreme Dream ~ Augusto Sandino*

For the Nicaraguan nationalist leader Augusto Sandino, fighting the power of outsiders in Central America was not just a matter of redefining cultural values; it was a matter of waging a guerrilla war against the U.S. Marines. In 1927, U.S. president Calvin Coolidge sent the Marines to Nicaragua to enforce the terms of a peace treaty between Nicaraguan parties; but the involvement of the U.S. armed forces in Nicaraguan affairs goes back at least to 1912. Sandino viewed Coolidge's move and the ongoing U.S. intervention as a violation of Nicaraguan sovereignty. So he formed what he called the Army in Defense of the National Sovereignty of Nicaragua to fight the Marines and restore Nicaraguan self-government. As the following excerpt from a 1929 Sandino letter to the president of Argentina makes clear, the guerrilla leader, invoking the name of the Liberator, wanted the support of other Latin American countries in his struggle against U.S. occupation. He proposed that a conference be held in Buenos Aires to gather support. Only a few of the plan's forty-four points are included here, as well as the preamble and conclusion. Notice that he uses the term "our America" in several places. Ultimately, his call for support went unheeded (there was no such "Congress of Representatives of the twenty-one states comprising the Latin American nationality"). The Marines left in 1933, but Sandino was killed in an ambush by the Nicaraguan National Guard in 1934.

Original Project that the Army in Defense of the National Sovereignty of Nicaragua Presents to the Representatives of the Governments of the Twenty-One Latin American States

Preamble

Various and diverse are the theories that have been conceived to accomplish, at one time an approachment, at another an *alliance*, and at yet another a federation, which, embracing the twenty-one divisions of our America, would integrate us into one *nationality*. But never before as much as today has that unification, unanimously longed for by the Latin American people, become so essential, nor have there been the urgent conditions or the facilities that now exist for the fulfillment of such a high purpose, historically prescribed as the maximum task to be accomplished by the citizens of Latin America.

*From Augusto Sandino, *Sandino: The Testimony of a Nicaraguan Patriot, 1921–1934*, comp. and ed. Sergio Ramírez, ed. and trans. by Robert Conrad (Princeton, NJ: Princeton University Press, 1990), 251–53, 261–62. © 1990 Princeton University Press. Reprinted by permission of Princeton University Press.

Profoundly convinced, as we are, that North American capitalism has arrived at its last stage of development, transforming itself as a result into imperialism; and that it now no longer has any respect for theories of right and justice, ignoring the inexorable principles of independence of the divisions of the Latin American nationality, we view as indispensable, and even more so, undelayable, the Alliance of our Latin American states a way to maintain that independence before the designs of U.S. imperialism, or before that of any other power that may wish to subject us to its interests.

Before entering into facts, I wish to be allowed to outline how, why, and in what circumstances we conceived the idea of the absolute need for Alliance among our Latin American states, which we are proposing in the present project.

The conditions under which our armed struggle against the forces of invasion of the United States and their allies have taken place have convinced us that our firm and prolonged resistance of three years could continue for another two, three, or four years, or who knows how many more, but at the end of our campaign the enemy, who possesses every kind of weapon and every type of resource, would necessarily record his victory, because we have found ourselves alone in our efforts, unable to rely upon the essential cooperation, official or extra-official, of any Latin American government, or of any other country. And it was this dark vision of the future which forced us to devise the best means to prevent the enemy from achieving victory. Our mind worked with the regularity of a clock, elaborating the optimistic panorama of our own America, triumphant on some future tomorrow.

We also agreed that the government of the United States would never abandon its inclination to succeed in its ambitious projects in this part of our America, violating Central American sovereignty, projects upon which the future maintenance of North American power largely depends, even though in order to accomplish this it must destroy a civilization and sacrifice countless lives.

On the other hand, an isolated Central America, even less, an abandoned Nicaragua, relying solely upon the anguish and collective suffering of the Latin American people, might possibly stop imperialist greed from constructing the interoceanic canal and from establishing their proposed naval base, tearing apart the lands of Central America.* At the same time, however, we clearly understood that the silence with which the Latin American governments looked upon the Central American tragedy implied their tacit approval of the aggressive and insolent attitude assumed by the United States against a huge part of this continent; an aggression which at the same time signified the collective decline of the right of self-determination of the Latin American states.

Laboring under the influence of these considerations, we have come to realize that it is absolutely essential that the intense drama experienced by Central

---

*Sandino is here referring to the two main conditions of the Bryan-Chamorro Treaty of 1916, which gave the United States permanent rights over any canal built across Nicaragua and a long-term option to construct a naval base in the country's Gulf of Fonseca.

American mothers, wives and orphans, deprived of those whom they loved most on the Segovian battlefields by North American soldiers of imperialism, should not be sterile or betrayed, but rather put to use in support of the Latin American nationality, by rejecting all the treaties, pacts, or conventions that have been entered into with an appearance of legality, which in one way or another impair the absolute sovereignty not only of Nicaragua but of the other Latin American states. To accomplish this, there is nothing more logical, nothing more decisive or vital, than the fusion of the twenty-one states of our America into one unique Latin American nationality, thereby making it possible to consider, as an immediate consequence, our rights over the canal route through Central American territory as well as our rights over the Gulf of Fonseca, also in Central American waters, as well as over all those other enclosed areas in the vast territory between the Rio Bravo in the north and the Strait of Magellan in the south, including the islands of Latin American heritage, which could be used as strategic points or as avenues of communication of common concern to the Latin American community. But, in association with other grave problems affecting the independence and stability of the Latin American states, what we hope to preserve for ourselves, without further delay, are the naval base in the Gulf of Fonseca and the interoceanic canal route across Nicaragua: places that one day not very distant will become the world's magnet as well as its key and therefore, finding themselves under Latin American sovereignty, will be bastions for the defense of its unrestricted independence, and a marvelous engine for the development of its full material and spiritual progress.

For these reasons the project presented to this great assembly confronts straightforwardly the solution to the problems stated in the following basic points:

Project

1. The Congress of Representatives of the twenty-one states comprising the Latin American nationality declares the abolition of the Monroe Doctrine* and, consequently, annuls the right that that doctrine pretends to confer to interfere in the internal and external politics of the Latin American states.
2. The Congress of Representatives of the twenty-one states comprising the Latin American nationality expressly declares its recognition of the right to form an alliance that belongs to the twenty-one states of continental and insular Latin America, and therefore the establishment of one nationality, to be called the Latin American nationality, thereby making effective Latin American citizenship.
43. The Congress of Representatives of the twenty-one states comprising the Latin American nationality adopts as the official motto of the Latin American Alliance, embodied in the Latin American Court of Justice

---

*The doctrine announced by U.S. president James Monroe in 1823 that prohibited future European imperialism in Latin America (the statement is excerpted and discussed further in chapter 10).

and in the sea and land forces of the Latin American Alliance, that which the vibrant new Mexican generation has chosen as the motto of its deep creative restlessness, interpreting therewith the fruitful destiny of our nationality surging into world history and charting new paths: *Let courage speak for my race.*

44. The Congress of Representatives of the twenty-one states comprising the Latin American nationality, which meets in a fraternal mingling of governments and peoples of the twenty-one states, acclaims as the name of the place where the Latin American Court of Justice will have its seat, that of Simón Bolívar, raising in the Hall of Honor of the Latin American Court of Justice, as homage of admiration to the memory of that eminent architect of Latin American independence, a monument crowned by the lofty figure of the greatest forger of free peoples.

Conclusion

Citizen Representatives of the twenty-one Latin American states:

Having revealed the original project that the Army in Defense of the National Sovereignty of Nicaragua is presenting to this great assembly with the high purpose of establishing an Alliance of undeferrable urgency among the twenty-one separate states of the Latin American nationality, we find ourselves fully aware of the enormous historic responsibility that we take upon ourselves with our America and with the world. For this reason, we have not intended to set forth a vain and risky plan, but rather, by interpreting our reality, we have tried to make of this project something effective and capable of finding solutions to our most immediate problems, facing above all else the imperative necessity of achieving the unanimously desired Latin American Alliance, which can be opposed only by theories of an unfortunate skepticism and of small value to the domestic and foreign policies of our states.

Basing our acts upon reality, we are proposing an alliance and not a confederation of the twenty-one states of our America. We understand that to reach this great goal, what is needed more than anything else is the establishment of a primary foundation, which the Alliance gives us. This is not, then, the culmination of our aspirations. It constitutes only the first definitive step toward new and fruitful endeavors of our nationality in times to come.

Perhaps men possessing advanced and universalist ideas will think that our dreams have collided with too many frontiers in the geographic expanse bordered by the Rio Bravo in the north of our America and the Strait of Magellan in the south. But they must also ponder the vital necessity for our Latin America to establish an alliance prior to a confederation of the twenty-one states that compose it, thereby assuring our

domestic freedom and independence, now threatened by the most vora-
cious of all imperialisms, to fulfill in time the great destiny of the Latin
American nationality, now already consummated, as a land of promise
for people of every nation and race.

[Posted from] El Chipotón, the Segovias, Nicaragua, Central America, the
twentieth day of the month of March of nineteen hundred and twenty-nine.

5. The Shark and the Sardines ⁓ Juan José Arévalo*

*This chapter's final selection comes from the populist era of the 1940s and
1950s, the era that is the subject of chapter 8 in this book. Suffice it to say for
now that the populist era had a strong nationalist bent. Coming after the collapse of the neocolonial order in the 1930s, populist governments were often
strong supporters of the emerging new nationalisms. In the following excerpt
from the book* The Shark and the Sardines, *we are introduced to the writing of
Juan José Arévalo, a former philosophy professor who became Guatemala's
first populist president (1945–1951). The book was published in 1956, just
a few years after the coup d'état that overthrew Arévalo's successor, Jacobo
Arbenz. The 1954 coup was directed by the U.S. government, in particular
the Central Intelligence Agency, and was strongly encouraged by the United
Fruit Company, which was aggrieved by Arbenz's land reform program. This
passage of the book, addressed to "the [North] American reader," comes from
the introduction to the English translation. In it he sketches the outlines of U.S.
history from a Latin American perspective and asserts the difference between
Anglo-American and Latin American culture.*

In your hands you hold a controversial book—a book that speaks out against
your State Department's dealings with the peoples of Latin America during the
twentieth century. It intends neither insult nor offense to the United States as a
nation. The future of your country is identified with the future of contemporary
democracy. Neither does this book seek to cast blame on the North American
people—who, like us, are victims of an imperialist policy of promoting business,
multiplying markets, and hoarding money.

Very different was the ideology of the men who first governed your country. It
was as thirteen widely varying former colonies inspired by ideals of individual freedom, collective well-being, and national sovereignty that the United States came
into existence in the world. Protestants, Catholics, and Masons alike, those men
of the eighteenth century were moved by an ardent sense of dignity that won for

*From Juan José Arévalo, *The Shark and the Sardines*, trans. June Cobb and Raul Osegueda (New
York: Lyle Stuart, 1961), 9–13.

them and for their cause the sympathy and the admiration of the entire world. They recognized worth in all kinds of work, they welcomed to their shores foreigners of every origin, and when their crops and their homes were threatened, they defended their crops and their homes just as they defended the privacy of the individual conscience. They went to church with their heads held high and they founded colleges so that their children might advance along the road to self-improvement.

Moral values served as a motivating force in the days of your independence. Those same values, confirmed by the civilian populace of the young republic, figured among the norms of government. The nation was characterized by its grandeur of spirit and indeed great were the military accomplishments and the thesis of the new law. Amazed, the world applauded.

But as the twentieth century was dawning, the White House adopted a different policy. To North America as a nation were transferred the know-how, sentiments, and appetites of a financial genius named [John D.] Rockefeller. Grandeur of spirit was replaced by greed. The government descended to become a simple entrepreneur for business and protector of illicit commercial profits. From then on, accounting was the science of sciences. The new instrument of persuasion was the gunboat. Now the United States had become different. It was neither a religious state nor a juridical state but, rather, a mercantile state—a gigantic mercantile society with all the apparatus of a great world power. The European juridical tradition was abandoned and North American morality was forgotten. The United States thenceforth was to be a Phoenician enterprise, a Carthaginian republic. Washington and Lincoln must have wept in shame in their graves.

The immediate victim was Latin America. To the North American millionaires converted into government, Latin America appeared an easy prey, a "big moneymaker." The inhabitants of this part of the world came to be looked upon as international *braceros*.* This multiple-faceted exploitation was carried out with intelligence, with shrewdness, with the precision of clockwork, with "scientific" coldness, with harshness, and with great arrogance. From our southern lands, the river of millions began to flow northward, and every year it increased. The United States became great while progress in Latin America was brought to a halt. And when anything or anyone tried to interfere with the bankers or the companies, use was made of the Marines. Panama, 1903. Nicaragua, 1909. Mexico and Haiti, 1914. Santo Domingo, 1916. Along with the military apparatus, a new system of local "revolutions" was manipulated—financed by the White House or by Wall Street, which were now the same. This procedure continued right up to the international scandal of the assault on Guatemala in 1954, an assault directed by Mr. [Secretary of State John] Foster Dulles, with the okay of Mr. Eisenhower, who was your President at that time. North American friends, this is history, true history, sketched here as briefly as possible.

---

*Mexican agricultural workers allowed to enter the United States as part of a U.S.-sponsored labor program during World War II.

We Latin Americans, who, more than anybody else, suffered from this change in political philosophy and its consequences, could no longer be friends of the government of the United States. The friendship certainly could be reestablished. But to do so, it would be necessary for the White House to alter its opinion of us, and it would be necessary for its conduct to change. We expect a new political treatment. We do not want to continue down this slope that takes us straight to colonial status, however it may be disguised. Neither do we want to be republics of merchants like the African trading stations of old.

We Latin Americans are struggling to prevent the business mentality from being confused with, or merged into, statesmanship. The North American example has been disastrous to us and has horrified us. We know that a government intimately linked to business and receiving favors from business loses its capacity to strive for the greatest possible happiness for the greatest number of its people. When businessmen become rulers, it is no longer possible to speak of social justice; and even the minimum and superficial "justice" of the common courts is corrupted.

In our resistance to the business mentality, we are still Spanish, stubbornly Spanish. Also, we have not stopped being Catholic, nor have we stopped being romantic, and we cannot conceive of private life without love, nor of public life without chivalry, nor of our children's education without ideals.

If you want to be our friends, you will have to accept us as we are. Do not attempt to remodel us after your image. Mechanical civilization, material progress, industrial techniques, wealth, comfort, hobbies—all these figure in our programs of work and enjoyment of life. But, for us, the essence of human life does not lie in such things.

These lines, my North American friends, are meant to explain why I wrote the fable of *The Shark and the Sardines*. This book was written with indignation—indignation wrapped from time to time in the silk of irony. It declares that international treaties are a farce when they are pacted between a "shark" and a "sardine." It denounces the Pan-American system of diplomacy as an instrument at the service of the shark. It denounces the Pan-American idea of "allegiance to the hemisphere"—a juridical device that will inevitably lead to the establishing of an empire from pole to pole. It denounces the relentless and immense siphoning-off of wealth from south to north. It denounces the existence of the terrible syndicate of millionaires, whose interests lie even outside the United States.

It denounces the subordination of the White House to this syndicate. It denounces the conversion of your military into vulgar policemen for the big syndicates. And for the purpose of analysis, it takes up the case of Nicaragua, compelled by the United States to sign (in 1914–1916) a treaty that goes against all written and all moral laws.

This book, friends of the North, has been read all over Latin America. Read it now, yourselves, and accept it as a voice of alarm addressed to the great North American people who are still unaware of how many crimes have been committed in their name.

VII

Women and Social Change

Given the male-dominated character of political and military affairs in nineteenth-century Latin America, it is easy to forget that women made up half of the new Latin American nations. While women were certainly involved in the patriot movements of the 1810s, their lives, as the selection from Sarah Chambers in chapter 1 pointed out, did not necessarily improve in the aftermath of independence. During the subsequent struggles over abolition, caudillos, the Church, scientific racism, and nation building, women were always there, always a presence, even when they did not always show up directly in the historical record as active participants. Historians who study the experiences of women in modern Latin America have identified a clear pattern when it comes to the movement for women's equality: the movement got started in the late 1800s, underwent important further developments in the first half of the 1900s, and then matured and achieved some successes in the late 1900s. This is not to suggest that the work of the women's movement is over. As Benedita da Silva, the author of the final selection of this chapter, points out, sexism and sexual inequality were alive and well in late twentieth-century Brazil.

Creating social change has thus been a problem that has occupied Latin American women for more than a century. Women in the region initiated a campaign for equal rights in the late 1800s, but progress has been slow. The early generation of women's rights activists (mostly white, middle class, educated, and urban) began a new political dialogue that included women and their concerns for the first time. These pioneers considered themselves to be part of a movement that transcended national boundaries and made connections with similar movements in Europe and North America. In their program, education in matters of marriage, finances, and family law was an especially important goal. Women's rights activists and their supporters in contemporary Latin America recognize the need to continue this struggle.

Recall for a moment that colonial Latin America was based on patriarchal foundations. Colonial women, except for some widows and nuns, faced legal subordination to their fathers or their husbands. They had limited options in life. The dictates of the honor code meant that "decent" women were always chaperoned when away from home. Their chastity could not be put at risk. Yet poor women often had to work outside the house, sacrificing their honor to help feed their families. Middle- and upper-class women stayed home, made the parish church the center of their public lives, and protected their honor (which, by extension, was also the family's honor). Furthermore, despite its lofty promises about freedom and equality, independence did little to transform the conditions of women's lives. Some historians have even argued that the creation of the independent Latin American republics did more harm than good to the cause of women's rights. In so doing, these authors pointed to the reactionary gender content of Europe's Enlightenment (which gave birth to republican ideology), particularly its emphasis on the "domesticity" of women.

The early movements for women's rights thus challenged more than four centuries of patriarchy. To build movements on this issue in various nations, Latin American women, like their North American and European counterparts, raised fundamental questions about their roles in society and their relationships with men. In a word, the women's movement gave us a more complicated understanding of *gender*, meaning the extensive set of qualities associated with being male or female. Gender should always be seen in the proper historical context. Masculinity and femininity, the qualities of maleness and femaleness, are constantly shifting in our world. They change over time (consider the gender expectations placed on your grandparents' generation versus your own), and they change from one society to another (consider the recent debate about women and education in some Islamic countries). In other words, gender roles are socially constructed, which is to say that they are created by human history, not generated by the biology of our sexual differences. Today's turn toward gender studies adds depth to the goal of earlier historians, who wished to "restore women to history" by filling in an essentially blank space in the historical record.

To explore the problem of women and social change in modern Latin America, this chapter is organized chronologically, beginning with the origins of the women's movement across the region in the 1870s and concluding with a spokeswoman of 1990s Brazil. Along the way, perceptive students will note both continuities and changes in the movement as well as the remarkable ability of women to manipulate the traditional language, symbols, and images of Latin America's patriarchal, Catholic heritage. Readers will also be introduced to the fascinating Evita Perón, who will reappear in chapter 8 as part of the problem of populism. Here, as a woman of tremendous power as well as contradictions, she serves as a guide to some of the extremes of gender identity in modern Latin America. By the end of this chapter, students should have a clear understanding of the issues that have driven Latin American women reformers into action and the obstacles they faced in achieving their goals.

QUESTIONS FOR ANALYSIS

1. How far have Latin American women advanced—socially, economically, and politically—during the last century?
2. How have these advances been achieved? What sorts of strategies have women social reformers devised in Latin America?
3. What remains to be done if women are to become fully equal partners in society?

1. Women and Education ~ Francesca Miller*

When Latin American women began to organize the campaign for women's rights in the nineteenth century, they started with female education. In this selection, historian Francesca Miller explains the early history and character of the Latin American women's movement. According to Miller, since the colonial era, women's education had been controlled by the Church, but independence (especially its notion of classical liberalism) introduced some changes to the status quo. Gradually, upper-class women and an increasing number of urban, middle-class women developed a reform agenda that put female education high on the list of priorities. Liberal governments across the region, Miller argues, had their own reasons to support some of these demands, which coincided with their own reform agendas. Note the influence of the North American educational model and the references to Argentine liberal Domingo Sarmiento's educational endeavors.

The examination of the education of women in a given time and place provides a vivid indicator of what women's proper roles in the larger society are perceived to be and of how those roles—economic, intellectual, cultural, social, political—differ from or coincide with those of the women's male peers. First, to properly measure who in a society was educated and who was not, we must understand what was meant by education in a particular time and place. Then we may ask how access to special kinds of education differed for socioeconomic groups and for women and men.

Female teachers, who are overwhelmingly the teachers of young women in Latin America, come from two distinct traditions: that of the *normalista* (the women trained in normal, or teaching, schools) and nuns and lay members of Catholic female teaching orders. In each country the history of public female

*From Francesca Miller, *Latin American Women and the Search for Social Justice* (Hanover, NH: University Press of New England, 1992), 35–51. © 1992 University Press of New England. Reprinted with permission.

education is intimately linked with attempts to secularize, or modernize, the state. Thus, in mid-nineteenth-century Mexico, Benito Juárez's government, which sought to weaken the church, passed legislation providing for public secondary schools for girls; in Argentina, Domingo Sarmiento and the Liberals placed the training of female teachers near the top of their national agenda—a move that incited furious opposition from Catholic female teaching and nursing orders, who regarded education and health care as their domain.

In addition, there is a strong correlation between the advent of public female education, the appearance of *normalistas*, and the rise of feminism in certain Latin American nations. At the end of the nineteenth century in Argentina, Uruguay, Chile, Brazil, Mexico, and Cuba, it was the female schoolteachers who formed the nucleus of the first women's groups to articulate what may be defined as a feminist critique of society. Two factors are of great importance: First, the teachers represented a new group in Latin American society, the educated middle sector, which included skilled workers, clerks, and government employees, as well as educators, and they were well aware of their precarious social, economic, and legal status; second, these women were in touch with one another through their training institutions and through a number of *congresos femininos* which took place in this era from Mérida in the Yucatán to Buenos Aires, Argentina.

The story of the education of women in Latin America consists of three interwoven strands: first, the history of the idea of educating females; second, the debate over what the content of that education should be; and third, the establishment of educational institutions that admitted females.

The patterns for female education established in the colonial period, that of the private, usually Catholic, education of the daughters of the privileged classes and the moral and vocational instruction of the daughters of the poor, usually provided by Catholic charitable societies, persisted in nearly all areas of Latin America throughout the nineteenth century. The private education of the elite woman continues today in many countries; the vocational instruction of the lower-class woman is more apt to be under the auspices of the state.

The intellectual ferment that marked the period of the wars of independence included the discussion of the "rights of man," and Latin American women intellectuals joined their North American, British, and French sisters in expanding the debate to the rights of women. The passion for republican ideals and the increased secularization of the institutions of society, including schools and universities, raised the level of debate on the merits of female education to the national level in Argentina, Chile, Brazil, Uruguay, and Mexico. However, little was done to implement reform in the first half of the nineteenth century.

The wars of independence had a significant intellectual dimension, fostered in the secret meetings of the Freemasons and in the discussions of newly founded scientific societies. Although women were generally barred from these masculine enclaves, they did participate in the discussion of ideas and current politics in the salons of Mexico City, Lima, Caracas, and Rio de Janeiro. In the aftermath of the independence movements some changes occurred in formal education. The first was the decline in clerical control of education, a trend begun with the expulsion of the Jesuit teaching order in the 1760s and intensified in the secular climate of the wars of independence, a struggle in which the hierarchy of the colonial church sided with the mother country. Female teaching orders were not expelled from the colonies, but their political sympathies in general had also allied them with the Spanish and Portuguese loyalists; at the dawn of the national period, patriots looked to private finishing schools rather than convents for the instruction of their daughters.

A second trend was the establishment of national universities, a move in keeping with the ideals set forth in the constitutions of the new Spanish American republics. The universities at Buenos Aires (1821), Montevideo (1833), Santiago de Chile (1842), and those of El Salvador, Costa Rica, and Honduras date from this postrevolutionary period, as do the faculties of medicine and law in Brazil. In Mexico, which already possessed a central university, a number of state institutions, most of which offered a bachelor of law degree, were inaugurated. Women were excluded from these formal institutions of learning, which were intended as training grounds for the American-born male elite; however, the result of the broadening of the educated public, even though relatively slight, created a climate in which the subject of educating women could be broached.

Many of the constitutions of the newly independent countries contained articles that proclaimed the state's responsibility to create and support public education at all levels, as did Chile's (1833), which provided that "education is one of the subjects of primary importance of the states." The Brazilian constitution, drafted in 1822, declared the commitment of the nation to the education of children of both sexes, although this clause was deleted from the constitution imposed by the Emperor Dom Pedro in 1823. In Mexico the constitution of 1822 declared elementary education free, and a nascent public education system for the children of the poor was instituted, employing the "Lancastrian" method, where more advanced pupils taught younger students.

However, as has often been noted, these constitutions were more statements of the aspirations of the national leadership than programs that could be immediately put into practice. Even the long-established educational institutions struggled to survive in the political turmoil and economic disruption of the postwar period, which absorbed the attention of the leaders and the scarce resources of the societies.

At mid-century several patterns are visible in female education in the larger Latin American states. First, as had been true during the colonial era, most formal education had a significant religious content. Young women of the upper classes might be tutored at home or might attend a convent school, where the course of instruction was likely to stress accomplishment in the *belles artes*, such as an acquaintance with French, a little musical training in voice or piano, sketching, fine needlework, and religious instruction.

In addition, female charitable societies sponsored schools for female orphans and children of the poor. In Argentina all public education for girls was under the auspices of the Society of Beneficence. In Brazil in 1870, the Society for the Propagation of Instruction of the Working Classes celebrated the opening of a new school in Rio de Janeiro with premises spacious enough to allow separate classrooms for boys and for "the other sex" as girls are consistently referred to in the records. The school was free, and another charitable organization, Protectoresses of the Children of the Poor, provided uniforms and school materials. Similar societies, many with church affiliations, carried on comparable activities in Mexico, Colombia, Venezuela, and Peru. As was true in the colonial period, the charitable schools for girls emphasized training in household skills that would prepare them for domestic service.

The impetus for dramatic reform in the content, availability, and quality of female education—an impetus that in the twentieth century became the drive for universal education—came not from the socially elite women nor from the charitable schools they established but from the women of the emergent middle sectors. These reform-minded women were urban and tended to be the wives and daughters of professional men: lawyers, doctors, magistrates, professors. Their appearance in Buenos Aires, Santiago, Rio de Janeiro, and Mexico City in the 1860s and 1870s is directly proportionate to the degree of political stability and economic expansion attained by these societies by the late nineteenth century. Conversely, in the societies in which small oligarchies continued to exercise exclusive economic and political power and in areas where political instability was the norm, such as Bolivia, Ecuador, and the Central American states, there was little interest in educational reform.

The medium of expression for social criticism was the periodical. In Brazil, for example, as abolitionist and republican sentiments reached a crescendo in the 1870s, there were some 250 papers and journals in print, and though most of them issued from the major urban centers, no region was without its own. The numerous articles written by women represented the whole spectrum of Brazilian political thought, from monarchist to republican, and ranged in subject matter from romantic poetry to advice on childbirth; however, one theme was common to the women's articles: the commitment to education for women. Education is presented as the sine qua non, the road to greater control over their lives, in both the domestic and political spheres.

An excellent example of the spirit of the women's writings is evident in the following passage from *0 Sexo Feminino*, which was published intermittently in Rio de Janeiro between 1873 and 1889. It was dedicated to the principles of education for women and to the elimination of all forms of slavery in Brazil: "It is to you, *Os Senhores* [meaning men in general], that is owed our inadequacy;

we have intelligence equal to yours, and if your pride has triumphed it is because our intelligence has been left unused. From this day we wish to improve our minds; and for better or worse we will transmit our ideas in the press, and to this end we have *O Sexo Feminino*, a journal absolutely dedicated to our sex and written only by us. *Avante, minhas patricias!* [Forward, my country-women!] The pen will be our weapon."

A brief profile of the editor of *O Sexo Feminino*, Dona Francisca Senhorinha da Motta Diniz, gives an idea of the social and economic background of these literate women. She was married to a lawyer and widowed at a young age; in 1873 she became the directress of a school for girls in the province of Minas Gerais, where she inaugurated her journal. In 1874 she moved to Rio de Janeiro, continued publishing *O Sexo Feminino*, and became headmistress of a secondary school for young women. Motta Diniz had numerous counterparts in Cuba, Mexico, Argentina, Chile, and Uruguay.

The efforts of these early reformers resulted in the establishment of a number of primary schools and a few secondary schools for young women, but the effect for most women in most places of Latin America was negligible. By and large, education remained within the domain of the church and was restricted to a small sector of the population, the majority of whom were male. The more important contribution of these early reformers was in creating a more receptive atmosphere toward the idea of educating women.

It was the introduction of the government-supported normal school that broadened and strengthened the move to educate a larger sector of the population, male and female. From their inception normal schools were overwhelmingly female institutions, although a few should be noted as being among the first coeducational institutions in Latin America. Many were reserved solely for women students (who were identified from the first as "natural teachers") so that girls from good families would be attracted to them. Normal school students were drawn from the newly emergent middle classes; in the societies of the Southern Cone many of them were the children of European immigrants. Teacher-training schools were also open to men, but young men of this emergent middle class had job opportunities in industry, commerce, banking, government, the military, higher education—realms from which young women were excluded. The normal schools offered girls a chance to acquire an education for themselves and a respectable, if poorly remunerated, profession teaching primary school children. In nations where this emergent class did not exist, such as Peru, normal school programs had few advocates and no constituency. The presence or absence of educational opportunities for women in a society provides a valid litmus test of the extent of social change that the society has experienced.

Several factors combined to favor these new secular institutions in societies where education had traditionally been under the auspices of the Catholic church. One was the exemplary pace of economic growth and industrialization being enjoyed by the United States, where public education was widespread. A second factor was the gradual change in public opinion about the value of an educated society, male and female. Less tangible but significant was the belief that the New World experiments in political democracy, whatever their present imperfections, offered the opportunity to build better societies than had previously existed and that an educated citizenry was essential to the realization of this ideal.

Although there were parallel movements in Chile, Uruguay, Brazil, and Mexico, the most famous normal school program was carried out in Argentina. In 1870, President Domingo Sarmiento founded Argentina's first public, coeducational normal school at Paraná. Sarmiento's enthusiasm for educational reform influenced the development of public education, not only in Argentina but throughout Spanish America. His program was modeled on what he had observed in the United States. The school system was to encompass kindergarten through secondary school, and the curriculum, which was entirely secular, would emphasize physical fitness, responsible citizenship, vocational instruction, and skills in reading, writing, and arithmetic. The teaching staff would be drawn from the newly established normal schools, which he envisioned as the keystone of the projected public system. In a singular effort to assure a strong beginning for the system, Sarmiento recruited young women schoolteachers from the Midwestern United States, and between 1869 and 1886 some sixty-five graduates of normal schools in Minnesota and upstate New York went to teach in Argentina. Their dedication to and influence on the fledgling system was considerable; through their efforts and the efforts of those they trained, Argentina's literacy rate rose from less than one-third of the population in 1869 to more than two-thirds in 1914.

2. Women's Reform Issues in Late Nineteenth-Century Peru and Mexico ⁓ Carolina Freyre de Jaimes and *Violetas del Anáhuac**

The women's rights activists of late nineteenth-century Latin America advanced a broad agenda of reforms. The following selections provide three examples of this agenda. The first two, published in the Lima newspaper El Correo del Perú, *were written by the reformer Carolina Freyre de Jaimes, whose articles appeared in newspapers in several other Latin American countries. The third comes from an elite Mexican women's magazine,* Violetas del Anáhuac. *In all three cases, female authors pointed to the need for specific social changes. Note that the model*

*From Carolina Freyre de Jaimes, "Education and Women," *El Correo del Perú* (Lima, Peru), 1872 (trans. Gertrude Yeager); Carolina Freyre de Jaimes, "The Problem with Marriage," *El Correo del Perú* (Lima, Peru), 1871 (trans. Gertrude Yeager); and "Against Drunkenness," *Violetas del Anáhuac*, 1889 (trans. Daniel Castro). Special thanks to Gertrude Yeager for bringing this material to the second edition.

for these changes, particularly in Freyre's articles, is either North American or northern European. Apart from the specific demands they expressed, what makes these selections significant is the way their authors used elements of liberalism— such as anticlericalism and state activism—to challenge Latin American social traditions. Finally, students should be aware of the limited nature of the demands in this early stage of the women's movement. While Freyre wants to change the way Peruvian marriages are conducted, she still sees marriage as the corner- stone of society and women as the "messengers of civilization."

Education and Women (1872)

Women have been admitted to the University of Vermont, all of its classes, and others in Zurich have become doctors. What do you think, ladies? Woman is weak by nature and soft by character? A woman doctor an absurdity? Education and women have never been incompatible ideas to me. Some believe that to change the poetic mission of women for the prosaic occupation of men may be ridiculous.

But there are places where women exercise influence. In the United States they are teachers, journalists, and are demanding the vote. They say in Chile that women administer the post office and telegraph. We need to raise woman's intelligence to the level of men through education or she will continue to be housebound.

Women are those who are called on to regenerate society; they are messen- gers of civilization. Lima, a great South American city, presents a very sad con- trast from the moral perspective because its women lack education. It is available to those with money while ignorance reigns among the masses. The schools offer a rich and varied curriculum for the elites and intellectual misery for the more numerous poor. To form a free society we must elevate women, amplify their educational opportunities, give them professions if they need employment, and inculcate habits of work, sobriety, and good customs.

The Problem with Marriage (1871)

Marriage suffers because the Roman Catholic Church has the poor and incor- rect view of women (who were associated with evil). God also created a need for the family. To quote Saint Paul, he who does not give his daughter in marriage is he who would not improve himself. Marriage is necessary according to positivism and progress because it represents the basis of social order. Mar- riage is not only enjoyment and pleasure, although without sexual attraction it could not continue to function. It is the fulfillment of God's will that marriage is vital to social organization, to educate, to form an honorable society. Marriage is based on intimacy and identification, confidence, and reciprocal caring.

A man who does not have a legal capacity to marry will look for other forms of diversion. He may become a seducer. He would not love truly because he who dishonors does not love truly.

Marriage is a refuge for children and a relief from obligatory celibacy. It is the behavior of married couples which discredits marriage. The failure to complete vows tends to pervert the institution; lack of love is nothing more than mere selfishness. Adultery breaks vows and divides one flesh, but its greatest offense is that it kills love.

People who do not marry are egoists, mere passengers through life, incapable of understanding love and commitment.

Against Drunkenness (1889)

One of the initiatives that should be adopted in Mexico is the creation, at least in the main urban centers, of workshops where journeymen who are prevented from entering their regular place of employment because of tardiness or any other reason can go and spend the day productively. In Mexico it is well known that the workers whose workday is reduced for any reason spend the time going to different *pulquerías* [bars where *pulque* alcohol was served]. We believe that the rules and regulations about to be adopted in some European countries could not be more appropriate, and the following ones could be easily adopted in Mexico:

1. The authorization to open a place to sell alcoholic beverages can only be given to people of proven morality, and the locale must meet certain conditions of hygiene, as well as good light and ventilation;
2. The drinking and consumption of spirits by children and young people under sixteen years of age shall be forbidden in these establishments;
3. There should be official vigilance of these establishments and the drinks being sold therein;
4. [There should be] active vigilance to avoid clandestine sales, particularly in second-class establishments; and
5. Drunkenness must be considered a crime and should not be invoked as an extenuating circumstance, under any circumstances, in the commission of a crime.

Do not label us as pretentious, if we add our weak voices to the universal uproar being raised against such a degrading vice. We are only guided by the desire to see women suffer less, because they are the targets of the excesses of their husbands or their children. Let us take the case of the worker's wife who anxiously awaits her spouse to come to the house with a week's worth of wages. In the course of the day, she will build innumerable castles in the air. She will envision thousands of projects which she will rework constantly to make the money go further. She will buy shoes for the oldest child, who is barefoot and is already going to school, and the littlest one needs a coat, because he is cold crawling on the floor (the mother cannot pick him up because of her household chores). The husband desperately needs another shirt, and whatever is left over will be used for the limited weekly budget of the home. For herself? . . . Oh, well! Next time. The hour when the husband normally comes home rolls around. He does not come . . . at half past . . . six o'clock; she feeds the children and puts them to bed, more than anything to avoid the spectacle that the father will provide soon, because undoubtedly he will be drunk, scandalously drunk. It was payday, after all!

Finally the hour arrives, no longer anxiously awaited but feared, when the head of the household appears, but in such a condition. My God! The wife does not dare say a word for fear of unleashing a storm. If she asks for the money, aside from justifying the use he found for it, he will argue that "this is why I work," and it is very much *his* to spend with his friends or in whatever way he wants.

The hapless woman can hardly find a voice to ask him if he wants to eat. He does not even answer. He throws himself on the bed and begins to shake the whole house with his loud snoring. The next day, he gives his wife what remains of his salary and leaves as if nothing had happened, as if he had fulfilled his duty as a husband and as a father.

The next Saturday, there will be a repeat performance until the wife is driven to the limit of her patience, and she will demand with harsh words. Then he will abuse her, because he has spent the week working like a dog, and he is not allowed even a single moment of leisure, and they want him to be there under all circumstances. . . . Come on!

There is a different kind of drunk. These are the middle-class ones in frock coats and top hats. Pity the clothes, as the poor would say. These gentlemen do not give a plugged nickel about the death of their ascendants and descendants when they have a bottle and a glass in front of them. These are the ones who drink everything from maguey juice to hard liquor.

---

3. The Lady of Hope and the Woman of the Black Myth ~ Julie M. Taylor*

María Eva Duarte de Perón ("Evita" to those who adored her) is one of the most controversial women in modern Latin American history. Half a century after her death from cancer, she was still the object of both praise and scorn in her native Argentina. Born into a poor, provincial family, Eva Duarte became a successful

*From Julie M. Taylor, *Eva Perón: The Myths of a Woman* (Chicago: University of Chicago Press, 1979), 75–81. © 1979 University of Chicago Press. Reprinted by permission of the publisher.

radio actress as a teenager. She then began a romantic liaison with politically ambitious Colonel Juan D. Perón. Eventually they married and Perón was elected president of Argentina. As first lady, Eva was extremely active. She helped women secure the right to vote, organized the Peronist Feminist Party (to make sure that they voted for her husband), created and administered the charitable Eva Perón Foundation, and made countless speeches on behalf of her husband's government. These activities resulted in the controversy surrounding her. In the following selection, anthropologist Julie M. Taylor presents two competing versions of Eva Perón's life and character. On one hand is the "Lady of Hope," the positive version promoted by her admirers and supporters. On the other hand is the "Woman of the Black Myth," the negative version put forth by her critics and detractors. Students should pay particular attention to the values used to judge Evita—either positively or negatively—and recall that the anthropologist is expressing the judgment of people on the street rather than her own.

The Lady of Hope

Claiming that she knew nothing about politics, Eva found in social work a sphere for which her womanly intuition and emotional life qualified her perfectly. She dedicated much of this work to children, as would be expected from such an ideally feminine, thus deeply maternal, woman. A woman may involve herself in any area of activity to which her man directs her, but her place and the function for which she was born are in the home. Neither Eva's childlessness nor her death affects this theme in any way. Eva Perón had no sons and daughters of her own; she was mother to the children of Argentina. More than that, she was mother of the nation as a whole, particularly to the common people and the poor and needy of Argentina. It was maternal devotion that motivated her attendance on the poor, her work to raise money for her cause, her conferences with governors of the provinces, and her meetings with labor delegations. In grateful response, popular Peronism dubbed her its Lady of Hope and Good Fairy.

Not even the invitation of the Spanish government to visit her nation's Motherland could make Eva forget the workers and their cause. She continued to stress her interest in social work and to distribute alms throughout her journey. But the deeds of the Good Fairy of the poor now had to share the spotlight with the successful social contacts of the traveling First Lady. The Spaniards welcomed her with protocol usually reserved for royalty. Soon she had become as much a favourite with the Spanish aristocrats as with the hundreds of thousands of anonymous Spaniards who lined the streets to catch sight of her. In Italy, too, she fascinated both the crowds and high society. Only her decision to change her itinerary prevented her arrival in London from being, as sumptuous preparations for it promised, one of the most important events of high society's year. The innumerable rooms of a mansion in the heart of the London frequented by English aristocracy awaited her in vain.

Europe, even France, the supreme authority on matters of feminine taste, marveled at the beauty of Argentina's emissary of good will. She encountered admiration everywhere, confirming her position as a paragon of elegance. Her followers memorized the details of her every change of dress—the fittings, the designers, the gold lamé, the hats, mantillas, even a tiara—and never tired of the rainbow of images that spread over the media of the time and continued glowing in the huge full-coloured photographs of magazines still dedicated, twenty-five years later, exclusively to her.

But Eva did not spend all her time dispensing charity, making calls, and planning her wardrobe. She made a point of visiting museums and attending cultural events, appreciating deeply these works and performances, which she went out of her way to see. As always properly hesitant to express inexpert opinions on politics, Eva Perón expatiated on her preferences in music and literature.

From her triumphal tour of Europe, the First Lady returned to throw herself immediately into her campaign for women's suffrage in Argentina. A week after her arrival in Buenos Aires, she directed an open letter to Argentinian women from the front pages of the newspapers, announcing her plans and the needs for their fulfillment. Eva explicitly differentiated her movement from feminist movements in other, especially Anglo-Saxon, countries, where the Peronists felt that feminism had become a form of competition with men. Eva and Peronism rejected earlier Argentinian campaigns on behalf of women's civil rights as copies of foreign ideas, considering them not only mistaken in content, but the result of ingrained social snobbery and cultural imperialism.

The virtue of the Peronist woman lay in never aspiring to supplant the opposite sex. Rather, Peronist feminism represented an effort to take advantage of women's own special identity and talents in order better to fill their particular place in the world. Peronist women carefully emphasized the point that they had no intention of denying their domestic nature now that they had obtained full citizenship.

Eva Perón's position in the nation exemplified the position of the ideal woman in the home. She, on her level, like the housewife on hers, assumed a role as the chief agent responsible for the transmission of the values which uphold society as a whole. Both carried out functions broader than spiritually and physically nutritive ones. The watchfulness of the Peronist woman over domestic economy and morality extended beyond the home to become one of her special political functions: it was she who, qualified by her feminine nature, could best take up a unique watch against treachery within the Peronist movement and threats arising from without. Evita, chief protector of the movement, kept watch as well over its leader and her husband, Juan Perón himself. He, realizing her importance as his shield against betrayal and evil, acknowledged that "Eva . . . with her marvelous judgment has been the guardian of my life, confided to her intelligence and loyalty."

With her successes in Europe and in the campaign for women's rights behind her, Eva's activities grew in importance and number. Her influence depended on her all-enveloping aura more than on specific actions affecting particular political situations, despite the fact that the Peronist press of the time offered reports on her activities or particulars of personages, organizations, schedules, gifts, and honours. Eva defined the tone of Peronism as a movement even more than as a party.

As she wore herself out in her office day by day, the symptoms of her final disease began to appear, bearing witness to the gruelling sacrifice that Eva insisted on offering up for her people. "Poor thing," stated a Peronist, referring to the widely known fact that sexual relations were impossible for Eva for two years before her death; "she gave up even her happiness as a woman for us." In her attempts to continue working through her long illness, the Lady of Hope was making her conscious and voluntary sacrifice.

Her renunciation of the vice-presidency formed part of this process. In the mass demonstration of the Cabildo Abierto, the Open Town Hall, Eva's people and her party offered her the highest honour which they could bestow. When she refused this honour, her disappointed followers dedicated the nearby anniversary of October 17 to her in recognition of her selfless renunciation. The words "*Santa Evita*" appeared for the first time in the press in connection with this celebration.

Her death, which loomed before her immediately after the Renunciation, made her martyrdom incontrovertible. Her brokenhearted followers responded to the dead Eva in the only way appropriate to her saintly act: they worshipped her as a saint. They erected altars to her; offered her prayers; called her their Spiritual Chief, Saint Eva, and Spiritual Protector of the Argentine University; believed in her miraculous powers; and waited for her return.

The Woman of the Black Myth

"That woman," "*esa mujer*," was born in the ill-disguised brothel of her mother. During a childhood and adolescence spent helping to run and maintain her family's "boarding house" or "*pensión*," Eva early began to attract the attention of passing clients as well as the townspeople in general. Already aggressive and ambitious at fifteen, she linked herself to the troupe of a tango singer whom she had probably seduced, and travelled to Buenos Aires to establish herself as a prostitute. Her professed occupation on the stage was no more than a disguise of her real activities.

The capital offered Eva a whirlwind of affairs with actors, producers, industrialists, and political figures. She possessed a coarse, dark attraction, a typically provincial prettiness. But beyond this, she demonstrated sexual appetites and habits that contributed spectacularly to her notoriety. Exploiting both her liaisons and the special talents that attracted them, Eva was frantically scrambling up the social ladder when she met Juan Domingo Perón and immediately moved in with him. Recognizing his rising star, she held on to this catch—with success which amazed even her: anti-Peronists say that when Perón proposed marriage, Evita Duarte was so astounded that she nearly fell out of bed.

Sometimes the account differs. Eva could magnetize Perón because she, like him, lacked sexuality. Either she was frigid and he, impotent, or both valued power over all. Even sexual attraction became unimportant beside this all-consuming passion. Their distorted values led them to center their lives entirely around the interests of their regime, to the extent that they did not sleep together—Perón, the military man, rising early, and Eva, the bohemian, retiring as he rose.

However she attracted him, Eva Duarte married Juan Perón and immediately began to wear the pants in their relationship. Unlike women such as Eleanor Roosevelt of the United States or Madame [Vincent] Auriol of France who knew how to play "the role of second violin which every woman of real tact assumes," Eva took up the first violin or even the baton of the orchestra. She contrasted dramatically with the ideal wife who "has neither youth, nor fur coats, nor [knows] how to harangue over the radio, but knows how to knit, cooks well, darns the socks and bakes pastries which make you lick your fingers." This perfect wife satisfies any man simply by being "a woman who is quiet, intuitive, and who does not make speeches."

The dominance of this upstart soon extended beyond her marriage. She involved herself in all aspects of government. Perón meekly endorsed her growing interference by asserting that wherever Eva appeared, she represented his own presence and carried his authority. The sun of a radiant Eva began to eclipse Juan's fading moon. Eva was converting the nation into a matriarchy.

Inexorably, she stretched her web of control over the other men in her husband's regime. Some she dominated through the fascination of her own eroticism or through secret sexual practices. Others, Eva Perón castrated—sometimes figuratively and sometimes literally: she dealt with her own underlings by rendering them political eunuchs, and she tortured her opponents with electric shocks that left them impotent. Eva took direct responsibility for the castration of rebel leaders and others, making flamboyant displays of her satisfaction with her deed. She kept a glass receptacle preserving the testicles of her victims in the office where she leaned, young and exquisitely clad in her Parisian suits, over a desk to attend the needs recited by ministers, union delegations, and the poor alike.

Meanwhile, the new First Lady attempted in vain to shoulder her way into social circles closed to her. When her efforts failed, she determined to outdo the aristocratic women who would not accept her. Her envy of these inaccessible social circles had decided her marriage to Perón, a rising young military figure. Now that she was First Lady, her bitter resentfulness intensified. It sent her to Europe; drove her to establish the vast Eva Perón Foundation; goaded her into the acquisition of houses, jewels, and clothes; and, finally, kindled her frustrated appeal to the masses for the recognition denied her by high society.

Early in her husband's regime, she had attended an exclusive fashion show in Harrod's department store, only to be ignored or, according to some accounts, to be left alone with her small party of friends as the distinguished ladies swept out. The same women refused her the traditional honor bestowed upon Presidents' wives, the office of president of their charity organization, the Society of Benefi-cence. Their acts only exacerbated Eva's long-standing resentment towards those whose social position she could never attain. This rancor became unbearable and prodded her into expressing it in every aspect of her life, accounting for most of her projects; she knit even the beneficial works of her charity into her elaborate plots of retaliation.

Her petty desire for vengeance far outweighed any political convictions or motivations Eva might have claimed. An anti-Peronist with a nondescript sur-name would run no risk from the same activities for which Eva would jail anyone with one of the aristocratic surnames of Buenos Aires. It was Eva Perón who imprisoned upper-class women and adolescents accused of demonstrating against the government. Knowing that this would inflict greater cruelty on the sheltered members of the upper classes than on middle-class anti-Peronists, Eva jailed the women with prostitutes and drug addicts. In some cases, the First Lady threatened to interfere with the funerals of older women of the aristocracy, preventing their relatives from burying them with their illustrious forebears. However, if the ladies in question invited her to tea in their homes, she promised that the funeral plans would go through.

Eva's drive to obtain the marks of her enemies' social status found its most complete and extravagant expression in her tour of Europe. However, as would have been expected, the lamentable cultural deprivation inherent in her disrepu-table origins foiled her prodigious efforts.

On her wardrobe alone, in her attempts to surpass her enemies, she lavished millions of dollars. Before Eva's trip to Europe, an anti-Peronist took the trouble to count her different outfits and reported to the press that during the 270 days between June 4, 1946, and April 30, 1947, the First Lady had donned 306 dresses.

Original models began to arrive by official airplane from Paris. Some of these bouffant, gala gowns occupied an entire plane, which the Argentinian gov-ernment sent to France and brought back at public expense, containing the dress arranged on a solitary standing mannequin.

All of this could not change the Eva who had peered out of one of her first publicity posters, smiling under "a funny little hat from the movies." This Evita, shamelessly and gaudily voluptuous, lurked forever behind the later, more streamlined image that diet and expensive clothes created. At the time of her European trip she still revealed her own true penchant for a wardrobe that was distinctly Hollywood-esque, her taste expressing itself in elaborate falls and rolls of blonde hair and in an addiction to fur wraps even in the hottest Spanish and Italian weather. Even when her clothes lost the stamp of her early career, she could not hide the tell-tale signs of her vulgar origins: her wide hips and thick ankles.

---

4. Peronist Feminism in Argentina 〜 Eva Perón*

Eva Perón's political activities, as we saw in the previous selection, inspired powerful feelings among Argentines. She never flinched when it came to putting herself on public view. During her years as first lady, she not only gave numerous speeches on behalf of her husband's government but also had her views on Peronism and Argentine society published for all to read. The following selection is taken from My Mission in Life, *a collection of short essays covering various aspects of Peronism, particularly with regard to the role of women in the movement. Two passages have been chosen to indicate the complicated, seemingly contradictory nature of Peronist feminism (at least as it was articulated by the self-proclaimed leader of the Peronist feminist movement). While Argentine women are being called to action, their efforts are still firmly grounded in the traditional feminine ideal of self-sacrifice.*

Women and My Mission

My work in the woman's movement began and grew, just like my work of social service and my trade-union activities, little by little, and more by force of circumstances than through any decision of mine.

This may not be what many imagine to be the case, but it is the truth.

It would be more romantic or more poetic or more literary, and more like fiction, if I said, for example, that all I do now I had felt intuitively . . . as a vocation or a special decree of fate.

But such is not the case.

All I brought by way of preparation to the scene of these struggles were those same feelings which had made me think of the problems of the rich and the poor.

But nothing more.

I never imagined it would fall to my lot someday to lead a woman's movement in my country, and still less a political movement.

Circumstances showed the way.

---

*From Eva Perón, *My Mission in Life*, trans. Ethel Cherry (New York: Vantage, 1953), 181–83, 205–6.

Ah! But I did not remain in my comfortable position of Eva Perón. The path which opened up before my eyes was the path I took if by it I could help [Juan] Perón's cause a little—the cause of the people.

I imagine many other women have seen the paths I pursue long before I did.

The only difference between them and me is that they stayed behind and I started. Actually, I should confess that if I girded myself for a struggle it was not for myself but for him . . . for Perón!

He encouraged me to rise.

He took me out of "the flock of sparrows."

He taught me my first steps in all my undertakings.

Afterward I never lacked the powerful and extraordinary stimulus of his love.

I realize, above all, that I began my work in a woman's movement because Perón's cause demanded it.

It all began little by little.

Before I realized it I was already heading a woman's political movement . . . and, with it, had to accept the spiritual leadership of the women of my country.

This caused me to meditate on woman's problems. And, more than that, to feel them, and to feel them in the light of the doctrine with which Perón was beginning to build a New Argentina.

I remember with what extraordinary fondness, as friend and master, General Perón explained to me innumerable women's problems in my country and in the world.

In these conversations I again became aware of the kindliness of his nature.

Millions of men have faced, as he has faced, the ever more acute problem of woman's role in humanity in this afflicted century; but I think very few of them have stopped, like Perón, to penetrate it to its depths.

In this, as in everything, he showed me the way.

The world's feminists will say that to start a woman's movement in this way is hardly feministic . . . to start by recognizing to a certain extent the superiority of a man!

However, I am not interested in criticisms.

Also, recognizing Perón's superiority is a different matter. Besides . . . it is my intention to write the truth.

Women and Action

I firmly believe that woman—contrary to the common opinion held by men—lives better in action than in inactivity.

I see this every day in my work of political service and social welfare.

The reason is very simple. Man can live exclusively for himself. Woman cannot.

If a woman lives for herself, I think she is not a woman, or else she cannot be said to live. That is why I am afraid of the "masculinization" of women.

When that occurs, women become even more egoistic than men, because we women carry things to greater extremes than men.

A man of action is one who triumphs over all the rest. A woman of action is one who triumphs for the rest. Isn't this a great difference?

Woman's happiness is not her own happiness, but that of others.

That is why, when I thought of my feminist movement, I did not want to take woman out of what is so much her own sphere. In politics men seek their own triumph.

Women, if they did that, would cease to be women.

I have not wanted women to look to themselves in the woman's party . . . but rather that right there they should serve others in some fraternal and generous form.

Woman's problem everywhere is always the deep and fundamental problem of the home.

It is her great destiny—her irremediable destiny.

She needs to have a home; when she cannot make one with her own flesh, she does so with her soul, or she is not a woman!

Well, for this very reason I have wanted my party to be a home that each basic unit should be something like a family . . . with its great loves and its small disagreements, with its sublime fruitfulness and its interminable laboriousness.

I know that in many places I have already attained this. Above all, where the women I have appointed are most womanly!

More than political action, the feminist movement has to develop social service. Precisely because social service is something that we women have in the blood!

Our destiny and our vocation is to serve others, and that is social service.

Not that other "social life" . . . which is contrary to all service!

5. Women's Reform Issues in Late Twentieth-Century Brazil ⁓ Benedita da Silva*

The right to education, to work, and to vote, according to Benedita da Silva, have been the achievements of the Latin American women's movements. But, da Silva adds, there is still a long way to go before the rights of women can be said to be truly equal to those of men. Da Silva should know. As a black woman in a country where blackness is still a disadvantage, she once worked as a domestic servant. However, as the first Afro-Brazilian woman to serve in her country's

*From Benedita da Silva, *Benedita da Silva: An Afro-Brazilian Woman's Story of Politics and Love*, as told to Medea Benjamin and Maisa Mendonça (Oakland, CA: Institute for Food and Development Policy, 1997), 103–9. Reprinted by permission of the publisher.

senate, da Silva has seen the full range of late twentieth-century Brazilian social life. Her experiences have led her to continue the struggle begun more than a century earlier by women such as Carolina Freyre de Jaimes. Specifically, as she explains in the following selection, da Silva has promoted legislation to eliminate the most abusive aspects of sexism in Brazil. Her words remind us that double standards, sexual and otherwise, remain a troubling aspect of contemporary life in Latin America.

Back in sixteenth-century Brazil, the Jesuit priest Antonio Vieira preached that a woman should only leave her home three times in her life—when she was baptized, married, and buried.

Since then, Brazilian women have certainly gotten out of the house. We've struggled for the right to education, and today 60 percent of university graduates are women. We've struggled for the right to work, and today almost half of the workforce are women. We've struggled for the right to vote, and today we are even running for office and winning elections.

Women in Brazil have come a long way, but not far enough. We're still relegated to less prestigious professions—teachers, secretaries, clerical and domestic workers—and we earn half the pay that men do. We may be winning elections, but only 6 percent of the congressional representatives are women.

While few men today dare to openly defend the idea that women are inferior, sexism still permeates our society. In the media, women are portrayed as sexual objects and their bodies are used to sell all kinds of products. Sometimes sexist attitudes appear in more subtle ways—disguised in our schoolbooks or in the words of popular songs. The message is that girls should be well behaved, cute, and sweet, and boys should be smart, sharp, and competitive.

Gender roles are not natural or determined by biological differences. They're socially constructed roles, and vary according to the culture and the time period. Intuitively, I have always questioned these stereotypes since the time I was a child. I liked to build my own toys and do the same things boys did. I played marbles. I climbed trees to pick fruit. I was one of the few girls who worked in the market.

But many women are influenced by the stereotypes promoted by the media. They obsess about their weight—going on crash diets, then gaining the weight back and dieting again. I don't worry about my weight. I'm not going to kill myself because someone thinks I should be skinny. Plus, who says that fat people are ugly? I also don't kill myself doing exercises that are too hard on my body. For me, taking care of my body means taking a shower. I love taking hot showers; that's my kind of exercise.

I'm not interested in looking like everyone else. I refuse to buy certain clothes just because they're in style. I'm also not the type of woman who worries about wrinkles and is afraid of getting old. I'm proud of being a grandmother. I enjoy my age, I don't try to hide anything.

Many times women in positions of power feel they have to act like men to gain respect. We have an expression to describe someone who is assertive. We say they "*põe a pau na mesa*," which literally means they "put their pecker on the table." I consider myself a feminist, but I don't want to have to act like a man to gain respect. I believe I can be assertive and a true feminist without losing my femininity.

I also don't think that feminist women have to be stiff and hide their emotions. Strong women are women who know how to laugh and cry, women who love with passion, women who nurture. I'm an extremely warm and caring lover. I have a very strong personality but in the privacy of my own home, I express all my feelings, including those considered by some to be a sign of weakness.

I know how to flirt and use my charm. I like to dress well and I know that men admire well-dressed women. I admire men who look sharp, too. Sometimes when I see an attractive man, I think of the romantic song "Girl from Ipanema" that goes, *Olha que coisa mais linda, mais cheia de graça*—Look at that beautiful thing, how full of charm. . . . I certainly appreciate a handsome man, a muscular body. But that doesn't mean that I would ever use a man as a sexual object, like men do to women. The most important thing in a relationship is to feel an intellectual affinity. When that happens, that first impression based solely on physical attraction becomes secondary.

And just because I look at other men doesn't mean I'm unfaithful to Pitanga. I'm faithful to him because I respect and trust him. For me, fidelity has to be a mutual agreement. I can't stand this double standard where people think it's acceptable for men to cheat on their partners, but if women do, it's a big scandal. If it's adultery when a woman sleeps with another man, then it's adultery when a man sleeps with another woman.

In Brazil, the concept of "conjugal fidelity" is actually written into the Civil Code. It's supposed to work both ways, but in reality it only applies to women and so it becomes an instrument to preserve male domination. That's why I'm trying to change the wording of the Civil Code, eliminating any reference to "conjugal fidelity" and replacing it with "mutual respect and consideration." The latter is a more advanced concept and reflects women's struggle for juridical equality. It also reflects my own feelings that the most important element for a good partnership is not fidelity but mutual respect.

You wouldn't believe the controversy that my suggested revision provoked. Some men in Congress were scandalized and said, "If you're going to get rid of fidelity, you might just as well get rid of marriage." They accused me of advocating free love and attacking marriage as an institution. But I really believe that fidelity in marriage should come from reciprocal love, not from the imposition of punitive laws or obsolete rules that are only applied to women.

I have a very liberated attitude when it comes to sex. I always talked to my children about everything. When they wanted to know how babies were born, my husband didn't know what to tell them, so I explained everything. I gave them all kinds of information about sex. One time my son came home with gonorrhea and my husband was horrified. I was the one who had to take care of him, and I had no problem with that. I also don't have a hang-up about my body or nudity. Even today, I take off my clothes in front of my children.

I never put pressure on my daughter to be a virgin when she married, even though that kind of pressure was very common when I was growing up. Most parents were really uptight. They were constantly fretting over whether their daughters "*pularam a cerca*"—jumped the fence. If the girls got caught with their boyfriends, the parents would create a big scandal and sometimes even throw their daughters out of the house. My parents had this type of mentality and my sisters suffered because of it. One of my sisters became a prostitute and had to leave the house. I felt sorry for her, and we continued to have a good relationship.

Although I've always tried to pass these liberal values on to my children, my daughter Nilcea is more conservative than I am. My granddaughter Ana Benedita, however, takes after me. Nilcea says, "This child is going to give us a headache." And I say, "Of course she is, *ela vai botar pra quebrar*—she's going to drive us crazy." She's already very assertive, and I'm sure she's going to be a very independent woman. But I want her to go out in the world with her eyes open to the difficulties that women face.

One of the real difficulties that many women confront is sexual harassment. Sure, it's nice to feel desired by a man. A sexual advance, if it's done respectfully, makes you feel good and is simply part of the game between the sexes. I'm not offended if a man admires me sexually, but I won't accept an aggressive come-on. I know how to throw a bucket of cold water on a guy's advances when I have to, but not all women are able to protect themselves. Many times women have to perform sexual favors in order to get a job. And to get ahead professionally, they have to put up with come-ons and lewd behavior from their bosses.

Sexual harassment not only exists in the workplace, but any place where men and women get together. When men first look at women, they're usually undressing them with their eyes. Men feel powerful through sex, especially if they have sex with a lot of different women.

Many men want to have their "*mulher de casa*"—woman at home—and "*mulher da rua*"—woman on the street. The prostitute is seen as someone with whom they can be more sexually intimate and get greater sexual pleasure. Their wives are expected to be more modest. Taboos and dogmas don't allow the wives to fully explore their sexuality. This pushes the men to play out their sexual fantasies with prostitutes, whom they feel they can exploit in whatever ways they please.

Black women bear the brunt of this exploitation, particularly when it comes to white men. There is this impression that black women are "*mais quentes*"— hotter, so men feel free to exploit them more. Black women are considered

more pleasing sexually, but these men usually don't want to make a commitment to them. Black women are considered good enough for screwing, but not
good enough to marry.

These sexist attitudes lead to one of the most serious problems in Brazil
today, which is violence against women. When I was a federal deputy, I helped
organize a special Congressional commission to investigate this issue, and we
were shocked by our findings. We discovered that over 300 cases of violence
against women were reported every day. In fact, we discovered that Brazil was
the world champion in terms of violence against women!

VIII

Populism

The twentieth century was a period of great changes in the traditional societies of Latin America. In the early 1900s, middle-class women and people of color initiated profound changes throughout the region as they pressed their claims for full and equal citizenship. As the century progressed, yet another new social group emerged to challenge the guardians of social order: the industrial working class.

Workers had always been the majority in Latin American societies. They toiled on the haciendas and plantations, labored in the mines and on the docks, sweated in the workshops, and moved merchandise in the streets and markets. But beginning in the twentieth century, a new type of worker was being created by the industrialization of the region's economies. This new, industrial working class was different. For one thing, these men and women were found primarily in large factories that required expensive machinery and produced vast quantities of manufactured goods. For another, such factories tended to be located in or on the outskirts of large cities, leading to an increased concentration of workers in those areas. Given the dense, mostly urban organization of Latin American industrial development, it is no wonder that the new labor force possessed greater class consciousness than any previous one in Latin American history.

This chapter, in examining the political and social consequences that accompanied Latin America's industrial growth, focuses primarily on a political phenomenon known as populism. In the 1930s and 1940s, varieties of populism also appeared in Europe and the United States. At the core of twentieth-century populism was a relationship between a charismatic leader and the industrial working class. Benito Mussolini's Fascist movement in Italy and Franklin Roosevelt's New Deal in the United States both had populist aspects. What linked these movements together was the worldwide crisis of capitalism that began with the Great Depression in 1929.

The Great Depression devastated national economies that depended on international trade. Nowhere was this shock worse than in Latin America, whose countries were completely dependent on the exportation of basic raw materials. As markets for exports shriveled, Latin American economies were thrown into free fall. One example of this trend occurred in the port of São Paulo, Brazil, where tons of handpicked coffee beans had to be burned for lack of buyers. To deal with the impact of the depression, Latin America needed to transform its entire approach to economic development, but such a transformation also required a radical change in political leadership.

Beginning in the 1930s (and carrying through until the 1950s), effective assaults on the political power of Latin America's traditional oligarchies were carried out by populist leaders such as Juan Perón of Argentina, Jorge Eliécer Gaitán of Colombia, and Getúlio Vargas of Brazil. Populist leaders often came from relatively humble origins, had a background in the military, and knew how to stir a crowd of workers with rhetoric based on nationalism, class struggle, and traditional gender relations. In their speeches, the populists created opportunities for workers to identify with the nation in ways that would have been unimaginable only decades earlier. Taking advantage of the latest communications technologies like radio, populists blasted the corruption and privilege of traditional oligarchies closely linked to the shattered import-export system. By equating the oligarchs with the economic devastation brought about by the Great Depression, populists rode to electoral victory.

Once in office, the populists attempted to implement a set of core policies aimed at the further industrial and social development of their countries. On the economic front, they pursued import-substitution industrialization, a key element of twentieth-century Latin American nationalism. Aggressively protecting fledgling national industries, populists ignored the tenets of laissez-faire liberalism. They also promoted state control over vital sectors of the economy. Many foreign investors lost capital in the "nationalization" of these industries (as the expropriation of industry by the state was called), which generated powerful enemies abroad for the populists. On the social front, their program favored the interests of the urban middle class and the industrial working class. Trade unionism flourished, and though most populist leaders manipulated the unions, Latin American workers generally felt more equitably treated in their relations with management than ever before. The first social security systems were established along with such important benefits as modern labor codes and welfare programs.

There is no better example of the problem of populism than Juan Domingo Perón of Argentina, whose rise to power is explored in three of the selections that follow. Together with his myth-making wife Eva (Evita), Perón defined the populist era in Argentina. The key moment in the Peróns' political ascendency occurred on October 17, 1945, when Juan Perón was released from military confinement after having been declared a threat to society by the military regime then governing Argentina. In the preceding years, the dashing young colonel, using his position as minister of labor, had built up his own base of power in the country's industrial labor unions. On October 17 (henceforth known as Loyalty Day in the Peronist ranks), the unionists of the industrializing outer bands of Buenos Aires—many of them first- or second-generation immigrants from southern Europe—came out of their neighborhoods to demand Perón's release. Late that night, Perón was released by the authorities; the workers won. When Perón finally came to the balcony in Buenos Aires' main plaza to speak, the crowd numbered in the hundreds of thousands. As we will see below, it was a defining moment for the Peronist movement. By the end of this chapter, students will be able to explain what connected leaders like Juan Domingo Perón to workers like Doña María Roldán.

QUESTIONS FOR ANALYSIS

1. How did populist leaders such as Perón, Gaitán, and Vargas attempt to achieve their goals? What strategies did they employ?

2. What were the limits on the goals and strategies of the populists? What, if anything, were they unwilling to do?

3. Decide for yourself. Were populist leaders legitimate heroes for the working class or authoritarian demagogues whose main goal was keeping themselves in power?

1. The Peronist Political Vision ~ Daniel James*

The career of Juan Perón of Argentina presents a fascinating case study of the problem of populism. Like the other populists, Perón was a powerful orator and manipulator of imagery. In this selection, historian Daniel James writes about Perón's successful linking, in his political rhetoric and symbolism, of Argentine nationalism with the "concrete, material aspects" of working-class life. Such aspects of workers' daily lives constituted the field in which Peronist language grew and included specific words (such as "los descamisados," the "shirtless" and thus penniless) and cultural references (such as lyrics from tangos). To begin, James grounds his interpretation of Peronism in the basic schools of thought regarding workers' motivations for participating in the Peronist movement.

The relationship between workers and their organizations and the Peronist movement and state is clearly vital for understanding the 1943–1955 period. Indeed, the intimacy of the relationship has generally been taken as defining the uniqueness of Peronism within the spectrum of Latin American populist experiences. How are we to interpret the basis of this relationship, and beyond that,

*From Daniel James, *Resistance and Integration: Peronism and the Argentine Working Class, 1946–1976* (New York: Cambridge University Press, 1988), 12–14, 21–24. © 1988 Cambridge University Press. Reprinted by permission of Cambridge University Press.

the significance of the Peronist experience for Peronist workers? Answers to this question have increasingly rejected earlier explanations which saw working-class support for Peronism in terms of a division between an old and new working class. Sociologists like Gino Germani, leftist competitors for working-class allegiance, and indeed Peronists themselves explained worker involvement in Peronism in terms of inexperienced migrant workers who, unable to assert an independent social and political identity in their new urban environment and untouched by the institutions and ideology of the traditional working class, were *disponible* (available) to be used by dissident elite sectors. It was these immature proletarians who flocked to Perón's banner in the 1943–1946 period.

In the revisionist studies working-class support for Perón has been regarded as representing a logical involvement of labor in a state-directed reformist project which promised labor concrete material gains. With this more recent scholarship the image of the working-class relationship to Peronism has shifted from that of a passive manipulated mass to that of class-conscious actors seeking a realistic path for the satisfaction of their material needs. Political allegiance has, thus, been regarded, implicitly at least, within this approach as reducible to a basic social and economic rationalism. This instrumentalism would seem to be borne out by common sense. Almost anyone inquiring of a Peronist worker why he supported Perón has been met by the significant gesture of tapping the back pocket where the money is kept, symbolizing a basic class pragmatism of monetary needs and their satisfaction. Clearly, Peronism from the workers' point of view was in a fundamental sense a response to economic grievances and class exploitation.

Yet, it was also something more. It was also a political movement which represented a crucial shift in working-class political allegiance and behavior, and which presented its adherents with a distinct political vision. In order to understand the significance of this new allegiance we need to examine carefully the specific features of this political vision and the discourse in which it was expressed, rather than simply regard Peronism as an inevitable manifestation of social and economic dissatisfaction. Gareth Stedman Jones, commenting on the reluctance of social historians to take sufficient account of the political, has recently observed that "a political movement is not simply a manifestation of distress and pain; its existence is distinguished by a shared conviction articulating a political solution to distress and a political diagnosis of its causes." Thus if Peronism did represent a concrete solution to felt material needs, we still need to understand why the solution took the specific political form of Peronism and not another. Other political movements did speak to the same needs and offer solutions to them. Even programmatically there were many formal similarities between Peronism and other political forces. What we need to understand is Peronism's success, its distinctiveness, why its political appeal was more credible for workers—which areas it touched that others did not. To do this we need to take Perón's political and ideological appeal seriously and examine the nature of Peronism's rhetoric and compare it with that of its rivals for working-class allegiance.

The issue of credibility is crucial for understanding both Perón's successful identification of himself with certain important symbols such as industrialism and, more generally, the political impact of his discourse on workers. Gareth Stedman Jones, in the essay to which we have already referred, notes that to be successful "a particular political vocabulary must convey a practicable hope of a general alternative and a believable means of realizing it, so that potential recruits can think in its terms." The vocabulary of Peronism was both visionary and believable. The credibility was in part rooted in the immediate, concrete nature of its rhetoric. This involved a tying down of abstract political slogans to their most concrete material aspects. . . . In the crucial years 1945 and 1946 this was clearly contrasted with a language of great abstraction used by Perón's political opponents. While Perón's rhetoric was capable of lofty sermonizing, particularly once he had attained the presidency, and depending on the audience he was addressing, his speeches to working-class audiences in this formative period have, for their time, a unique tone.

They are, for example, framed in a language clearly distinct from that of classic radicalism, with its woolly generalities concerning national renovation and civic virtue. The language of "the oligarchy" and "the people" was still present but now usually more precisely defined. Their utilization as general categories to denote good and evil, those who were with Perón from those against, was still there, but now there was also a frequent concretizing, sometimes as rich and poor, often as capitalist and worker. While there was a rhetoric of an indivisible community—symbolized in "the people" and "the nation"—the working class was given an implicitly superior role within this whole, often as the repository of national values. "The people" frequently were transformed into "the working people" (*el pueblo trabajador*): the people, the nation, and the workers became interchangeable.

A similar denial of the abstract can be found in Peronism's appeal to economic and political nationalism. In terms of the formal construction from the state of Peronist ideology, categories such as "the nation" and "Argentina" were accorded an abstract, mystical significance. When, however, Perón specifically addressed the working class, particularly in the formative period, but also after, one finds little appeal to the irrational, mystical elements of nationalist ideology. There was little concern with the intrinsic virtues of *argentinidad* nor with the historical precedents of *criollo* culture as expressed in a historical nostalgia for some long-departed national essence. Such concerns were mainly the province of middle-class intellectuals in the various nationalist groups which attempted, with little success, to use Peronism as a vehicle for their aspirations. Working-class nationalism was addressed primarily in terms of concrete economic issues.

Moreover, Peronism's political credibility for workers was due not only to the concreteness of its rhetoric, but also to its immediacy. Perón's political vision of a society based on social justice and on the social and political integration of workers into that society was not premised, as it was, for example, in leftist political discourse, on the prior achievement of long-term, abstract structural transformations, nor on the gradual acquisition at some future date of an adequate consciousness on the part of the working class. It took working-class consciousness, habits, life styles, and values as it found them and affirmed their sufficiency and value. It glorified the everyday and the ordinary as a sufficient basis for the rapid attainment of a juster society, provided that certain easily achievable and self-evident goals were met. Primarily this meant support for Perón as head of state and the maintenance of a strong union movement. In this sense Peronism's political appeal was radically plebeian; it eschewed the need for a peculiarly enlightened political elite and reflected and inculcated a profound anti-intellectualism.

The glorification of popular life styles and habits implied a political style and idiom well in tune with popular sensibilities. Whether it was in symbolically striking the pose of the *descamisado* (shirtless one) in a political rally, or in the nature of the imagery used in his speeches, Perón had an ability to communicate to working-class audiences which his rivals lacked. The poet Luis Franco commented cryptically on Perón's "spiritual affinity with tango lyrics." His ability to use this affinity to establish a bond with his audience was clearly shown in his speech to those assembled in the Plaza de Mayo [in Buenos Aires] on 17 October 1945 at a mass demonstration that marks the rise of the Peronist movement. Towards the end of that speech Perón evoked the image of his mother, "*mi vieja*": "I said to you a little while ago that I would embrace you as I would my mother because you have had the same griefs and the same thoughts that my poor old lady must have felt in these days." The reference is apparently gratuitous, the empty phraseology of someone who could think of nothing better to say until we recognize that the sentiments echo exactly a dominant refrain of tango—the poor grief-laden mother whose pain symbolizes the pain of her children, of all the poor. Perón's identification of his own mother with the poor establishes a sentimental identity between himself and his audience; with this tone of nostalgia he was touching an important sensibility in Argentine popular culture of the period. Significantly, too, the speech ended on another "tangoesque" note. Perón reminded his audience as they were about to leave the Plaza, "remember that among you there are many women workers who have to be protected here and in life by you same workers." The theme of the threat to the women of the working class, and the need to protect their women, was also a constant theme of both tango and other forms of popular culture.

Perón's use of such an idiom within which to frame his political appeal often seems to us now, and indeed it seemed to many of his critics at the time, to reek of the paternalistic condescension of the traditional *caudillo* figure. His constant use of couplets from "Martin Fierro,"* or his conscious use of terms taken from *lunfardo* slang can grate on modern sensibilities. However, we should be careful to appreciate the impact of his ability to speak in an idiom which reflected popular sensibilities of the time. In accounts by observers and journalists of the crucial formative years of Peronism we frequently find the adjectives *chabacano* and *burdo* used to describe both Perón himself and his supporters. Both words have the sense of crude, cheap, coarse and they also implied a lack of sophistication, an awkwardness, almost a country bumpkin quality. While they were generally meant as epithets they were not descriptions Peronists would necessarily have denied.

Indeed, this capacity to recognize, reflect, and foster a popular political style and idiom based on plebeian realism contrasted strongly with the political appeal of traditional working-class political parties. The tone adopted by the latter when confronted by the working-class effervescence of the mid-1940s was didactic, moralizing, and apparently addressed to a morally and intellectually inferior audience. This was particularly the case of the Socialist Party. Its analysis of the events of 17 October is illustrative of its attitude and tone:

> The part of the people which lives for its resentment, and perhaps only for its resentment, spilled over into the streets, threatened, yelled, and, in its demon-like fury, trampled upon and assaulted newspapers and persons, those very persons who were the champions of its elevation and dignification.

Behind this tone of fear, frustration, and moralizing lay a discourse which addressed an abstract, almost mythical working class. Peronism on the other hand was prepared, particularly in its formative period, to recognize, and even glorify, workers who did "threaten, yell, and trample with a demon-like fury." Comparing Perón's political approach to that of his rivals one is reminded of Ernst Bloch's comment concerning Nazism's preemption of socialist and communist appeal among German workers that "the Nazis speak falsely, but to people, the communists truthfully, but of things."

Perón's ability to appreciate the tone of working-class sensibilities and assumptions was reflected in other areas. There was in Peronist rhetoric, for example, a tacit recognition of the immutability of social inequality, a commonsense shrug-of-the-shoulders acceptance of the reality of social and economic inequities, a recognition of what Pierre Bourdieu has called "a sense of limits." The remedies proposed to mitigate these inequities were plausible and immediate. Perón, in a speech in Rosario in August 1944, had emphasized the apparently self-evident reasonableness of his appeal, the mundaneness behind the abstract rhetoric of social equality: "We want exploitation of man by man to cease in our country, and when this problem disappears we will equalize a

---

*The Argentine national epic poem.

little the social classes so that there will not be in this country men who are too poor nor those who are too rich."

This realism implied a political vision of a limited nature but it did not eliminate utopian resonances; it simply made such resonances—a yearning for social equality, for an end to exploitation—more credible for a working class imbued by its experience with a certain cynicism regarding political promises and abstract slogans. Indeed, the credibility of Perón's political vision, the practicability of the hope it offered, was affirmed on a daily basis by its actions from the state. The solutions it offered the working class did not depend on some future apocalypse for confirmation but were rather directly verifiable in terms of everyday political activity and experience. Already by 1945 the slogan had appeared among workers which was to symbolize this credibility: "*Perón cumple!*" (Perón delivers).

2. Declaration of Workers' Rights ～ Juan Perón*

Populist leaders such as Perón did more than just talk about the working class and its needs. They also created a vast array of new programs and policies aimed at improving the lives of workers. In this primary source selection, many aspects of the Peronist agenda come together as an official "Declaration of Workers' Rights" ("solemnly proclaimed in public on the 24th of February, 1947, by His Excellency, General Juan Perón, President of the Republic"). Note the particular rights granted in the document. What exactly is being promised—and what is not? As with all such declarations and manifestos, students must distinguish between the ideological principles espoused and the practical application of those principles. The document does, nevertheless, reveal a key component of Peronist populism.

I. The Right to Work

Work is the indispensable means of satisfying the spiritual and material necessities of the individual and the community. It is the cause of all the conquests of civilization and the basis of general prosperity. Therefore the right to work should be protected by society, by giving it the dignity it deserves and by providing occupation to all.

II. The Right to a Fair Wage

As wealth, rent, and the interest on capital are the exclusive results of human labor, the community should organize the sources of production and guarantee the

---

*Adapted from Juan Domingo Perón, *Perón Expounds His Doctrine* (Buenos Aires, 1948; repr., New York: AMS Press, 1973), 201–5.

worker a moral and material reward to satisfy his vital needs and to compensate him for his efforts.

III. The Right to Training

The improvement of the condition of mankind and the preeminence of spiritual values make it imperative to raise the standard of culture and professional ability, so that all intellects should be led towards every branch of knowledge; and it is the concern of society to stimulate individual effort by supplying the means which will enable every individual to have an equal chance to exercise the right to learn and perfect his knowledge.

IV. The Right to Proper Working Conditions

The consideration which is due to any human being, the importance of work as a social function, and the reciprocal respect inherent in the productive relationships confer the right of individuals to demand fair and proper working conditions and oblige society to see that these conditions are strictly regulated.

V. The Right to the Preservation of Health

The physical and moral health of the individual should be a constant concern of society. Society is responsible for the hygiene and security of the workplace. Working conditions should not exact excessively heavy effort and should enable the individual to recover his energy through rest.

VI. The Right to Well-Being

Workers have the right to well-being. The minimum expression of this right is an adequate dwelling place and adequate clothing and food. A worker should be able to satisfy his and his family's necessities, work with satisfaction without too heavy toil, rest free of worry, and enjoy spiritual and material freedom. The right of well-being imposes the social necessity of raising the standard of living as far as our level of economic development allows.

VII. The Right to Social Security

The right of the individual to be protected in cases of disability or unemployment requires society to take unilaterally into its charge matters such as social security and workman's compensation insurance.

VIII. The Right to the Protection of the Family

The protection of the family is a part of the natural destiny of the individual, since it is here that his most elevated affections have their origin. The worker's well-being must be stimulated and favored by the community to encourage the improvement of humanity and the consolidation of our spiritual and material principles.

IX. The Right to a Better Economic Situation

Productive capacity and the zeal to excel find their natural initiative in the possibility for economic improvement. Therefore society must support economic initiatives and stimulate the formation and utilization of capital insofar as it constitutes an active element for production and contributes to general prosperity.

X. The Right to the Defense of Professional Interests

The right to group together freely and to participate in other legal activities which promote the defense of their professional interests constitutes an essential right of the workers.

---

3. Doña María Remembers Perón ~ María Roldán*

In this third selection dealing with the Argentine populist Perón, historian Daniel James takes us deeper into the world of Peronist workers. In particular, James conducted extensive oral history research with workers in the town of Berisso, a meatpacking town south of Buenos Aires. The focus of James's study was a remarkable woman named María Roldán, whose life experiences as a woman, a union worker in a meatpacking plant, and a Peronist bring the book to life. In the following excerpt from the testimony given by Doña María (as James respectfully refers to her), she remembers the experience of participating in the protest/celebration of October 17, 1945. What is especially interesting to consider here is the way Doña María remembers this defining event in Peronist history. According to James, much of her understanding of Argentine history is based on this singular moment. As we will see in this book's final chapter, the act of remembering such a historic event must always be approached critically by the reader.

Before 17 October it was all just talk, but Perón appeared that night in the Plaza de Mayo and everything was different.

The idea of 17 October was growing because [Cipriano] Reyes† went by plane, by mule, by bus, however he could, visiting all the unions and all the fac-

*From Daniel James, *Doña María's Story: Life History, Memory, and Political Identity* (Durham, NC: Duke University Press, 2000), 58–63. © 2000 Duke University Press. All rights reserved. Republished by permission of the copyright holder, Duke University Press. www.dukeupress.edu/.
† A key leader in the effort to unionize workers in the meatpacking industry and cofounder of the Argentine Workers Party, which worked for Perón's election in 1946.

tories, cooking oil factories, textile factories, every sort of factory, arguing that there had to be a strike, that there had to be a 17 October. This started before they imprisoned Perón. We knew definitely that there was going to be a seventeenth on 12 October. On the twelfth Reyes disappeared. "Where is he?" we asked his wife. "He's in La Rioja, he's in Tucumán, he went to Catamarca." He was talking to all the trade unionists so that they would strike the seventeenth. They had to get to the Plaza de Mayo however they could, and everyone who could come somehow got to the plaza.

You know why we went that day? Nobody sent me the seventeenth of October to the Plaza San Martín to ask for Perón, but I felt a tremendous pain, I saw pregnant women crying, asking for help in the streets. In October 1945 there was still awful poverty here, as God is my witness. The union used to ask for meat in the butchers, to give out. "How many kids do you have?" Three kilos of potatoes for you. Then the next, "How many do you have?" Well then four kilos of potatoes. We lived liked that, making do here and there, as best we could. So the seventeenth arose from our pain. Let me repeat it, it came from the great poverty. There were conventillos in the Nueva York where seven or eight families lived, twenty kids playing on the sidewalk, the only yard they had was the sidewalk. What sort of men were they going to be tomorrow?

We set out from Berisso on that day with an old flag, torn. We had already heard from Reyes, that we had to go out into the street with the people, and nearly all the women had been told to be in the Calle Montevideo at such and such a time. We went to Los Talas on foot, that's about twenty blocks along the Calle Montevideo, and from there we came back with the flag. That's when we met the mounted police. The police didn't let us pass so easily like they say now. No, there was gas, they chased us, a little of everything, they wouldn't let us shout "Viva Perón." We got to the Sportman bar at the corner of Montevideo and Rio de Janeiro, two blocks from the Swift. When we arrived there the streets were full of people. We were some seven thousand souls. We formed a caravan on foot. We went to La Plata on foot. Some women who couldn't walk, they got rides in a truck, a car. We arrived in the Plaza San Martín in La Plata. In the Plaza San Martín there seemed to be almost the entire province of Buenos Aires. The plaza was full and the crowd flowed over into the diagonals. I spoke from a stairway leading into the government house. From there you could see more. There were people in the side streets, up in the trees, on the balconies. It was like the taking of the Argentine Bastille. I never saw the French Revolution, but for me it was the taking of the Argentine Bastille. Everyone was happy, nobody fought, people didn't insult each other: "We're going to win. Peroncito is going to come."

DJ: I read that there were some fights that night.

DM: Well, when there are men who drink. You know there are people who drink. There were some who broke windows and took beer, wine, those sorts of people are never absent, then they get into fights. But this is a very small part of the people that has nothing to do with decent working people who get up at four in the morning to be in the *frigorífico** at five. But you're right, there was a little of everything that day, you can't deny it. But people were happy, especially when we heard by phone that Perón was going to be in the Plaza de Mayo at midnight. In my speech in the Plaza San Martín I had said that if Perón wasn't in the Plaza de Mayo alive and well by midnight the workers would continue with arms crossed, that we wouldn't work. Then we went on to the Plaza de Mayo. We went in a truck. I don't know how many of us, forty or so. The truck driver said, "I won't take children, I don't want problems, I'll take adults," and even so Ricardo Giovanelli, who was a man from the union who was worth his weight in gold, was telling everyone who got on the truck not to bring sticks, arms, not to bring anything, we were going in peace, we were going to wait for Perón, that night we would have Perón with us, and that's the way it turned out.

When we arrived at the Plaza de Mayo, we pushed our way to the front, rubbing up against the people, we lost buttons on our clothes, there were so many people. We had also taken a lot of our clothes off. It was so hot. Imagine it, spring, and yet it was so hot. The people, euphoric, they were throwing shoes in the air, hats, they were taking their shirts off, the men were naked up to here, all of them. Later, several of us from Berisso spoke, Ricardo Giovanelli, myself. Reyes wasn't there. He didn't appear all day. When it was my turn I said that the moment of the social demands had arrived, that the people have their moments, their dates, their day, their hour and their minute, and this is our minute, twelve o'clock on the night of 17 October:

"The colonel has to come here because we in the Sindicato de la Carne† have sworn that if he isn't here by twelve midnight among us, we will continue without working, as will all the Argentine people, come what may, we offer our lives for Perón, and we will take inspiration from the statue of General San Martín, that man who gave everything for freedom and received nothing, and who is carved in stone and in bronze by great sculptors with his finger raised in the air warning us, "Beware Argentines, so that the gains that we have made shall be eternal." And I say this because what is in play here is the future of Colonel Perón. Because here there is talk of a Señor Braden‡ whom we do not know. He may be a great man, a great father, but he is not Argentine. May those who are not Argentines forgive me, but I as an Argentine must say this. Let us remember San Martín at this moment. Let us ask above all for liberty, peace, and work, but this work must be rewarded with salaries that allow us all to live in peace and love." It was more or less with those words that I spoke. It was spoken spontaneously, without preparation. On all the walls, wherever there was propaganda there was the shape of a pig, and next to it they wrote the word Braden, and then alongside an image of Perón and a flower beside it. That sort of thing that the people invented, the

---

*A meatpacking plant.
†The meatpackers' union.
‡U.S. Ambassador to Argentina Spruille Braden.

people is extraordinary, there were little songs that really were like small poems, incredible, with just the right words, they were very well received.

Well, when I finished, Edelmiro Farrell, General Farrell, the de facto president, asked me who I was, because my husband and Ricardo Giovanelli were supporting me with their hands.

So I said, "I am a woman who cuts meat with a knife that's bigger than I am in the Swift packing house."

"But who are you, señora?"

"My name is María Roldán."

"Pleased to meet you, señora. Please be patient, Perón will be here." It must have been about eleven o'clock.

In fact, when Perón arrived Farrell was speaking, and the people started to applaud, and he says, "One minute, please, I am still the president and I'll speak first, then Perón will talk." After his words he and Perón embraced, patting one another on the back the way military men do. And then Perón started to talk, and he would have to stop, and he would start again and then have to stop, he couldn't communicate with the people, they wouldn't let him, they kept interrupting. Then there were the *bombos* [big drums], beating away. It was something so tremendous. It was almost four in the morning, and when they let him talk for a moment he said, "Muchachos, if you let me I'll talk, if not I'm going to leave because I am very tired." When he said, "I'm going," they finally got quiet. And the speech he gave that night was for us the most memorable, the most sublime that we could have experienced as trade unionists. That night in the Plaza de Mayo, when he arrived all tired, all agitated, the speech was for us who knew that our country was in a bad way, that working people were completely defeated, humiliated if you want, by the bosses, not only in the frigoríficos here, but all the bosses, the words will remain ingrained in my mind until the day God calls me to him. Because he delivered the speech as if he were transported outside himself: "I am a mortal, I may be here and in a short time cease to exist. I feel very bad, but God will know how to give me the strength to continue with what I have determined to do. I promise you nothing, but I know that you need me." The people were almost beside themselves.

"You need me, and I will join you in this project. I will follow what my heart of an Argentine citizen tells me to do. I have very good intentions. I am going to work first for the workers who are those who keep the nation moving, and then I will work for all the Argentines. But first I will work for you. I know how you are living, because I have seen you weep in the Secretaria de Trabajo,* because I have seen you on your knees say to me, 'Please, colonel, do something. We can't bear anymore.' I have never allowed a man to go down on his knees before me, but you did so. I know that Berisso is like a weeping shawl, I know that since 1917 you have struggled, because I am no neophyte, I am old enough to know. I will fight first for you, who suffer most. First, I will raise up the weakest, then I

---

*The Department of Labor.

will see if I can raise my country up. I think I will be a good leader, but you will have to accompany me muchachos and muchachas, because we have to rescue the Argentine people from the pain in which it is submerged."

When he finished speaking we started to leave. The people went back to their homes, to work, half naked some of them, without shoes, without sleeping. We got back to Berisso about seven in the morning.

I think that Perón, without the support of the people, wouldn't have been Perón. Let's start with October seventeenth. If we hadn't been in the plaza on 17 October and all the people in the streets, Perón would have stayed in prison, and I don't know if they wouldn't have killed him. Perón's life was hanging by a thread, because the armed forces had already realized that the Argentine people were with Perón, and that he had a majority of the people. It wasn't just a gift. Nobody gave us anything. It's the people who did everything.

DJ: Because that is a very common idea about what happened. That the people just passively received everything.

DM: I know, and that's what I want to explain to you. The Argentine people needed a man to follow, and Perón was that man. Semana Santa [Easter Week, 1987, the week of a military rebellion against the Radical Party government] in the Plaza de Mayo was not like the 17 October for one basic reason. The people went to the Plaza de Mayo this time because they were frightened for themselves and their families. But we went into the streets because we were afraid that they would kill a man, whom we already wanted for president. Look at the difference. The people went into the streets for a man. You have to analyze that. Because at 7:50 I was on a platform in the Plaza de Mayo, and we said that if Colonel Perón doesn't appear there was an order from the union, tomorrow nobody works and we won't work until they give us Colonel Juan Domingo Perón. And Perón was there at twelve midnight. That's what people don't realize.

---

4. Words as Weapons ~ Herbert Braun*

Colombia was another country where populism flourished in the 1940s. There, the new breed of politician was named Jorge Eliécer Gaitán, a lawyer who carried forward the populist challenge to the traditional oligarchy in Bogotá. Due to a unique power-sharing arrangement between the Liberals and the Conservatives, the country maintained a fragile stability from the early twentieth century until the late 1930s, when Gaitán burst onto the scene. He served as mayor of Bogotá and minister of labor and education, and almost won the presidency in 1946. His assassination in Bogotá two years later brought about the riot known

*From Herbert Braun, *The Assassination of Gaitán: Public Life and Urban Violence in Colombia* (Madison: University of Wisconsin Press, 1985), 99–103. © 1985 by the Board of Regents of the University of Wisconsin System. Reprinted by permission of the University of Wisconsin Press.

as the Bogotazo *and initiated the long period of violent confrontation,* la Violencia, *between armed Colombian factions. In this selection, historian Herbert Braun examines Gaitán's unsurpassed ability to connect with the working people of his city during his 1946 run for the presidency.*

Jorge Eliécer Gaitán became an orator who never doubted his rhetorical abilities and knew that his power resided in his words. Gaitán was not responsible for the prominent place of oratory in Colombian politics. He adopted a traditional practice to create a symbiotic relationship between himself and the crowd.

Gaitán understood that linguistic shock had a subversive quality in Colombia's highly verbal and formalistic culture. He was aware that the baroque and aristocratic texture of the *convivialistas'* orations intimidated barely literate audiences,* and he could sense the liberating effect of direct and popular forms of expression on those audiences. Yet his vulgarity was carefully measured. Gaitán was known as the "orator of the *mamola.*" The term, a rather mild expletive with a meaning similar to the verb "to chuck" in English, was personally insulting and physically aggressive. It was also a play on words and conjured up images of human and animal sucking. Gaitán used it, to the obvious delight of the crowd, every time the convivialistas intimated that he ought to lay his presidential aspirations to rest. The convivialistas were outraged and claimed that they would not permit their children to listen to him.

Tonality and intonation were important ingredients of Gaitán's oratory. Prolonging the vowels and crisply sounding the consonants of key expressions, he made the words fly out of the side of his mouth. *"Pueeeblooo,"* he intoned at the end of his speeches, *"aaa laa caargaa!"* ("Common people, charge!"). Gaitán's heavy and growling delivery was in a marked contrast to the melodic, calm, and lyrical rhetoric of the convivialistas. He appealed to the emotional, subjective sensibilities of his audience. Although he was capable of delivering reasoned and logical arguments on technical subjects before select groups, more often he spoke to fantasies that sparked the imagination of the crowd. To search for a clear line of argumentation in Gaitán's more political speeches is to misunderstand them. The orations were designed for dramatic effect, not intellectual consistency. He often returned to the same point, taking his listeners back and forth from one theme to another, reaching rapid conclusions, and supporting them much later or not at all.

Gaitán's speeches were filled with social and political content. His emotionalism and spontaneity and the simplicity of his words did not mean that he had thrust aside his ideology in order to transfix the crowd. Quite the contrary. His easily understandable phrases were a remarkably complete expression of his world view and a condensation of the ideas he had consistently held since writing *Las ideas socialistas* twenty years earlier. They also tellingly reflected his middle

---

*The *convivialistas* were the leaders of the rival Liberal and Conservative parties who sought to reduce potential conflict in Colombia.

place in society. Few of Gaitán's slogans were his own, as his opponents quickly pointed out, but when they came from his mouth they held new meanings.

Gaitán's words require close attention. He played astutely on the contrasting worlds of the convivialistas and the pueblo. He was best known for popularizing the distinction between the *país político* and the *país nacional** and using it to demonstrate the distance that separated leaders from followers: the convivialistas inhabited the former, the pueblo the latter. But Gaitán reversed the places these two "countries" had for the convivialistas. Gaitán's populist ideology pitted a small, unproductive, and meritless elite against a large majority defined by its need and ability to work. Gaitán returned to his favorite organic image. He likened the país político to a putrefied organism whose head, voice, and tentacles were strangling the productive impulses of the pueblo. Politics, Gaitán said, was simply "mechanics, a game, a winning of elections, knowing who will be the minister, and not what the minister is going to do. It is plutocracy, contracts, bureaucracy, paperwork, the slow, tranquil usufruct of public office, while the public pueblo is conceived of as grazing land and not a place of work that contributes to the grandeur of the nation."

Gaitán referred to the leaders of the país político as oligarchs, a term they used to accuse one another of the use of public office for private gain. Gaitán thereby added an economic dimension to his political critique of the convivialistas. As a result of the public corruption and nepotism that characterized the current López regime, the term gained a particular bite during the war years. Coming from Gaitán, the accusation had an added sting. For Gaitán was an outsider, and he was using public office, if not for financial gain, for something much worse: to move from the bottom to the top of society. The crowds understood, on the other hand, that the leader used the term to refer to the system of decision making represented by the closed conversations of the convivialistas as well as the boardroom meetings of corporations, or, as Gaitán referred to them, "monopolies."

Gaitán's slogan "*El pueblo es superior a sus dirigentes*" ("The pueblo is superior to its leaders") took the reversal to its logical conclusions. It was the most far-reaching of all his slogans, for it pointed to an overturning of the social order. The slogan is consistent with Gaitán's habit of speaking highly of the pueblo. In an impromptu speech in Caracas, he went so far as to say that "we have learned to laugh at those decadent generations that see the multitudes of our tropics as beings of an inferior race." He also claimed that Gaitanismo was a "great movement of the Colombian race," and that the crowds on the streets "were exactly the opposite of anarchy," a "normal part of a true democracy." In his oratory the feared *chusma* (mob) became the "*chusma heroica*," and the despised *gleba* (tillers of the soil) became the "*gleba gloriosa*." But Gaitán was not a demagogue who promised his followers the impossible. He was harsh and demanding of them, urging them to be honest, moral, and hardworking. He never promised them a

*Roughly, the politicians' country versus the real country.

reversal of the social order that would place them suddenly at the top, living a life of luxury at the expense of toiling politicians. He was too committed to social order, and too conscious of the dangers of such promises.

Gaitán did not believe, moreover, that followers were naturally superior or equal to their leaders. In a speech to medical doctors, he explained what he meant by the superiority of the pueblo. He admitted that some individuals were able to excel on their own. But "with the multitude the phenomenon is different. . . . Separate, they are insignificant; together, they are the strong basis without which the apex does not exist. . . . If collective processes mediocratize the mind and reduce it, those same processes raise the minimal men and place them at the level of mindfulness." Thus, Gaitán believed that participation in a cohesive and purposeful crowd could make individuals more social. The crowd could civilize the pueblo. He shared the convivialistas' hierarchical vision of society, but his vision of the social pyramid was broader.

Yet another masterfully crafted slogan—"*Yo no soy un hombre, soy un pueblo*" ("I am not a man, I am an entire people")—reunited the two worlds that Gaitán had separated and reversed. He represented a new order with himself as head of the país nacional. The slogan contradicted the traditional distinction between private and public life. Gaitán was claiming to be an entirely public figure for reasons that were precisely the opposite of those of the convivialistas: they separated themselves from the pueblo; he was giving himself over to it. For his followers the slogan meant that their leader, a distinguished man with the character to challenge the convivialistas, was returning to the pueblo from which he had come.

Gaitán's other major slogan, "*Por la restauración moral y democrática de la república*" ("Toward the moral and democratic restoration of the nation"), succinctly captured the elusive ideal of a return to a social order that the convivialistas had betrayed. It must have produced an intense feeling of racial isolation in the white elite, which saw any restoration, any return to the past that was not led by them, as a return to the indigenous, pre-Hispanic origins of the nation.

Even Gaitán's simple call to arms—"*A la carga*"—contained a meaning that is not readily apparent. The word *carga* also signifies a physical burden, a heavy weight to be carried. Every time Gaitán called the pueblo to action at the end of his orations, he was eliciting images of the daily world of labor. Gaitán ended most of his speeches by repeating these slogans. As the crowds grew accustomed to the ritual, he would call out, "*Pueblo*," and the crowds responded: "*A la carga!*" "*Pueblo!*" "*Por la restauración moral y democrática de la república!*" "*Pueblo!*" "*A la Victoria!*" "*Pueblo!*" "*Contra la oligarquía!*"

The power of Gaitán's oratory was not lost on the convivialistas. Azula Barrera wrote that he "was the first to speak to the national proletariat in direct language, creating an aggressive class consciousness without the obscure Marxist phraseology, and a more elevated concept of its own worth." Through Gaitán's oratory, the Conservative historian concluded, the poor realized that "behind politics there existed the zone of their rights, the real range of their economic aspirations, the concrete world of misery, and of their collective victory." The Liberal politician Abelardo Forero Benavides could only agree. "He spoke [to the multitude] in a language that could be its own. . . . The boundary of the theater was transposed through the microphones into all the homes, shops, and attics." According to the Conservative Mario Fernández de Soto, Gaitán's oratory did not win him a place in the Academy or the Atheneum. But his "power resided primarily in his extraordinary ability to create between himself and the masses who followed him a community of spirit and emotions and aspirations so intimate that [the crowd] delivered itself completely to him." After the May 5, 1946, election, *Calibán* wrote that Gaitán was a "born caudillo of the multitudes."

Gaitán's oratory was a complete representation of the man. He stood above the crowd, demonstrating his prowess. He forged a unity with the pueblo to lead the nation to a new compromise, a balance between leaders and followers. He spoke proudly and passionately, for he believed that the warmth of emotion was as much the basis of society as was the cold reason of the convivialistas. And he revealed both his public and private selves, for he had nothing to hide. The new order would be built around individuals who stood up openly for their beliefs. Gaitán was like the corner grocer who stood proudly in front of his windows displaying the staples of daily life.

---

5. Father of the Poor? Robert M. Levine*

Like Juan Perón of Argentina, Getúlio Vargas of Brazil employed a radically new vocabulary of class-conscious rhetoric and imagery in his long and influential political career. Vargas defined the populist era in Brazil (which created opportunities for bold nationalist thinkers like Gilberto Freyre). In this selection, historian Robert Levine begins by posing a puzzling contradiction: the Vargas years are remembered by most poor Brazilians as a time of great progress, yet the standard measures of most workers' material lives showed little sign of improvement. The author looks for explanations in two related areas of Brazilian culture. According to Levine, Vargas's political connection to the daily lives of the workers in his country was similar to the traditional Brazilian kinship role known as padrinho, *or godfather, of an extended family and other dependents. Levine also examines the Catholicism of the urban poor as a dimension of Vargas's relationship with the workers. Along the way he also allows several supporters of Vargas to explain their reasons for doing so. How do they explain their support for Vargas?*

*From Robert M. Levine, *Father of the Poor? Vargas and His Era* (New York: Cambridge University Press, 1998), 100–106. © 1998 Robert M. Levine. Reprinted by permission of Cambridge University Press.

Throughout the Vargas years, the unmistakable division separating the social classes remained essentially untouched by government reforms. Brazil's "haves," in fact, employed more maids and domestic servants than any country in the Western world, because labor was so cheap. Whether remaining in the rural interior or as migrants to urban areas, these men and women were barely above subsistence level, hidden, in that sense, from the everyday world of the affluent. That the "have-nots" on the whole tended to accept their lot caused them to be treated as if they were children, a by-product of the paternalistic legacy of Brazilian society. They used good-naturedness and resignation as coping mechanisms, although when they snapped, mobs smashed and burned streetcars (*quebra quebra*) or looted storehouses for food. The lower classes, Spanish journalist Ricardo Baeza pontificated, are a "garrulous and laughing people, who do not yet know the poison of thought or the curse of work."

Vargas maintained a sharp distance in his mind between himself and the people he called *populares* in his diary. They loved him nonetheless. During the 1930 election campaign pro–Liberal Alliance crowds overturned streetcars in Salvador. After the Liberal Alliance triumph, thousands lined the tracks to watch Vargas's train proceed from the South to Rio de Janeiro, where he would take office. Street poets called Getúlio the *defensor dos marmiteiros*, the protector of the workers who carried their tin lunchboxes of rice and beans with them to their jobs. At the same time, the growing migration of rural families to the cities of the coast in a desperate search for jobs spawned ever larger slums: foul *mocambos* on the river banks of Recife, shanties in Salvador and Pôrto Alegre, *favelas* (shantytowns) sprouting in São Paulo for the first time, between 1942 and 1945, and a proliferation of new and larger favelas on the hillsides of Rio de Janeiro.

Carolina Maria de Jesus, an indigent black girl in rural Minas Gerais living at the lowest rung of poverty, scorned by the "good families" in her small city and condemned to deprivation, describes in her autobiographical memoirs what the 1930 Revolution meant to her:

> One day I awoke confused to see the streets filled with soldiers. It was a revolution. I knew only revolutions of ants when they moved about. Revolutions by men are tragic. Some killing others. And the people only talked about Getúlio Vargas and João Pessoa. It was the union of the State of Paraíba with the State of Rio Grande do Sul. And the military rebels asked people to arm themselves, that men shouldn't be absent in the hour of their country's litigation. These seditions occur because of the arrogance of those who want to govern the nation. With Getúlio Vargas we will have more work.

The soldiers spread through the streets with green, yellow, and white banners with Getúlio's face in the center. Those who saw the portrait liked him and said: "Now, Brazil will be watched over by a man!" This will move the country forward. We are a country without a leader. We have to wake up. Countries cannot

lie down eternally in a splendid cradle. Our country is very backward. The girls
who were domestic servants didn't leave their employers' houses. I was working
in Dona Mimi's house, the wife of the *gaúcho*.* He was happy it was his state
that would bring order to Brazil.

> I walked the streets. I heard the soldiers sing:
> Long live our Revolution
> Brazil will ascend like a balloon
> With Getúlio, Brazil moves ahead
> With Getúlio, Brazil won't fall
> Let's have more bread on the table
> Getúlio is a friend of the poor.

When she was eighteen or nineteen, in the early 1930s, Carolina went to a
charity hospital. She wrote:

> In the ward the women only spoke about the [1930] Revolution, that it was
> beneficial for the people. That it had changed the rules of the game for workers.
> Salaries were better; they now were able to have bank accounts and other ben-
> efits from the working-class legislation. A worker is able to retire when he is old
> and be paid for full-time work. Workers were content with the laws. And Getúlio
> was becoming known as the "father of the poor." The people were disciplined.

Carolina, who wrote her memoirs during the last years of her life in the
mid-1970s, did not remember that Vargas's social legislation came into effect
only over decades. Unskilled workers were initially excluded from benefits.
Still, Carolina remembered that Getúlio gave young men the opportunity to join
the army and therefore leave the hardscrabble interior. Many of them got jobs
in São Paulo, she said; in their letters home to their relatives they convinced
them to come to São Paulo also. They came to believe that São Paulo was the
paradise for poor people. This was the moment in which she decided that when
she could, she would go to São Paulo herself, a place that for her, in her words,
was "Heaven's waiting room."

Men in rural Minas Gerais, Carolina said, when they got together, started to
speak about Getúlio being the great protector of the poor. She later wrote that
she thought, "Will this be the politician who is going to improve Brazil for the
Brazilians? . . . He had reanimated the people, that people who were lukewarm,
apathetic, leave-it-for-tomorrow idealistic dreamers, now moving into action
because they believed that this government would not deceive them." Planners,
she claimed, said that they were going to Sao Paulo to get a loan from Getúlio
and open a plant with fifty workers because Getúlio said that if workers have
jobs they won't have time to go astray. "Not only does he give us loans," she

---

*A nickname for people from Vargas's home state of Rio Grande do Sul.

wrote, "but his goal is to make workers the beneficiaries. Industry in São Paulo brings immediate profits."

Almost from the outset of his arrival in the public eye, millions of these men and women revered Vargas as a father figure. One reason for this was the importance of fictive kinship in Brazilian society. The descendants of slaves became kin of African tribal ancestors through initiation into spiritist cults. Landless peasants traditionally took powerful figures as godparents [*padrinhos* or *madrinhas*] for their newborn children. In the northeastern backlands in the late nineteenth century, for example, parish birth records list the Virgin Maria as madrinha for thousands of baby girls and the northeastern charismatics Antonio Conselheiro or Father Cícero as padrinhos. Many more families elicited permission of the local landlord to god-father (and therefore protect) their offspring. In the same way, Getúlio Vargas, the first national politician to reach out to all Brazilians, became the nation's padrinho. For ordinary people, Getúlio was accessible, all-powerful, demanding of their loyalty, and willing to intervene on their behalf if they proved him worthy.

Many lower-class Brazilians, including Carolina de Jesus, mixed spiritism with the penitential Roman Catholicism prevalent in the hinterlands. For people with such beliefs, Getúlio was a miracle-working saint, with whom one could commune spiritually. They decorated personal shrines with his photograph, and asked him for personal intervention, as they did to clay statues for Father Cícero, the miracle-working defrocked priest whose backlands Ceará religious community in Joaseiro coexisted with Vargas's government during the 1930s and who exerted considerable influence in state politics.

The life histories of ordinary Brazilians who reached adulthood during the 1930s and 1940s demonstrate incontestably that the Vargas era was pivotal in changing their lives, even if the new opportunities for mobility were more incremental than dramatic. Consider the case of Maurílio Tomás Ferreira, born in 1915 in rural Espírito Santo:

I had six brothers, most of them older. I even have a photograph of them. Three were drafted into the Guard, all at once, and they had to go even though they were married and had small children. . . . Before the Vargas government things were out of hand. . . . We lived on my father's land he had bought, everyone in the family had a little house and a small plot. . . . He distilled *cachaça* [rum] from sugar cane. . . . I had four sisters also. My father was angry because he now had to take care of his three daughters-in-law and their kids. My father had to pay for their uniforms, shoes—in the countryside you had to provide everything yourself.

I went to a rural school, very rudimentary. After primary school I studied with a teacher my father hired for all of us. Getúlio regulated lots of things. Before that, things were disorganized. I was now the oldest boy living at home. My father decided to send me to the army too, to get it over with, so I lied about my age. . . . I served in the army in 1930 when I was fifteen. . . . I was sent first to Vitória and then to Rio, to the Praia Vermelha barracks. I got out in December. I returned to work with my father and when I was twenty-two I married, in 1937.

I grew corn and potatoes and coffee beans and raised pigs. There was no place to sell things, so I had to transport my produce, and this was expensive. We made very little money. Things grew well; my father sometimes harvested ten thousand sacks of coffee. But we had too little land for all of my brothers and their families. All of my family were *crentes* [evangelical Protestants]. There was a church in Córrego Rico. We went. I directed a choir. We were baptized. I met my wife there when she was twelve years old.

[In 1942] I decided, overnight, to leave. We had two children already. We went to [the town of] Muniz Freire and bought a house with my savings. I had no job, nothing. I worked as a barber but didn't make very much; the town was too small. I worked for the mayor's office. I got one job through one of my brothers-in-law who was a driver for an Arab. I became foreman on his farm but he didn't pay me. I stayed for a year and then left for another foreman's job. Then I got a job with the railroad. I got it [in 1945] when I went to Cachoeiro to sell chickens. A fellow I sold them to told me to try and get a railroad job, that they were hiring many people. He introduced me to some officials of the Leopoldina Railroad. They hired me. I liked the idea of living in Cachoeiro because there was a school there my kids could attend. My children all studied, one as far as the fifth grade, the others to high school. And railroad workers were eligible for pensions; [we were] one of the first. . . . When I started working they registered me in the railroad pension institute. There was an enormous union building in Cachoeiro. The union sold provisions and merchandise to us at cheaper prices. Later on the union gave a scholarship for my youngest son to study at high school.

Starting in 1945 my wife and I always voted in elections, every year. I joined the PTB [Workers' Party] . . . and became active in the union. . . . I admired Getúlio Vargas, always voted for him. . . . He named the state interventors. He was leading Brazil forward. . . . When he killed himself it was an enormous shock. . . . I kept his photograph [the union had given to us] and a copy of his suicide letter, to remind me of what he did for poor Brazilians. . . . He was the chief organizer of this country.

Looking back on his life nearly a half century later, Maurílio recognized that this was the turning point in his life. Employment by a state agency meant school for his children, a future. To have a government job meant security and a pension. Perhaps because he understood that so few other workers received these benefits, Maurílio idolized Vargas, considering him his personal benefactor. He would have scoffed at social scientists writing that Vargas's labor measures were enacted to control the labor force, because he knew that he and his family benefited. As long as he belonged to the union, his wife would receive food at reduced prices at the union-run store. He would receive a pension, and his children would be eligible for scholarships available to families of union members. He considered voting for Vargas a natural obligation and something that gave him satisfaction. The union allowed him to advance: when Maurílio started, he was an apprentice brakeman. When he retired in 1970, he held the position of "chief of the train." Such upward mobility would have been impossible before 1930.

IX

Social Revolution

Latin America saw many "revolutions" before 1950, but none was a social one. Before 1950, the word "revolution" in Latin America usually referred to any forceful regime change, the replacement of one leader by another. Social revolutions, by contrast, bring more fundamental changes to the way countries operate; they seek to alter the social order in some essential way. If a society is like a house in need of repair, then fixing rusted pipes, frayed electrical wiring, or a leaky roof is *reform*. Tearing the house down to redesign and rebuild it is *revolution*. In twentieth-century Latin America, the inspiration for this kind of revolution came overwhelmingly from Marxism-Leninism (albeit in a Latin Americanized form).

For many decades Latin Americans have confronted the challenge of social revolution, whether as proponents or opponents. While the region experienced numerous episodes of crisis and reform in its first century of independence, the revolutionary challenges that began in the 1950s were more profound, larger in scale and ambition, more organized, and more ideologically driven. But if social revolutionary movements were widespread in Latin America from the 1960s through the 1980s, successful social revolutions were few. Only in Cuba did a lasting revolution occur, although several other movements achieved real power in their countries for months or even years at a time.

Factions of traditional Latin American elites came together with international allies (primarily the U.S. government) and the military to combat revolutionary outbreaks. The connection between U.S. and Latin American armed forces figures prominently in the next chapter in this book. For now, let us focus on another critical aspect of the problem: how and why Latin Americans themselves participated in the social revolutionary movements of the twentieth century.

Following the lead of Bolívar, Martí, and others in the nationalist tradition, Latin American revolutionaries drew deeply from the well of European social thought, but they also revised existing theories to match the unique social conditions and histories of their own national societies. Classical Marxist doctrine suggested that social revolutions would begin in the industrial working class, whose experience and working conditions would be particularly conducive to revolutionary mobilization. As we have seen, industrial workers did play an important political role in the mid-1900s, but more a populist than a revolutionary one. Seeking an alternative strategy, Latin American revolutionaries turned to the countryside. Cuba's Fidel Castro and Argentina's Ernesto "Che" Guevara, for example, started the hemisphere's most successful social revolution in the remote Sierra Maestra mountain range on the southern coast of Cuba, an island with one main city and hundreds of villages. The revolutionary model that seemed more relevant in most parts of Latin America was Chinese, not Russian. As Chinese Communist Party chairman Mao Zedong said, revolutionary guerrillas could become like fish swimming in the water of the rural peasantry.

After revolutionaries marched into Havana in January 1959, the Cuban example created great excitement in Latin America. Cuban revolutionaries were bolstered by their alliance with the Soviet Union and by the overall strength of the global Communist bloc (including Communist Eastern Europe, the People's Republic of China, North Korea, and North Vietnam as well as some African and Middle Eastern states). Indeed, the Cubans even went so far as to develop an informal Ministry of Exporting Revolution headed by Guevara, who traveled from the Congo to Bolivia to assist fellow insurgents. Revolutions broke out in the Dominican Republic, Guatemala, Colombia, and Nicaragua, to name only a few of the major cases. Che announced the famous goal of creating "100 Vietnams" to challenge the U.S. armed forces. The 1960s were, without doubt, a decade of revolutionary advance in Latin America.

The 1980s, as we will see in the next chapter, was a decade of revolutionary reversals. Between local defeats at the hands of Latin American military governments and the collapse of the international Communist bloc, social revolution in Latin America suffered a punishing blow. After years, sometimes decades, of guerrilla warfare revolutionary movements throughout the region sought peace (or a cease-fire, at the minimum) and reconciliation in the 1990s.

In their heyday, social revolutionary movements in Cuba and elsewhere had a profound impact on the history of Latin America. Yet as the selections in this chapter illustrate, there was no single path to revolution in this period, no single model of how to achieve the goal of revolution along socialist lines. While Che advocated for one revolutionary path, Chile's Salvador Allende, whose ideas are also examined in this chapter, advocated a different one. Every institution in Latin America, including the Catholic Church, was forced to deal with the challenge of socialist revolution in this period. As we will see below, the revolutionary impulse divided the Church and raised fundamental questions about the meaning of Christianity. By the end of this chapter, students should be able to recognize the different approaches to social revolution that were developed in this period and explain some of the reasons ordinary Latin Americans might consider supporting or even joining the numerous revolutionary organizations that appeared in the region beginning in the 1960s.

QUESTIONS FOR ANALYSIS

1. Historians often discuss the implications of revolution "from above" versus revolution "from below." What do the terms mean, and how does leadership "from above" or "from below" affect a revolutionary movement?

2. Why did these revolutionary movements inspire such a devoted following? With what cultural ideals did they connect?

3. What kind of oppression, if any, justifies the use of violence to end it? Can oppression that is institutionalized (that is, legal), such as slavery once was, be a kind of violence?

1. Essence of Guerrilla Warfare ~ Che Guevara*

Ernesto "Che" Guevara, born in Argentina in 1928, was one of the most influential and inspiring revolutionary figures in Latin America in the 1960s. He became an icon of social revolution for a generation of young Latin Americans and young people around the world. His ideas and personal example had a powerful impact in Cuba, where he served as a medical doctor and military commander in the peasant-based rural insurgency that defeated the dictatorship of Fulgencio Batista. His book, Guerrilla Warfare, *published in the year after the Cuban Revolution of 1959, condenses Che's experiences in Cuba and offers practical advice to would-be revolutionaries from across the region. Of particular importance was Guevara's message about how guerrilla soldiers should build relationships with the rural peasant communities. After the Cuban experience, Guevara attempted to export his brand of revolution to Africa's Congo, which utterly failed, and later Bolivia, where he was captured and killed by the Bolivian army. Yet to this day his iconic standing lives on. Why do you think that is?*

The armed victory of the Cuban people over the Batista dictatorship was not only the triumph of heroism as reported by the newspapers of the world; it also forced a change in the old dogmas concerning the conduct of the popular masses of Latin America. It showed plainly the capacity of the people to free themselves by means of guerrilla warfare from a government that oppresses them.

*From Ernesto Guevara, *Guerrilla Warfare*, with an introduction by Major Harries-Clichy Peterson, USMCR (New York: Praeger, 1961), 3–10.

We consider that the Cuban Revolution contributed three fundamental lessons to the conduct of revolutionary movements in [Latin] America. They are:

1. Popular forces can win a war against the army.
2. It is not necessary to wait until all conditions for making revolution exist; the insurrection can create them.
3. In underdeveloped [Latin] America the countryside is the basic area for armed fighting.

Of these three propositions the first two contradict the defeatist attitude of revolutionaries or pseudo-revolutionaries who remain inactive and take refuge in the pretext that against a professional army nothing can be done, who sit down to wait until in some mechanical way all necessary objective and subjective conditions are given without working to accelerate them. As these problems were formerly a subject of discussion in Cuba, until facts settled the question, they are probably still much discussed in [Latin] America.

Naturally, it is not to be thought that all conditions for revolution are going to be created through the impulse given to them by guerrilla activity. It must always be kept in mind that there is a necessary minimum without which the establishment and consolidation of the first center is not practicable. People must see clearly the futility of maintaining the fight for social goals within the framework of civil debate. When the forces of oppression come to maintain themselves in power against established law, peace is considered already broken.

In these conditions popular discontent expresses itself in more active forms. An attitude of resistance finally crystallizes in an outbreak of fighting, provoked initially by the conduct of the authorities.

Where a government has come into power through some form of popular vote, fraudulent or not, and maintains at least an appearance of constitutional legality, the guerrilla outbreak cannot be promoted, since the possibilities of peaceful struggle have not yet been exhausted.

The third proposition is a fundamental of strategy. It ought to be noted by those who maintain dogmatically that the struggle of the masses is centered in city movements, entirely forgetting the immense participation of the country people in the life of all the underdeveloped parts of [Latin] America. Of course, the struggles of the city masses of organized workers should not be underrated; but their real possibilities of engaging in armed struggle must be carefully analyzed where the guarantees which customarily adorn our constitutions are suspended or ignored. In these conditions the illegal workers' movements face enormous dangers. They must function secretly without arms. The situation in the open country is not so difficult. There, in places beyond the reach of the repressive forces, the inhabitants can be supported by the armed guerrillas.

We will later make a careful analysis of these three conclusions that stand out in the Cuban revolutionary experience. We emphasize them now at the beginning of this work as our fundamental contribution.

Guerrilla warfare, the basis of the struggle of a people to redeem itself, has diverse characteristics, different facets, even though the essential will for liberation remains the same. It is obvious—and writers on the theme have said it many times—that war responds to a certain series of scientific laws; whoever ignores them will go down to defeat. Guerrilla warfare as a phase of war must be ruled by all of these; but besides, because of its special aspects, a series of corollary laws must also be recognized in order to carry it forward. Though geographical and social conditions in each country determine the mode and particular forms that guerrilla warfare will take, there are general laws that hold for all fighting of this type.

Our task at the moment is to find the basic principles of this kind of *fighting* and the rules to be followed by peoples seeking liberation; to develop theory from facts; to generalize and give structure to our experience for the profit of others.

Let us first consider the question: Who are the combatants in guerrilla warfare? On one side we have a group composed of the oppressor and his agents, the professional army, well armed and disciplined, in many cases receiving foreign help as well as the help of the bureaucracy in the employ of the oppressor. On the other side are the people of the nation or region involved. It is important to emphasize that guerrilla warfare is a war of the masses, a war of the people. The guerrilla band is an armed nucleus, the fighting vanguard of the people. It draws its great force from the mass of the people themselves. The guerrilla band is not to be considered inferior to the army against which it fights simply because it is inferior in firepower. Guerrilla warfare is used by the side which is supported by a majority but which possesses a much smaller number of arms for use in defense against oppression.

The guerrilla fighter needs full help from the people of the area. This is an indispensable condition. This is clearly seen by considering the case of bandit gangs that operate in a region. They have all the characteristics of a guerrilla army: homogeneity, respect for the leader, valor, knowledge of the ground, and, often, even good understanding of the tactics to be employed. The only thing missing is support of the people; and, inevitably, these gangs are captured and exterminated by the public force.

Analyzing the mode of operation of the guerrilla band, seeing its form of struggle, and understanding its base in the masses, we can answer the question: Why does the guerrilla fighter fight? We must come to the inevitable conclusion that the guerrilla fighter is a social [revolutionary], that he takes up arms responding to the angry protest of the people against their oppressors, and that he fights in order to change the social system that keeps all his unarmed brothers in ignominy and misery. He launches himself against the conditions of the reigning institutions at a particular moment and dedicates himself with all the vigor that circumstances permit to breaking the mold of these institutions.

When we analyze more fully the tactic of guerrilla warfare, we will see that the guerrilla fighter needs to have a good knowledge of the surrounding country-side, the paths of entry and escape, the possibilities of speedy maneuver, good hiding places; naturally, also, he must count on the support of the people. All this indicates that the guerrilla fighter will carry out his action in wild places of small population. Since in these places the struggle of the people is aimed primarily and almost exclusively at changing the social form of land ownership, the guerrilla fighter is above all an agrarian revolutionary. He interprets the desires of the great peasant mass to be owners of land, owners of their means of production, of their animals, of all that which they have long yearned to call their own, of that which constitutes their life and will also serve as their cemetery.

It should be noted that in current interpretations there are two different types of guerrilla warfare, one of which—a struggle complementing great regular armies such as was the case of the Ukrainian fighters in the Soviet Union—does not enter into this analysis. We are interested in the other type, the case of an armed group engaged in a struggle against the constituted power, whether colonial or not, which establishes itself as the only base and which builds itself up in rural areas. In all such cases, whatever the ideological aims that may inspire the fight, the economic aim is determined by the aspiration toward ownership of land.

The China of Mao begins as an outbreak of worker groups in the South, which is defeated and almost annihilated. It succeeds in establishing itself and begins its advance only when, after the long march from Yenan, it takes up its base in rural territories and makes agrarian change its fundamental goal. The struggle of Ho Chi Minh [in Vietnam] is based in the rice-growing peasants, who are oppressed by the French colonial yoke; with this force it is going forward to the defeat of the colonialists. In both cases there is a framework of patriotic war against the Japanese invader, but the economic basis of a fight for the land has not disappeared. In the case of Algeria, the grand idea of Arab nationalism has its economic counterpart in the fact that nearly all of the arable land of Algeria is utilized by a million French settlers. In some countries, such as Puerto Rico, where the special conditions of the island have not permitted a guerrilla outbreak, the nationalist spirit, deeply wounded by the discrimination that is daily practiced, has as its basis the aspirations of the peasants (even though many of them are already a proletariat) to recover the land that the Yankee invader seized from them. This same central idea though in different forms, inspired the small farmers, peasants, and slaves of the eastern estates of Cuba to close ranks and defend together the right to possess land during the thirty-year war of liberation, 1868–1898.

Taking account of the possibilities of development of guerrilla warfare, which is transformed with the increase in the operating potential of the guerrilla band into a war of positions, this type of warfare, despite its special character, is to be considered as an embryo, a prelude, of the other. The possibilities of growth of the guerrilla band and of changes in the mode of fight, until conventional warfare is reached, are as great as the possibilities of defeating the enemy in each of the different battles, combats, or skirmishes that take place. Therefore, the fundamental principle is that no battle, combat, or skirmish is to be fought unless it will be won.

War is always a struggle in which each contender tries to annihilate the other. Besides using force, he will have recourse to all possible tricks and stratagems in order to achieve the goal. Military strategy and tactics are a representation by analysis of the objectives of the groups and of the means of achieving these objectives. These means contemplate taking advantage of all the weak points of the enemy. The fighting action of each individual platoon in a large army in a war of positions will present the same characteristics as those of the guerrilla band. It uses secretiveness, treachery, and surprise; and when these are not present, it is because vigilance on the other side prevents surprise. But since the guerrilla band is a division unto itself, and since there are large zones of territory not controlled by the enemy, it is always possible to carry out guerrilla attacks in such a way as to assure surprise; and it is the duty of the guerrilla fighter to do so.

"Hit and run," some call this scornfully, and this is accurate. Hit and run, wait, lie in ambush, again hit and run, and thus repeatedly, without giving any rest to the enemy. There is in all this, it would appear, a negative quality, an attitude of retreat, of avoiding frontal fights. However, this is consequent upon the general strategy of guerrilla warfare, which is the same in its ultimate end as is any warfare: to win, to annihilate the enemy.

Thus, it is clear that guerrilla warfare is a phase that does not afford in itself opportunities to arrive at complete victory. It is one of the initial phases of warfare and will develop continuously until the guerrilla army in its steady growth acquires the characteristics of a regular army. At that moment it will be ready to deal final blows to the enemy and to achieve victory. Triumph will always be the product of a regular army, even though its origins are in a guerrilla army.

Just as the general of a division in a modern war does not have to die in front of his soldiers, the guerrilla fighter, who is general of himself, need not die in every battle. He is ready to give his life, but the positive quality of this guerrilla warfare is precisely that each one of the guerrilla fighters is ready to die, not to defend an ideal, but rather to convert it into reality. This is the basis, the essence of guerrilla fighting. Miraculously, a small band of men, the armed vanguard of the great popular force that supports them, goes beyond the immediate tactical objective, goes on decisively to achieve an ideal, to establish a new society, to break the old molds of the outdated, and to achieve, finally, the social justice for which they fight.

Considered thus, all these disparaged qualities acquire a true nobility, the nobility of the end at which they aim; and it becomes clear that we are not speaking of distorted means of reaching an end. This fighting attitude, this attitude of not being dismayed at any time, this inflexibility when confronting the great problems in the final objective is also the nobility of the guerrilla fighter.

---

2. Cuba's Revolutionary Literacy Campaign ⁓ Jonathan Kozol*

The Cuban Revolution of 1959 inspired a great deal of revolutionary idealism among the youth of Latin America. Charismatic figures like Fidel and Che had a powerful influence on the refashioning of youth identity, right down to the beards and rugged clothes (like Fidel's famous fatigues and Che's black beret) that symbolized the changes brought about by the revolution. In 1961, the idealism of the Cuban youth was put to the test when Castro declared to the world that Cuba would wipe out adult illiteracy on the island in one year. It was an audacious proposal. In the following selection, U.S. educational researcher and activist Jonathan Kozol explains the basic plan for Cuba's 1961 literacy campaign. Kozol travelled to Cuba in 1976 to conduct research on what is still considered to be the world's most successful literacy campaign. What he found was that the huge number of young people who volunteered to serve in the campaign (referred to as brigadistas *below) was motivated by a desire to participate in the guerrilla experience of living with and serving the poorest, most disadvantaged Cubans.*

On September 26, 1960, less than two years after coming to power, Fidel Castro stood before the General Assembly of the U.N. in New York to present his first significant address before an audience which (because of radio, press and TV) would reach at least five hundred million people in almost one half of the nations of the world.

In a brief passage of this speech Dr. Castro spoke approximately one hundred words that marked the start of one of the most extraordinary educational events of recent times.

"In the coming year," said Fidel, "our people intend to fight the great battle of illiteracy, with the ambitious goal of teaching every single inhabitant of the country to read and write in one year, and with that end in mind, organizations of teachers, students and workers, that is, the entire people, are [now] preparing themselves, for an intensive campaign. . . . Cuba will be the first country of America which, after a few months, will be able to say it does not have one person who remains illiterate."

Newspapers do not record whether any of those world figures who were present—Nikita Khrushchev, of the U.S.S.R., for example, or Adlai Stevenson of the

---

*From Jonathan Kozol, *Children of the Revolution: A Yankee Teacher in the Cuban Schools* (New York: Delacorte, 1978), 4–7, 12–14, 20, 22–23.

United States—responded to this portion of the speech or to the back-breaking challenge which in two brisk sentences Fidel had just established for his nation. What is well known is that back home in Cuba the words of Fidel—above all, the promise of complete success in less than one year—came as a great surprise.

It is the truth, however, as a number of organizers of the literacy struggle recollect today, that the promise of Fidel was in general accepted with both energy and zeal by a Cuban population which had already been led by him to consider education—along with land reform and health care—to be one of the three most serious struggles which the revolution had to undertake.

Whether they were forewarned or not, the challenge that faced the Cuban educators was of very great proportions. According to the latest census, that of 1953, 1,032,849 Cubans were illiterate out of a population of a bit more than 4,000,000 adults. One out of four adults in Cuba, most of them farmers in small, isolated mountain villages far from town or city, could not read or write. The total teaching force in the Cuban classrooms on the day Batista fled (December 31, 1958) was thirty-six thousand. These teachers, moreover, were in large part obligated to remain in their jobs as teachers of children in the public schools.

The initial question, then, was not one of "approach" or "method"—but of logistics and manpower. Cuban educators were convinced that traditional teacher-pupil ratios could not bring the reading skills of middle-aged and older campesinos up to a functional level in the course of only eight or nine months. The ideal ratio, they felt, was one-to-two—although they were prepared to settle for a ratio of one-to-four at most.

Where could Cuba find two hundred and fifty thousand teachers for approximately one million people, living in the least developed and most isolated sections of Las Villas, Oriente, and Pinar Del Río provinces, where the highest rates of mass illiteracy conspired with the highest and most rugged mountain ranges to compound the task?

The answer—then, as many times again during the years ahead—came from young people. Cuba is, in demographic terms, a youthful nation, with almost half its population younger than eighteen. Only by the active intervention of young men and women could the nation possibly achieve its goal.

A call went out for student volunteers.

The call was answered by one hundred thousand pupils, almost all between ten years of age and seventeen. Exact statistics compiled by the Literacy Commission at the end of 1961 indicate that of this number, forty percent were ten to fourteen years of age. Forty-seven percent were between fifteen and nineteen. Virtually all the rest were under thirty. (The youngest "teacher" listed, a child named Elan Menéndez, was eight years old. The oldest "student," by way of contrast, was a woman of 106 who had been born—and grown up—as a slave.)

The student volunteers would soon be reinforced by over one hundred and forty thousand men and women, achieving a total teaching force of a quarter-million people. In the face of these remarkable statistics one obvious question is quite often posed: Why would so many Cuban students answer an appeal for work which (as Fidel warned them in advance) would not be easy, but would call for infinite patience, and would offer only gradual and piecemeal satisfaction?

The anti-Castro critic can provide a glib response: "slave-labor . . . who can argue with a gun?" A mindless booster of the Cuban revolution might propose the opposite answer: "This is the magic of a socialist revolution." The answer does unquestionably have to do with revolution—but neither with magic, miracles, or guns.

As veterans of the literacy struggle reminisce today, it seems apparent that the basic—or, at least, initial—motivation had a lot to do with the desire of kids (most of them urban, many middle-class) to share in an adventure which appeared in certain graphic ways to carry on the work-and-struggle-in-the-mountains symbolized by Che Guevara and Fidel. A kind of "ethical exhilaration," modeled upon these heroes, seems to have been the overwhelming impetus, rather than a tough, consistent, well-developed Marxist dedication.

The preparation given to each unit of the youth brigades was concentrated and extremely brief: seven to ten days at Varadero—an elegant former tourist spot about one hour from Havana, reserved in earlier times for foreign visitors, corporation representatives, and their Cuban friends, forbidden to blacks, whether North American or Cuban.

Students were given instruction in the use of two essential teaching aids: a book of "oral readings" which would also function as a teacher's manual (*Alfabeticemos*) and the learner's primer (*Venceremos*). Both are papercover booklets that the government prepared, after extensive research, under the direction of a well known Cuban scholar, Dr. Raúl Gutiérrez. (The press-run of the primer was one million five hundred thousand copies.)

In preparation of the primer, an exhaustive search was made for "active" words—words that bore associations of emotion, love or longing, ecstasy or rage among the campesinos. Using these words as starting points, the technical experts wrote the primer in the form of fifteen lessons, each lesson somewhat more difficult than the one before but each one reiterating basic sounds and themes. Each of the fifteen lessons was presented as a story or discussion of one of the "active" topics. Each was preceded by a photograph of Cuban life which served both to provoke discussion and to clarify the main theme of the chapter: an agricultural collective with three farmers briefly resting from their work; children and teenagers planting a sapling in the midst of an unforested terrain; Cuban fishermen holding up the catch from a day's work for "the cooperative"; a man walking out of the doorway of "the People's Store," his arms loaded with heavy bags of food and other goods; a couple standing in the doorway of their own small but attractive house; a mother receiving a child-care lesson from the doctor in a neighborhood prenatal class; a composite photo of a rifle, farmer's shovel, and the cheerful cover of the primer—symbolizing victory on all three fronts. . . .

In a brief guidebook, *Orientations for the Brigadista*, students were instructed prior to the lesson itself to use the photographs to initiate informal conversation. "Avoid giving orders!" the young teacher was advised. "Say to the pupil: 'We are going to work. We are going to study. . . .' Avoid the authoritarian tone. Never forget that the work of learning how to read and write is realized and achieved in common."

The brigadistas had to learn much more, however, than the way to use the primer. They also had to be prepared for life in the distant, largely unelectrified and unfamiliar rural areas to which they would be sent to teach and live. They had to be prepared to share in every aspect of the daily work—whether it was that of farmers in the fields or that of mothers in their one-room homes. The sense of solidarity that grew out of these periods of shared labor seems frequently to have become the key to motivation, trust, and perseverance for the teacher and the learner both.

Each brigadista was given a number of copies of the primer and the manual, two pairs of socks, two pairs of pants, two shirts, a pair of boots, a blanket and beret, as well as a sophisticated multi-purpose version of the Coleman lantern. Hammocks also were provided to the brigadistas. (This was to avoid embarrassing the campesino families, few of whom would have an extra bed.)

The lantern was essential, not just to provide a light by which to travel on the country roads from house to house, but also to provide the light by which to carry on the reading lessons in the hours before sunrise or during the evening when the farmers and their families had assembled at the kitchen table.

One former brigadista, Armando Valdez, now a member of the Cuban foreign service, summarized his own reactions in the course of conversation in September 1976: "I never could have known that people lived in such conditions. I was the child of an educated, comfortable family. Those months, for me, were like the stories I have heard about conversion to a new religion. It was, for me, the dying of an old life and the start of something absolutely new. I cried, although I had been taught men must not cry, when I first saw the desperation of those people—people who had so little. . . . *No, they did not have 'so little,' they had nothing!* It was something which at first I could not quite believe.

"I did not need to read of this in Marx, in Lenin, in Martí. I did not need to read of what I saw before my eyes. I cried each night. I wrote my mother and my father. I was only twelve years old. I was excited to be part of something which had never happened in our land before. I wanted so much that we would prove that we could keep the promise that Fidel had made before the world. I did not want it to be said that we would not stand up beside Fidel."

3. Chile's Revolution from Below ⁓ Peter Winn*

Chile, unlike Cuba, had a proud tradition of electoral democracy and civilian rule going back to the nineteenth century. The views of its most important revolutionary leader, Salvador Allende, differed greatly from those of Che Guevara on how to achieve socialism. Put simply, Allende believed in the power of the ballot over the bullet. He thus founded a revolutionary electoral coalition, the Unidad Popular *or Popular Unity, and called his strategic vision* la vía chilena, *the Chilean Road. In this selection, historian Peter Winn discusses the way Allende's victory in the 1970 presidential election radicalized the workers at the Yarur cotton mill outside Santiago, a bastion of Allende's support. Ultimately, Winn suggests that President Allende's controlled revolution from above was not possible once the uncontrollable revolution from below gained momentum at places such as Yarur.*

On the twenty-fifth of April 1971, the workers at the Yarur cotton mill in Santiago seized control of their factory and demanded "socialism." There had been strikes before at the Yarur mill—for better wages, for an independent union, against the Taylor System†—but this was different: This was a strike to rule. Three days later, President Allende reluctantly bowed to their demands and Yarur, Inc., became the first Chilean industry to be requisitioned by the Popular Unity government "for the simple fact of being a monopoly."

It was a historical role that took the workers themselves by surprise. All they had hoped to do was "liberate" themselves from "the yoke of the Yarurs." All they thought they were doing was fulfilling the Popular Unity program and redeeming Allende's campaign pledge. But what they did was enact their own understanding of the Chilean revolution—a model other workers then followed.

In only five months of Popular Unity government, the workers' movement at the Yarur mill had fulfilled its historic agenda and gone beyond it to pose questions of worker power that challenged Amador Yarur's control over his own factory. The Yarur workers may have been bywords for political backwardness in the past, but during the five months of Allende's presidency they had leaped into the vanguard of an accelerating and deepening revolution from below, one significantly different from Salvador Allende's revolution from above.

---

*From Peter Winn, *Weavers of Revolution: The Yarur Workers and Chile's Road to Socialism* (New York: Oxford University Press, 1986), 139–43. © 1986 by Oxford University Press, Inc. Reprinted by permission of Oxford University Press.
†Philadelphia engineer and efficiency expert Frederick Winslow Taylor's scientific approach to factory operations.

The Popular Unity program and the authors of its economic strategy envisioned a carefully controlled revolution from above. The structural changes that would pave the way for socialism were to be carried out legally, using the instruments created by the bourgeoisie and the powers granted the state. At the same time, mandated price controls and wage increases would redistribute income "from the infinitesimal minorities to the overwhelming majority" of Chileans. Together with the Popular Unity government's vastly expanded social programs, the resultant raised real incomes would "solve the basic needs of the people" and make possible Allende's promised "revolution with meat pies and red wine."

These measures—and successes—were also central to the Popular Unity's political strategy, which was to produce an electoral majority for socialism by the end of Allende's six-year presidential term. It was a strategy that counted on the growing support of Chile's workers, peasants, and *pobladores* [urban underclass], who would be won over by the material benefits that they would receive and persuaded by their experience that socialism was a superior system that was in their own self-interest. But in order to succeed, *la vía chilena* also required the support of a sizable sector of the middle classes, who wanted the benefits of *los cambios* ("the changes") that both Allende and [Radomiro] Tomic had proposed but feared the personal and societal costs of a Marxist-led revolution. Most of them had voted for Tomic and change in 1970, rather than for [Jorge] Alessandri and the status quo, and their support could give the Popular Unity the majority that it sought. The solution was to produce the promised revolution without sacrifice while allaying their fears of a violent or authoritarian revolution in which they might become victims.

This required a carefully controlled and phased revolutionary process, which was also necessary for the successful implementation of the Popular Unity's program of structural change. Here the strategy called for dividing the Chilean bourgeoisie, confronting one sector at a time, and enlisting the cooperation or neutrality of the smaller and medium-sized enterprises by confining leftist attacks to the "monopolies." In this delicately balanced strategy of economic and political change, the role of the "masses"—workers, peasants, and pobladores—was to provide political and social support when called on, but otherwise to await patiently the advances and benefits of the revolution from above.

Allende's "popular triumph," however, had a different meaning to his mass base than it had to the politicians and planners of the Popular Unity. To Chile's workers, peasants, and pobladores, the election of a "Popular Government" was a signal for them to take the revolution into their own hands and fulfill their historic aspirations through direct action from below. Allende's promise that he would never use the security apparatus of the state against "the people" freed them from fear of governmental repression, and the Popular Unity's commitment to structural change, redistribution of wealth, and meeting the basic needs of Chile's poor persuaded many that, in acting for themselves, they were fulfilling the Popular Unity program and advancing the revolutionary process. For them, the underlying meaning of Allende's election was that they were now free to pursue their long postponed dreams.

The result was the unleashing of a revolution from below, which sometimes coincided with or complemented, but increasingly diverged from, the legalistic and modulated revolution from above. More spontaneous, it emerged from the workers, peasants, and pobladores themselves, although through a complex process in which certain political groups played an important role. Workers, peasants, and pobladores, however, were the protagonists of this other revolutionary process, and they infused it with their own concerns, style, and worldview. Their aims tended to be concrete—objectives that responded to problems in their daily lives but that they equated with advancing "the revolution." It was an uneven process, with varying dynamics, but it was sufficiently powerful to call into question the speed, priorities, and character of the overall revolutionary process. It was never completely autonomous nor totally spontaneous, but from a passive political base the Chilean masses began to transform themselves into active agents of change, the protagonists of their own destiny.

The hallmark of this revolution from below was the *toma*—the seizure of the sites where people lived or worked—or hoped to live or work. Allende's election was followed by a wave of suburban land seizures by homeless urban workers and recent rural migrants desperate for the housing that successive governments had promised to provide but failed to deliver. Led by leftist activists, squatters seized vacant lots on the edge of Chile's cities, raising the national flag and building cardboard shacks as symbols of legitimacy and signs of possession.

Equally dramatic and even less compatible with Allende's phased revolution from above was the wave of farm seizures that began in the Mapuche Indian areas of the Alpine south and spread rapidly to the rural laborers and poor peasants of the fertile Central Valley, Chile's breadbasket and the economic and political base of Chile's traditional elite. Whether it was "the running of the fences" by Indians to reclaim the lands that European settlers had taken from them during the preceding century or the toma of large estates by peasants who had been disappointed by the speed and scope of [1960s president Eduardo] Frei's agrarian reform, the message was the same. The deprived of Chile had taken Allende's victory as their own and were acting out its meaning in their own direct action. It was at once a sign of faith in the Popular Unity and suspicion of all governmental bureaucracy.

For Chile's industrial workers, Allende's election and inauguration were also a signal: a time to organize, to press for big wage increases, to prepare for the socialization of one's workplace. For the most part, the industrial workers were better organized and better paid, more disciplined and more committed to the Popular Unity than the peasants and pobladores. They interpreted the advent of a Popular Unity government as an opportunity to press for their historic aspirations—higher real wages, an economist orientation ingrained by years of struggle within the legalistic Chilean Labor Code and a politicized labor movement. The workers took the Allende government's wage guidelines—a 36 percent raise, equal to the previous year's inflation—as a starting point for contract negotiations. Taking advantage of their new bargaining leverage—management awareness that government representatives on the tripartite mediation boards would now side with the workers and fear that a labor conflict might lead to a strike that would provoke a factory seizure or government takeover—industrial workers won the largest real wage raises in Chilean history, leading the way to the 30 percent average increase in real incomes that Chilean workers secured for 1971.

For such workers, peasants, and pobladores, the meaning of Allende's presidency was the license to fulfill their aspirations and pursue their dreams. Some were conscious of the broader implications of their actions; others, conscious only of the opportunity to realize the goals of a lifetime. Together, their individual actions transformed Allende's narrow electoral victory into a profound revolution from below. It was a social revolution that confirmed the fears of the elite and awoke the anxieties of the middle classes even as it raised the hopes of the most "revolutionary" factions within the Popular Unity and factions to its left.

The Popular Unity leaders had banked on the increasing radicalization and support of Chile's workers, peasants, and pobladores on their democratic road to socialism, but they had not bargained for a revolution from below. The problem for the Allende government was how to reward the expectations of its mass base while keeping wage increases within non-inflationary bounds and land seizures from threatening its political strategy of class coalition.

Although the large raises for 1971 might cause economic problems later on, it was the tomas that most worried the Popular Unity leadership. There had been land seizures before the election of Allende, but never on such a scale. The rural revolution from below, in particular, was playing havoc with the Popular Unity's timetable and image of legality and was threatening the governing coalition's political strategy of class coalition by raising the anxieties of small landowners, a central social base of the Radical party.

Still more worrying to many Popular Unity leaders was the prospect of a deepening revolution from below among the industrial working class. Except for those few industries whose owners had abandoned the country, failed to meet payrolls, or shut down plants, factory seizures had been conspicuous by their absence before 1971. By March of that year, however, government officials were becoming aware that pressure from below for the socialization of industry was growing. If these pressures could not be contained, the Popular Unity might be forced to choose between its strategy for socialism and its central mass base.

By April 1971, it was becoming clear that Allende's election had set off processes that were calling into question his initial timetable and strategy. A surging revolution from below was threatening to leave the national leaders of the Left behind and to disrupt the Popular Unity's economic and political strategies in the process. Together with the unexpectedly rapid progress of the revolution from above, this unanticipated emergence of a revolution from below was forcing the Popular Unity leaders to reassess the scope, speed, direction, methods, and character of their road to socialism, posing with new urgency the old question: reform or revolution?

4. The Chilean Road to Socialism ⁓ Salvador Allende*

Allende's democratic road to socialism differed from the road of guerrilla warfare proposed by Che Guevara. In the following selection Allende explains what he calls the "five essential points" about the Chilean Road. The overall impression given is of a controlled, gradual transformation rather than immediate change. Having the electoral majority on his side was obviously crucial to his strategy. Allende believed that majority support allowed him to reorganize institutions such as the judicial system through the democratic legislative process. On the question of revolutionary violence, Allende clearly differentiated between the conditions his movement faced in Chile versus those found in military dictatorships such as prerevolutionary Cuba. One of Allende's most popular measures was the government takeover of foreign-owned copper companies, mentioned as his fifth point, despite furious U.S. opposition. Sadly, the Chilean military did not remain neutral in the political struggles of the early 1970s as it had in the past. A coup d'état ended Allende's life and the Popular Unity government in September 1973.

In the revolutionary process in which we are involved, there are five essential points upon which our political and social struggle turns—legality, institutionality, political freedom, violence, and the nationalization of the means of production. These are questions which affect the present and future of each citizen.

The Principle of Legality

The principle of legality now reigns in Chile. It was imposed after the struggle of many generations against absolutism and the arbitrary use of the power of the state. It is an irreversible triumph as long as no distinction remains between the governing and the governed. It is not the principle of legality which is denounced by popular movements. Our protest is against a legal order whose principles reflect an oppressive social system. Our juridical norms, the tech-

---

*From Salvador Allende, *Salvador Allende on Chile's Road to Socialism*, ed. Joan E. Garces, trans. J. Darling, with an introduction by Richard Gott (Hammondsworth, UK: Penguin, 1973), 147–55.

niques which regulate social relations between Chileans, correspond today to the requirements of a capitalist system. In the transition to a socialist regime, the juridical norms will correspond to the necessities of a people struggling to build a new society. But legality there will be.

Our legal system must be modified. This is the main responsibility of the courts at the present time to see that nothing impedes the transformation of our juridical system.

It depends to a great extent on the realistic attitude of Congress whether or not the legal system of capitalism can be succeeded by a socialist legal system, conforming to the socioeconomic changes which we are planning, without there being a violent rupture in the juridical system, which could give rise to those arbitrary acts and excesses that we wish to avoid.

Institutional Development

The regard for law and order which marks the constitutional state extends through all our institutions. The struggle of the popular movements which now are represented in the government has contributed substantially to one of the most heartening facts on which the country can rely: we possess an open institutional system which has withstood attempts to violate the will of the people.

The flexibility of our institutional system allows us to hope that it will not present rigid opposition to our proposals, and that it will adapt itself, as will our legal system, to the new requirements in order to create the new concept of institutionality needed for the overthrow of capitalism in a constitutional manner.

The new institutional order will serve the principle which legitimizes and directs our action: that is, to transfer political and economic power to the workers. To make this possible, it is essential first of all for society to own the basic means of production.

At the same time it is necessary to accommodate the political institutions to the new reality. For that reason, at the proper time, we shall submit to the sovereign will of the people the question of the need to replace the present Constitution, which has a liberal framework, with a socialist-orientated Constitution, and to replace the two-Chamber system by a single Chamber.

We have promised that our governmental program will put its revolutionary aims into practice with full respect for the rule of law. This is not merely a formal assurance, but the explicit recognition that the principles of legality and institutional order are compatible with a socialist regime, in spite of the difficulties inherent in a period of transition.

To maintain these principles while transforming their class bias during this difficult period is an ambitious task, and of decisive importance for the new social order. Nonetheless, its fulfillment depends solely on our strength of will; it will depend fundamentally on the relationships in our social and economic structure, on their evolution in the short term, and on realistic political behaviour on the part of the people. At the present time, we believe that it is possible, and we are acting accordingly.

Political Freedoms

It is also important for us, as the representatives of popular forces, to remember that political freedom has been won by the people along their arduous road towards emancipation. It is part of what was positive in the historical period which we leave behind us, and it must remain, as our respect also remains for freedom of conscience and of all beliefs. For this reason we are pleased to note the words of the Cardinal Archbishop of Santiago, Raúl Silva Henríquez, in his speech to the workers: "The Church I represent is the Church of Christ, son of a carpenter. Thus the Church was born and thus we want her to remain. Our greatest sorrow is when men forget her birthplace, which was and is among the humble."

But we would not be revolutionaries if we were to limit ourselves to maintaining political freedom. The government of Unidad Popular will extend political freedom. It is not enough to proclaim it by word alone, for that leads to frustration and mockery. We shall make it real, tangible, and concrete, and exercise it in the measure that we master economic freedom.

The policies of the Unidad Popular government are inspired by a paradoxical situation. Classes and sectors exist in our society with hostile and exclusive interests, and disparate political levels exist within one and the same class or sector.

In the face of this diversity the government will attend primarily to the interests of all those who earn their living by their own work: labourers and professionals, technicians and artists, intellectuals and clerical workers. These people represent a group which is growing day by day as the result of capitalist development. They are becoming more and more united by their common situation as wage-earners. The government will also support small- and medium-scale businesses. Indeed we shall support all those sectors of society which, with varying degrees of severity, have been exploited by the minorities who own the means of production.

The multi-party coalition of the Unidad Popular government is very conscious of the problems in this situation. In the daily confrontation of its interests with those of the ruling class the government will make use of all the decision-making processes available within the institutional juridical system. We recognize the political freedom of the Opposition and we will conduct all our activities within the terms of the Constitution. Political freedom is the prized possession of all Chilean people.

It is fundamental to our policy to develop the political potential of our country to the maximum, so that in the stage of transition towards socialism we shall be able to dismantle the present system systematically. We shall abolish or reject its negative aspects and strengthen and reinforce its positive factors.

Violence

The people of Chile are acquiring political power without finding themselves forced to use arms. They are advancing on the road of its social liberation without having had to fight a despotic or dictatorial regime. They have had to resist only the limitations of a liberal democracy. Our people hope with deep sincerity to spend the period of transition to socialism without having to fall back on authoritarian forms of government.

Our attitude on this point is very clear. But the responsibility of guaranteeing political evolution towards socialism does not rest solely with the government and the movements and parties that compose it. Our people have risen against the institutionalized violence which the present capitalist system imposed upon them; that is why we are transforming this system at the base.

My government owes its existence to the freely expressed will of the people. It answers only to them. The movements and parties which compose it are the guides of the revolutionary consciousness of the masses and the expression of their hopes and interests. They are also directly responsible to the people.

Nonetheless I must warn you that there are dangers which could obscure the clear path of our emancipation and radically alter for the worse the way which a realistic assessment of our circumstances would recommend. Such a danger would consist of violence done to the decisions of the people.

If violence, internal or external, violence in any of its forms, whether physical, economic, social, or political, were to succeed in threatening our natural development and the achievements of the workers, then the continuity of our institutions, our constitutional state, political liberties, and the chance for pluralism would be in acute danger. The battle for social emancipation, for the free determination of our people, would be forced to take on very different features from those which, we can proudly and truthfully say now, constitute the Chilean road to socialism. The resolute attitude of the government, the revolutionary energy of the people, the democratic strength of the armed forces and police will be our defense in ensuring that Chile advances safely along the highway to socialism.

The unity of the popular forces and the good will of the middle classes represent that infinitely superior strength which ensures that the privileged minority will not easily take to violence. As long as violence is not used against the people, we shall be able to transform the basic structures where capitalism is entrenched in a democratic, pluralistic, and free manner. The transformation will come about without the use of unnecessary physical coercion, without institutional disorder, and without disorganizing production, at a pace set by the government in accordance with the needs of the people and the development of our resources.

Nationalization of the Means of Production

Citizens, during our six months of office, we have taken decisive action on all fronts. Our economic activities aim to remove the barriers which hinder the complete development of our human and material potential. In our six months of office, we have made vigorous advances along a path of irrevocable change. The report which we have just published contains details of our activities.

Chile has begun the definitive recovery of its basic wealth: copper. The nationalization of our copper is not an act of vengeance or of hate towards any group, government, or particular nation. On the contrary, we have taken the positive step of exercising the inalienable right of a sovereign people: the full use of our resources exploited by national labour and effort.

The recovery of our copper is Chile's decision and we have a right to the respect of all countries and governments for the unanimous decision of a free people. We snall pay for the copper if it is fair to pay, or we shall not pay if it is not fair to do so. We shall protect our interests. We shall be totally intransigent if we find that negligence or malevolent acts are being perpetrated by persons, or companies in order to damage the interests of the country.

---

5. Christianity and Revolution ~ Margaret Randall*

In the 1970s, the small island of Solentiname in Lake Nicaragua became the home of an experimental community inspired by "liberation theology," which had as its goal the liberation of Christian communities from all forms of oppression (both spiritual and material, the linkage between the two being crucial to their theological perspective). Liberation theology arose in Latin America in the wake of the Bishops' Conference at Medellín, Colombia, in 1968, which issued a call for the Catholic Church to take a more active role in demanding respect for human rights and social justice, even when such demands led to direct confrontations with state authorities. At that time, Central America's numerous Cuba-inspired revolutionary movements had produced high levels of government repression, especially among the peasantry. In this selection, several members of the Christian-based community at Solentiname talk to researcher Margaret Randall about the way the community took shape. A key figure mentioned by the participants is Ernesto Cardenal, a controversial Nicaraguan priest and

---

*From Margaret Randall, *Christians in the Nicaraguan Revolution*, trans. Mariana Valverde (Vancouver: New Star Books, 1983), 68–73.

revolutionary who helped create Solentiname. Notice also the references to the deceased Che Guevara.

MANUEL: Ernesto would celebrate the Mass and afterwards he would read the Gospel. Each person would get a book called *God Comes to Man*, which is a very clear translation of the Gospel. We would read it and then comment on it verse by verse. Each person would give their opinion. And we arrived at the conclusion that the system we were living under was bad and had to be changed.

NATALIA: Ernesto would ask, "What do you think of what it says here in the Gospel?" And he would listen to everyone's opinion. Some people said what they thought; others didn't say anything. Some didn't agree with Ernesto and would have died before saying anything. One time, someone mentioned Che Guevara. And I said: "Che died, but he didn't die. He remains alive because there are others who followed him."

OSCAR: When I began to participate in the dialogues I felt relief, I felt satisfied. Many people only preached the Gospel in Latin, and of course we didn't understand it. We were so happy to have the opportunity to hear Ernesto talk clearly and to participate ourselves.

I was brought up in a sect called the Seventh-Day Adventists. My family and my grandmother were of that religion. I would hear the Gospel and would pick up a few things about Christianity and the Word of God. But we never had the opportunity of discussing them with the priest or the pastor. They just preached. But Ernesto wanted everyone to discuss the Gospel. He didn't like just speaking or reading. When we participated, each person communicated their ideas, and the Holy Spirit was there in what was being said.

Ernesto tried to get to know the people better. Then he formed a group called "God's family" with the older people. From then on we had more confidence, as though we belonged to the same house. The group was both women and men. We lived as though in a seminary. Ernesto spoke about our vices; that was the kind of thing that he was concerned about. The group had discussions with comrades from Managua and from outside the country.

That experience was very beautiful. The Gospel was spoken there as Jesus Christ had wanted. Christ was a guerrilla fighter, not the sort of person to be kicked around, with the imperialist boot always on top of him. The Gospel was quite clear. It told of the suffering that Christ underwent for a group that was in a similar situation to ours in Nicaragua under [Anastasio] Somoza. Earlier we had thought we could always live like that, with the Book in our hands, without any change. Because many people, even the oldest men, believe that you can be saved by the Bible alone. After hearing the Gospel we saw more clearly what Jesus Christ wanted, what kind of love he had for his people. We saw that you had to overthrow imperialism to live a little better.

I used to think that Somoza had given us something. I didn't feel the need for change, the need to struggle to overthrow the dictatorship. I was quite mistaken. With time, I came to feel hatred against Somoza's rule here. I remember that we were very afraid of the National Guard. Through the Gospel, through dialogue, this fear went away. I also felt a different change. I began to see the possibility of a change for my people, for the human race, a future for Nicaragua and for all the peoples that have suffered.

TERESITA: Everything changed when we began to understand what it really meant to be a Christian. It wasn't so much the prayers and Masses and Communions, but something else. Love, really. Love for others. At the beginning we had daily Masses in Solentiname but afterwards Ernesto said that if we didn't want Mass, we shouldn't have it. He said we could ask him whenever we wanted. From then we didn't have Masses every day but only one or two a week, apart from Sunday Mass. And we never said the Rosary. We would recite the Psalms in the morning, and then read some other book. Prayer was still very important to me.

ALEJANDRO: Father de la Jara, who was active in the Christian base communities in Managua, gave us the idea of taping the commentaries and told us how to do it. Afterwards, Fernando, Ernesto's brother, came and wanted to tape us and make a book with the tapes. Because our commentaries concerned theological questions it was important to write them down. After we did the taping, we saw how we were developing politically. Within the context of the Gospel, we were overcoming theoretical problems. The tapes helped us improve our discussions and made us realize how important they were.

Other influences helped. We had a large library, and lots of visitors, although we were more and more selective. And that helped a lot. University students came with their Christian faith and their Marxism, and all their skills. We soon changed from receiving only Christians to receiving others, too. We discussed all that, and became more politically aware. In this way we kept growing.

OLIVIA: You see, before that I would read the Bible with my daughter and would try to be resigned in my misery, waiting for death in order to enjoy happiness. Now I see that is absurd.

MANUEL: Those who taught us the old religion, and said that we shouldn't hate anybody, had us supporting Somoza's government. In that sense we supported Somoza. Religion taught us that we had to have a dictator there, for God had put him there, that we had to spend our time praying for this man to be healthy. That's what religion taught us, to accept the conditions of life that we had.

OLIVIA: I believe that still happens, even in Nicaragua, in any place where some people still live in conformity, in their misery, expecting to go to their reward.

What will they enjoy then? What we have to enjoy is this life here and now, which God made for all of us. I got to the point where I could not live resigned to eating next-to-nothing, bringing up my children in such poverty, with all my childbirths, everything.

MANUEL: They would say: God wants it that way, we have to be on His side. This is a commandment of God. For instance, the evangelists read the verses from the Bible to teach you that each country has to have a government, and that we must help it, protect it, and pray for it. They said that it is a sin to kill a National Guardsman or to join the guerrillas, and if we agreed with the guerrillas or supported "assassins" who went around in the mountains killing, we would burn in Hell.

At that point, for me, Che Guevara was just a creep. But when Ernesto put some politics in the Gospel, we began to realize much of what we had learned was not true, that Che Guevara was better than a priest, better than a bishop, better than the Pope. That this man went around changing the system so we could live better.

Now, there were some people who accepted what Ernesto told them, but some people did not. They did not believe in Ernesto. For example, some didn't believe in the baptisms that he celebrated. When Ernesto was going to baptize a child he said: "Bring some water from the beach to baptize the child." People said that was not right, because the water had not been blessed. It wasn't holy water. And that would not do. But of course what really works are the words, the commitment that you make at a wedding or a baptism. In Christianity, that's what counts; not the rites, which are meaningless.

ERNESTO: Some people complained because we took the statues of saints away. We only left two of them, beautiful antique sculptures. But we burned the others. They were ugly, painted with lead.

NATALIA: Some people said they wouldn't go to Mass because Ernesto was a communist. They would say, "Everybody who goes there is a communist." Ernesto told the people in Mancarroncito that we would all go there in a boat and he would say Mass. They had said they could not come here, and when Ernesto went, there wasn't a soul to be seen. And when we saw that, we said, "Ernesto, let's go, what's the point?" We knew they were afraid to come because people said Ernesto was a communist. The rumor was that anybody coming to see Ernesto was going to end up in jail. Even some of the people here believed it, too.

And then I would ask them: Do you know what a communist is? If Ernesto asks you what it means to be a communist, you won't be able to answer. There are different kinds of communists. To be a communist is to be in a community together. But they would say, what does Natalia know anyway? Ernesto is brainwashing all the old women, after they've already sold their sons to him. They thought he was paying us and that he was turning our sons into communists. That's how they talked.

X

The Cold War

In order to combat the rising threat of social revolution in Latin America, the Cold War–era government of the United States went to extraordinary lengths. Alliances between the U.S. and Latin American governments became increasingly important in the context of the postwar, global struggle between the Communist East and the capitalist West, between Moscow and Washington. In the previous chapter, we explored the problem of Latin American social revolution from the point of view of its participants. In this chapter, we will shift perspectives and consider the role of the U.S. government in preventing social revolutionary change in Latin America, which it considered its primary mission in the region.

Since the end of the nineteenth century, the U.S. government had often acted aggressively toward the neighboring republics to the south. The Mexican-American War (1846–1848) and the Spanish-American War (1898) are two classic examples of this violent early history. As we saw in chapter 6's exploration of the problem of nationalism, armed intervention by U.S. forces (usually the Marines) was not unusual in the first half of the twentieth century in the Caribbean and Central America, although Franklin Roosevelt began to change the pattern of intervention prior to World War II with his Good Neighbor Policy. Nonetheless, the term "our backyard" became a fitting description of Latin America's standing relative to the United States.

The outcome of World War II presented a new set of global dynamics for U.S.–Latin American relations. By the late 1940s, old European empires were collapsing around the globe. The United States and the Soviet Union then became the world's two military superpowers, each with nuclear arsenals and extensive military alliances. U.S. policy makers were thrust into a position of responsibility for the preservation of what they saw as the "Free World," that is to say, the non-Communist world. So began the Cold War, so called because the two sides, though apparently locked in a life-and-death confrontation, never struck at each other directly. Although they came close to armed conflict, the war stayed cold—except in some areas of the Third World, where it got very hot indeed.

In their dealings with Latin Americans, U.S. policy makers looked at the region's upsurge in social revolutionary movements and saw, or thought they saw, the hand of the Soviet Union at work. Their approach to the region was therefore founded on fundamental tenets of Cold War thinking. First was the conviction that the Soviet Union was bent upon the destruction of the Free World and the imposition of global Communism. Second was a commitment to "containment," which dedicated U.S. resources to stopping the spread of Communism in Europe, East Asia, and the developing world. In Latin America, these tenets translated into staunch support for anti-Communist forces. And who better to combat Communist insurgency than the Latin American armed forces?

Washington's relations with the Latin American armed forces underwent a dramatic intensification during the Cold War decades. The United States provided money, weapons, special agents, advisers, and, occasionally, troops in the anti-revolutionary effort. Thousands of Latin American military officers underwent specialized "counterinsurgency" training at the U.S. School of the Americas in the Panama Canal Zone (later moved to Fort Benning in Georgia). Support for the region's military officers grew especially fast after the Cuban Revolution of 1959. Another wave of intensified funding and assistance came after Nicaragua's Sandinista Revolution of 1979.

In this context of extreme political and ideological polarization, U.S. policy makers sometimes encouraged the Latin American military to seize the reins of civil authority before it was too late. Beginning in Brazil in 1964 and continuing through the 1980s, the U.S. government declared its support for the temporary suspension of civilian democratic regimes in the region's hot spots of guerrilla conflict. Washington's National Security Doctrine justified anti-Communist dictatorships across the region. Chile, for example, which had a nearly unblemished record of democratic succession since the nineteenth century, was taken over by General Augusto Pinochet in 1973, with U.S. support. This was the coup that cost Salvador Allende his life. Not until 1990 would Chile see another elected president.

It is often said that the United States "won" the Cold War. There is no doubt that the U.S. government achieved its goal of stopping social revolutions (with the nagging exception of Cuba). For most foreign policy decision makers in Washington, victory was what mattered, at any cost to Latin America. The following selections ask students to think critically about that victory. What were its assumptions, costs, and implications? By the end of this chapter, students will be able to explain their own view of the role of U.S. foreign policy in Latin America during the Cold War.

QUESTIONS FOR ANALYSIS

1. What was the Cold War strategy of the U.S. government in regard to Latin America? How did the region fit into the bigger, geopolitical picture?
2. How does the Cold War period fit into broader patterns of the historical relationship between the United States and Latin America?
3. In the context of the Cold War, were the means used to combat social revolution in Latin America justified?

1. The Lesser of Two Evils ∼ David F. Schmitz*

With the coming of the Chinese Communist revolution in 1949 and the Korean War of the early 1950s, U.S. policy makers faced an uncertain era of global commitments. It did not take long for the Cold War to spread from East Asia to Latin America. In the following selection, historian David Schmitz offers a perspective on one of the major challenges facing the Eisenhower administration in this new age of American superpower—how to eliminate the root causes of Communist insurgency in the Third World. Schmitz argues that President Dwight D. Eisenhower and his cabinet (in particular, Secretary of State John Foster Dulles) decided that measures to reform decolonizing societies in Asia and Africa had to be sacrificed to preserve the more fundamental objective of anti-Communist stability. For this difficult task, military dictatorships seemed the only possible solution. The author also emphasizes the decision to develop the capability for covert (secretive and often illegal) action in pursuit of the anti-Communist victory.

As had all administrations since [Woodrow] Wilson's, Eisenhower's agreed that U.S. interests were best served by the existence of other stable democratic and capitalist nations and spoke publicly about promoting democracy and freedom abroad. The problem, as Eisenhower and Dulles understood it, was in areas lacking a history of free government. New democratic governments tended to be weak and faced a myriad of challenges in their efforts to establish order and create prosperity. It was, therefore, considered a gamble to support such governments when the Soviet Union appeared to be active in all areas and communists were apparently poised to take advantage of instability or nationalist reform movements. Dictators who protected Western interests, provided stability, and

*From David F. Schmitz, *Thank God They're on Our Side: The United States and Right-Wing Dictatorships, 1921–1965* (Chapel Hill: University of North Carolina Press, 1999), 181–87. © 1999 by the University of North Carolina Press. Used by permission of the publisher.

suppressed communism were a much better bet in such a context and had to be supported until their nations matured politically or, given the logic of the domino theory, whole areas would fall to communist forces. With their Manichean view of the Cold War, neither Eisenhower nor Dulles could tolerate revolutionary nationalism and other challenges to the status quo in the Third World.

The fundamental premise for this policy remained the idea that too many of the world's people were not yet trained or were unable to govern themselves democratically. With enough time and tutelage they could possibly develop democratic systems, but communist forces were waiting to take advantage of any signs of instability and the weaknesses of new democratic governments. The time necessary for the transition from colonial status or authoritarian government to democracy was a luxury the United States did not appear to have. In addition, an agent theory of communist activity and revolution saw all disturbances and radical movements as emanating from the Kremlin. Communist forces were seen as having a discipline and zealousness that democratic groups had difficulty matching.

The president mused in June 1953 that the "tricky problem that is posed these days is this: if firm opposition to the spread of Communism requires fighting, as in Korea and Indo-China [now Vietnam], how can the free world turn its attention to the solution of these great humanitarian problems which must be tackled in order to eliminate the conditions that promote Communism?" As Eisenhower's comments indicate, the administration understood the need for social change in the world and recognized that the United States had to adjust its approach to relations within the hemisphere and elsewhere in the Third World. Dulles told the Senate Foreign Relations Committee in April 1953 that he realized social problems and instability would be present in the world without the Soviet Union, "but what makes it a very dangerous problem for us is the fact that wherever those things exist, whether it is in Indo-China or Siam or Morocco or Egypt or Arabia or Iran . . . even in South America, the forces of unrest are captured by the Soviet Communists." In a peaceful world without the threat of the Soviet Union, the United States "could do very much more in the way of promoting . . . reforms and advancing self-government than we can do under present conditions." The secretary of state believed that it was necessary "to take a realistic view of the situation and recognize that at this time, to support a somewhat backward situation, it is the lesser of two evils, because the possibility of a peaceful change is very much diminished by the fact that you have constantly with you, for instance, the tactics of the Soviet Communist forces which take advantage of every opportunity to capture and lead the so-called reform and revolutionary movement." The United States was forced to back dictators. "Syngman Rhee [of South Korea], Chiang Kai-shek [of Nationalist China], and so forth . . . are not the people, under normal circumstances, that we would want to support." Others would be preferable, "but in times like these, in the unrest of the world today, and the divided spirit, we know we cannot make a transition without losing control of the whole situation."

The solution to the dilemma of how to bring about social change and an evolution toward democracy without setting off revolutions and aiding the spread of communism was to be found in supporting strong leaders who would heed American advice. The rule of various dictators, therefore, was viewed positively by the new administration. For example, Vice President [Richard] Nixon, discussing South Korea, exclaimed in 1953 that "they are hard to work with, but thank God they're on our side. With all the things that are wrong with Rhee, the Communists are a lot worse." Eisenhower commented in June that, given the recurring crises in Paris, "he himself was beginning to feel that only a strongman could save France." Favors and honors were extended to shore up the rule of certain dictators, such as Marcos Pérez Jiménez of Venezuela. The State Department found Venezuela to be an "outstanding example to the rest of the world of cooperation between foreign investors and the government" for the benefit of both sides. For his efforts, Jiménez was invited by Eisenhower for a state visit in Washington in 1956 where he was presented the Legion of Merit medal, the highest award the nation can bestow on a non-citizen. Advocates of greater military aid for [Anastasio] Somoza argued that Latin American military leaders, such as that Nicaraguan dictator, worked more closely with the United States than any other groups, and those who "come to this country and see what we have and what we can do are frequently our most useful friends in those countries."

To enhance this relationship, National Security Council (NSC) resolution 5432/1, adopted in September 1954, called for closer relations with military officers, recognizing that they "play an influential role in government." A National Intelligence Estimate noted that the United States faced a dilemma in the "conflict between 'democracy' and 'dictatorship' in the Caribbean." The dictators "present themselves as guarantors of stability and order and of cooperation with the United States. The reformists, by definition, are an unsettling influence, but they contend that the United States, as a progressive democracy dominant in the area, has a moral obligation to foster social and political development." Conversely, the region's dictators "resent any indication of U.S. support for reformist regimes as a betrayal of the 'true friends' of the United States." Early the next year, Secretary of State Dulles made it clear where the administration stood on this question when he instructed State Department officials to "do nothing to offend the dictators; they are the only people we can depend on."

In a February 1955 discussion on the progress of the implementation of NSC 5432/1, the National Security Council considered the question of communism and dictatorships in Latin America. Secretary of the Treasury George Humphrey told the council that it must realize "that a strong base for Communism exists in Latin America." Moreover, "wherever a dictator was replaced, Communists gained." The United States had to "back strong men in Latin American governments." Nelson Rockefeller responded that the "dictators in these countries are a mixed blessing. It is true, in the short run, that dictators handle Communists effectively. But in the long run, the U.S. must encourage the growth of democracy in Latin America" if it wished to defeat communism in the region. The discussion of relations with dictators reminded the president of a comment made by Portugal's Antonio Salazar, which he did not dispute: "Free government cannot work among Latins." Eisenhower noted his general agreement with Rockefeller "that in the long run the United States must back democracies" without providing any indication of when and how that would come about. It was, however, the short-run challenge of communism that had to be attended to.

In both the crises in Iran and Guatemala, Eisenhower and Dulles believed that the situation had moved from a theoretical problem to an actual danger of communist rule. Both governments exhibited all of the problems policymakers associated with weak and ineffective democratic governments. They were creating a climate of confusion that would either pave the way for a communist takeover or had already permitted communists to penetrate their governments. The evidence for this view was found in Iran's efforts to nationalize the oil industry and Guatemala's pursuit of land reform. These policies, the administration noted, were exactly the same ones that communist nations adopted. Even if the people in power were not communists, they were doing the work of the Kremlin. In these cases, the administration found it necessary to help remove the dangerous government and support leaders who would maintain order, suppress communism, and align the countries with American foreign policy. The Truman administration had allowed the situation in these nations to reach the crisis stage. Establishing and supporting right-wing dictators, covertly and through announced policy, appeared to be the only option outside of direct military intervention to prevent the creation of full-blown communist states.

The administration formally set out its policy on covert action in March 1954 when it adopted NSC 5412. Greater suspicion of nationalist movements required new measures to combat these forces and shore up traditional forms of authority. Based clearly on the bipolar worldview and concern that the Soviet Union had redirected its efforts from Europe to the Third World, the National Security Council believed that "in the interest of world peace and U.S. national security, the overt foreign activities of the U.S. Government should be supplemented by covert operations." The CIA's activities could expand beyond espionage and counterespionage actions to include discrediting and reducing the strength of international communism and its parties; countering "any threat of a party or individuals directly or indirectly responsive to Communist control to achieve dominant power in a free world country"; orienting peoples and nations toward the free world and the United States by increasing the "capacity and will of such peoples and nations to resist International Communism"; and developing resistance movements and covert operations in areas "dominated or threatened by International Communism." These actions were to be coordinated with the State and Defense Departments to ensure that "covert operations are planned and conducted in a manner consistent with United States foreign and military policies" and carried out in such a manner that "any U.S. Government responsibility for them is not evident . . . and that if uncovered the U.S. Government can plausibly disclaim any responsibility for them." The operations would include "propaganda; political action; economic warfare; preventive direct action, including sabotage, anti-sabotage, demolition; . . . subversion against hostile states or groups including assistance to underground resistance groups, guerrillas and refugee liberation groups; [and] support of indigenous and anti-communist elements in threatened countries of the free world."

At the same time, Eisenhower appointed a committee headed by General James Doolittle to conduct a study of the CIA [Central Intelligence Agency] and the need for covert activity. The committee's conclusion, which Eisenhower received in October 1954, set the issues out in stark and dangerous terms:

> It is now clear that we are facing an implacable enemy whose avowed objective is world domination by whatever means and at whatever cost. There are no rules in such a game. Hitherto acceptable norms do not apply. If the United States is to survive, long-standing American concepts of "fair play" must be reconsidered. We must develop effective espionage and counterespionage services and must learn to subvert, sabotage, and destroy our enemies by more clever, more sophisticated, and more effective methods than those used against us. It may become necessary that the American people be made acquainted with, understand, and support this fundamentally repugnant philosophy.

Covert activities were to fill the gap between the need to maintain order and prevent the spread of communism and the desire to avoid direct intervention. The United States was entering a new phase of the Cold War and relations with right-wing dictators.

In a 1956 interview, Secretary of State Dulles captured the intentions and problems confronting the administration. The secretary explained that American policy was designed to ensure freedom from communism for all the nations of the world. What nations did "with their freedom after they get it is a second problem. We naturally would like them to have the same kind of freedom and exercise it the way we do, with our same democratic processes." This was not, he realized, the case. Nor was it a major concern of the United States. Democracy was the best system, but it "is a system which can only be spread throughout the world gradually, and as I say, today there are not many parts of the world where that particular system prevails." To insist on it, then, would damage American interests and create openings for the Soviet Union to exploit. Better to stay with loyal friends than experiment with change and new people in a dangerous world.

2. Statements of U.S. Foreign Policy Doctrine ~ Presidents James Monroe, Theodore Roosevelt, and Harry Truman*

At various critical junctures in U.S. history, American presidents have articulated fundamental statements about the goals and methods of their foreign policy. Historians often refer to such statements as doctrines (or corollaries, when addenda to doctrines are made after the fact). The earliest and most deeply rooted of these doctrines was announced before Congress in 1823 by President James Monroe at the time of the Spanish-American Wars of Independence. Monroe called for a policy of noncolonization in the Americas, aiming his message at any European power that might be eyeing the territories soon to be liberated from Spanish control. The next major statement to impact Latin America came from President Theodore Roosevelt in the early twentieth century. Known as the Roosevelt Corollary (to the Monroe Doctrine), Roosevelt's announcement made in Congress in 1904 embraced the idea that the U.S. government would act as the hemispheric "policeman" of the Americas, settling any and all disputes among parties. Four decades later, the most important statement of U.S. policy during the Cold War was announced to Congress by President Harry Truman in 1946. At the time, the U.S. ally Greece was being menaced by an internal Communist insurgency, which was seen as part of a Soviet assault on the eastern Mediterranean. The Truman Doctrine pledged U.S. support and protection to Greece and any other government facing a Communist threat. In a word, Truman's doctrine of worldwide "containment" was the foundation of U.S. policy throughout the Cold War.

Monroe Doctrine (1823)

In the wars of the European powers in matters relating to themselves we have never taken any part, nor does it comport with our policy so to do. It is only when our rights are invaded or seriously menaced that we resent injuries or make preparation for our defense. With the movements in this hemisphere we are of necessity more immediately connected, and by causes which must be obvious to all enlightened and impartial observers. The political system of the allied powers [Europe's Holy Alliance] is essentially different in this respect from that of America. This difference proceeds from that which exists in their respective Governments; and to the defense of our own, which has been achieved by the loss of so much blood and treasure, and matured by the wisdom of our most enlightened

---

*From James D. Richardson, comp., *Messages and Papers of the Presidents*, 20 vols. (New York: Bureau of National Literature, 1897–1922); and U.S. Congress, Senate Committee on Foreign Relations, *A Decade of American Foreign Policy: Basic Documents, 1941–1949* (Washington, DC: U.S. Government Printing Office, 1950), 1270–71.

citizens, and under which we have enjoyed unexampled felicity, the whole nation is devoted. We owe it, therefore, to candor and to the amicable relations existing between the United States and those powers to declare that we should consider any attempt on their part to extend their system to any portion of this hemisphere as dangerous to our peace and security. With the existing colonies or dependencies of any European power we have not interfered and shall not interfere. But with the Governments who have declared their independence and maintained it, and whose independence we have, on great consideration and on just principles, acknowledged, we could not view any interposition for the purpose of oppressing them, or controlling in any other manner their destiny, by any European power in any other light than as the manifestation of an unfriendly disposition toward the United States. In the war between those new Governments and Spain we declared our neutrality at the time of their recognition, and to this we have adhered, and shall continue to adhere, provided no change shall occur which, in the judgment of the competent authorities of this Government, shall make a corresponding change on the part of the United States indispensable to their security.

Roosevelt Corollary to the Monroe Doctrine (1904)

Chronic wrongdoing, or an impotence which results in a general loosening of the ties of civilized society, may in America, as elsewhere, ultimately require intervention by some civilized nation, and in the Western Hemisphere the adherence of the United States to the Monroe Doctrine may force the United States, however reluctantly, in flagrant cases of such wrongdoing or impotence, to the exercise of an international police power. If every country washed by the Caribbean Sea would show the progress in stable and just civilization which with the aid of the Platt amendment* Cuba has shown since our troops left the island, and which so many of the republics in both Americas are constantly and brilliantly showing, all question of interference by this Nation with their affairs would be at an end. Our interests and those of our southern neighbors are in reality identical. They have great natural riches, and if within their borders the reign of law and justice obtains, prosperity is sure to come to them. While they thus obey the primary laws of civilized society they may rest assured that they will be treated by us in a spirit of cordial and helpful sympathy. We would interfere with them only in the last resort, and then only if it became evident that their inability or unwillingness to do justice at home and abroad had violated the rights of the United States or had invited foreign aggression to the detriment of the entire body of American nations. It is a mere truism to say that every nation, whether in America or anywhere else, which desires to maintain its freedom, its independence, must

---

*An amendment to Cuba's 1901 constitution that gave the United States the right to intervene in Cuban affairs.

ultimately realize that the right of such independence cannot be separated from the responsibility of making good use of it.

Truman Doctrine (1946)

One of the primary objectives of the foreign policy of the United States is the creation of the conditions in which we and other nations will be able to work out a way of life free from coercion. This was a fundamental issue in the war with Germany and Japan. Our victory was won over countries which sought to impose their will, and their way of life, upon other nations. To ensure the peaceful development of nations, free from coercion, the United States has taken a leading part in establishing the United Nations. The United Nations is designed to make possible lasting freedom and independence for all its members. We shall not realize our objectives, however, unless we are willing to help free peoples to maintain their free institutions and their national integrity against aggressive movements that seek to impose upon them totalitarian regimes. This is no more than a frank recognition that totalitarian regimes imposed on free peoples, by direct or indirect aggression, undermine the foundations of international peace and hence the security of the United States.

The peoples of a number of countries of the world have recently had totalitarian regimes forced upon them against their will. The Government of the United States has made frequent protests against coercion and intimidation, in violation of the Yalta Agreement in Poland, Romania, and Bulgaria. I must also state that in a number of other countries there have been similar developments.

At the present moment in world history nearly every nation must choose between alternative ways of life. The choice is too often not a free one.

One way of life is based upon the will of the majority, and is distinguished by free institutions, representative government, free elections, guarantees of individual liberty, freedom of speech and religion, and freedom from political oppression.

The second way of life is based upon the will of a minority forcibly imposed upon the majority. It relies upon terror and oppression, a controlled press and radio, fixed elections, and the suppression of personal freedoms.

I believe that it must be the policy of the United States to support free peoples who are resisting attempted subjugation by armed minorities or by outside pressures.

I believe that we must assist free peoples to work out their own destinies in their own way.

I believe that our help should be primarily through economic and financial aid which is essential to economic stability and orderly political processes.

The world is not static, and the status quo is not sacred. But we cannot allow changes in the status quo in violation of the Charter of the United Nations by such methods as coercion, or by such subterfuges as political infiltration. In helping free and independent nations to maintain their freedom, the United States will be giving effect to the principles of the Charter of the United Nations.

3. Alleged Assassination Plots Involving Foreign Leaders ⁓ Church Committee*

In 1975 and 1976, Idaho senator Frank Church held a series of hearings to look into the covert activities of the U.S. government in regard to the alleged assassinations of five prominent political figures in the Third World. The assassinations (four out of five of which were successful) spanned the years from 1960 to 1970 and took place from the Caribbean to Central Africa and Southeast Asia. What Church found was a shock to some Americans: the Central Intelligence Agency (CIA), set up in the late 1940s to coordinate the large-scale intelligence-gathering and covert operations of the Cold War, was indeed implicated (see, in particular, the summaries on Cuba's President Fidel Castro and Chile's General Rene Schneider). Moreover, a footnote to the report stated that the Church Committee had also received some evidence of CIA involvement in plans to assassinate President Sukarno of Indonesia and "Papa Doc" Duvalier of Haiti. The Church Committee eventually passed legislation curtailing the activities of the "rogue elephant," the senator's term for the out-of-control, unsupervised CIA of the 1950s and 1960s. Nevertheless, the record is clear about the lengths to which the U.S. government would go to stop the spread of Communism around the world.

1. The Questions Presented

The Committee sought to answer four broad questions:

ASSASSINATION PLOTS—Did United States officials instigate, attempt, aid and abet, or acquiesce in plots to assassinate foreign leaders?

INVOLVEMENT IN OTHER KILLINGS—Did United States officials assist foreign dissidents in a way which significantly contributed to the killing of foreign leaders?

AUTHORIZATION—Where there was involvement by United States officials in assassination plots or other killings, were such activities authorized, and if so, at what levels of our Government?

COMMUNICATION AND CONTROL—Even if not authorized in fact, were the assassination activities perceived by those involved to be within the scope of their

---

*From U.S. Senate, *Alleged Assassination Plots Involving Foreign Leaders: An Interim Report of the Select Committee to Study Governmental Operations with Respect to Intelligence Activities*, with an introduction by Senator Frank Church (New York: Norton, 1975), 4–7.

lawful authority? If they were so perceived, was there inadequate control exercised by higher authorities over the agencies to prevent such misinterpretation?

2. Summary of Findings and Conclusions on the Plots

The Committee investigated alleged United States involvement in assassination plots in five foreign countries:

Country	Individual Involved
Cuba	Fidel Castro
Congo (Zaire)	Patrice Lumumba
Dominican Republic	Rafael Trujillo
Chile	General Rene Schneider
South Vietnam	Ngo Dinh Diem

The evidence concerning each alleged assassination can be summarized as follows:

PATRICE LUMUMBA (Congo/Zaire)—In the Fall of 1960, two CIA officials were asked by superiors to assassinate Lumumba. Poisons were sent to the Congo and some exploratory steps were taken toward gaining access to Lumumba. Subsequently, in early 1961, Lumumba was killed by Congolese rivals. It does not appear from the evidence that the United States was in any way involved in the killing.

FIDEL CASTRO (Cuba)—United States Government personnel plotted to kill Castro from 1960 to 1965. American underworld figures and Cubans hostile to Castro were used in these plots and were provided encouragement and material support by the United States.

RAFAEL TRUJILLO (Dominican Republic)—Trujillo was shot by Dominican dissidents on May 31, 1961. From early in 1960 and continuing to the time of the assassination, the United States Government generally supported these dissidents. Some Government personnel were aware that the dissidents intended to kill Trujillo. Three pistols and three carbines were furnished by American officials, although a request for machine guns was later refused. There is conflicting evidence concerning whether the weapons were knowingly supplied for use in the assassination and whether any of them were present at the scene.

NGO DINH DIEM (South Vietnam)—Diem and his brother, Nhu, were killed on November 2, 1963, in the course of a South Vietnamese Generals' coup. Although the United States Government supported the coup, there is no evidence that American officials favored the assassination. Indeed, it appears that the assassination of Diem was not part of the Generals' pre-coup planning but was instead a spontaneous act which occurred during the coup and was carried out without United States involvement or support.

GENERAL RENE SCHNEIDER (Chile)—On October 25, 1970, General Schneider died of gunshot wounds inflicted three days earlier while resisting a kidnap attempt. Schneider, as Commander-in-Chief of the Army and a constitutionalist opposed to military coups, was considered an obstacle in efforts to prevent Salvador Allende from assuming the office of President of Chile. The United States Government supported and sought to instigate a military coup to block Allende. U.S. officials supplied financial aid, machine guns, and other equipment to various military figures who opposed Allende. Although the CIA continued to support coup plotters up to Schneider's shooting, the record indicates that the CIA had withdrawn active support of the group which carried out the actual kidnap attempt on October 22, which resulted in Schneider's death. Further, it does not appear that any of the equipment supplied by the CIA to coup plotters in Chile was used in the kidnapping. There is no evidence of a plan to kill Schneider or that United States officials specifically anticipated that Schneider would be shot during the abduction.

Assassination Capability (Executive action)—In addition to these five cases, the Committee has received evidence that ranking Government officials discussed, and may have authorized, the establishment within the CIA of a generalized assassination capability. During these discussions, the concept of assassination was not affirmatively disavowed.

Similarities and Differences among the Plots—The assassination plots all involved Third World countries, most of which were relatively small and none of which possessed great political or military strength. Apart from that similarity, there were significant differences among the plots:

1. Whether United States officials initiated the plot, or were responding to requests of local dissidents for aid.
2. Whether the plot was specifically intended to kill a foreign leader, or whether the leader's death was a reasonably foreseeable consequence of an attempt to overthrow the government.

The Castro and Lumumba cases are examples of plots conceived by United States officials to kill foreign leaders.

In the Trujillo case, although the United States Government certainly opposed his regime, it did not initiate the plot. Rather, United States officials responded to requests for aid from local dissidents whose aim clearly was to assassinate Trujillo. By aiding them, this country was implicated in the assassination, regardless of whether the weapons actually supplied were meant to kill Trujillo or were only intended as symbols of support for the dissidents.

The Schneider case differs from the Castro and Trujillo cases. The United States Government, with full knowledge that Chilean dissidents considered General Schneider an obstacle to their plans, sought a coup and provided support to the dissidents. However, even though the support included weapons, it appears that the intention of both the dissidents and the United States officials was to abduct General Schneider, not to kill him. Similarly, in the Diem case, some United States officials wanted Diem removed and supported a coup to accomplish his removal, but there is no evidence that any of those officials sought the death of Diem himself.

3. Summary of Findings and Conclusions on the Issues of Authority and Control

To put the inquiry into assassination allegations in context, two points must be made clear. First, there is no doubt that the United States Government opposed the various leaders in question. Officials at the highest levels objected to the Castro and Trujillo regimes, believed the accession of Allende to power in Chile would be harmful to American interests, and thought of Lumumba as a dangerous force in the heart of Africa. Second, the evidence on assassinations has to be viewed in the context of other, more massive activities against the regimes in question. For example, the plots against Fidel Castro personally cannot be understood without considering the fully authorized, comprehensive assaults upon his regime, such as the Bay of Pigs invasion in 1961 and Operation MONGOOSE in 1962.

Once methods of coercion and violence are chosen, the probability of loss of life is always present. There is, however, a significant difference between a coldblooded, targeted, intentional killing of an individual foreign leader and other forms of intervening in the affairs of foreign nations. Therefore, the Committee has endeavored to explore as fully as possible the questions of how and why the plots happened, whether they were authorized, and if so, at what level.

The picture that emerges from the evidence is not a clear one. This may be due to the system of deniability and the consequent state of the evidence which, even after our long investigation, remains conflicting and inconclusive. Or it may be that there were in fact serious shortcomings in the system of authorization so that an activity such as assassination could have been undertaken by an agency of the United States Government without express authority.

The Committee finds that the system of executive command and control was so ambiguous that it is difficult to be certain at what levels assassination activity was known and authorized. This situation creates the disturbing prospect that Government officials might have undertaken the assassination plots without it having been uncontrovertibly clear that there was explicit authorization from the Presidents. It is also possible that there might have been a successful "plausible denial" in which Presidential authorization was issued but is now obscured. Whether or not the respective Presidents knew of or authorized the plots, as chief executive officer of the United States, each must bear the ultimate responsibility for the activities of his subordinates.

where the move into Texas began at the very moment of Mexican independence. The Anglos who wanted Mexico's territory took advantage of the fledgling's weakness, cloaking their acquisitive behavior in the mantle of improving upon Hispanic civilization. As Theodore Roosevelt would write years later, "it was inevitable, as well as in the highest degree desirable for the good of humanity at large, that the American people should ultimately crowd out the Mexicans from their sparsely populated Northern provinces."

So it was that the mental mold of U.S. policy toward Latin America was firmly set by the time that the United States descended into its own Civil War. Then late in the nineteenth century, when the United States had recovered and was beginning to renew its interest in Latin America, this mold was once again used to fashion policy by the Young Turks [advocates of change] of Theodore Roosevelt's generation. Identifying Latin America as a convenient site for demonstrating that their adolescent nation had matured into an international power, the United States became involved in disputes in Peru, Chile, Venezuela, Cuba, Colombia, Panama, the Dominican Republic, Haiti, and Nicaragua. In each case, U.S. policy can be explained by a mixture of security concerns, domestic politics, and economic interests, but it was the underlying belief in Latin American inferiority that guided U.S. officials to the specific policies known as the Big Stick and Dollar Diplomacy. In particular, the belief in Latin American inferiority dictated Washington's turn-of-the-century assumption of responsibility for solving Latin Americans' problems, be it their inability to end a war, draw a boundary line, achieve independence, or stabilize their economies.

The decision to help Latin Americans with their foreign debt was especially significant. Shouldering this burden was originally justified by a security argument (the need to keep European creditors out of the Caribbean), but this justification was based on the underlying belief that the region's profligate leaders were unable to manage their own money. Poised at the top of a slippery slope, U.S. officials argued that security required economic control, took one step in that direction, and immediately slid into the conclusion that economic control required political tutelage, a requirement based on the assumption that Latin America's corrupt, chaotic politics were the cause of the region's economic problems. Having learned from Europe how a powerful nation should behave, U.S. leaders seemed almost eager to accept their share of the White Man's Burden,* which in Latin America manifested itself in the appointment of proconsuls, often accompanied by detachments of Marines.

As this proconsular policy gathered momentum, it quickly became the norm. By 1913, when Woodrow Wilson entered office, the new President saw nothing unusual about assuming responsibility for teaching Mexicans not simply how to handle their economy, but how to behave democratically, a task that the preceding generations—Benjamin Harrison or a Grover Cleveland—would never have con-

---

*Rudyard Kipling's famous phrase justifying European imperialism in Africa and Asia.

sidered for a moment. Wilson instructed his new secretary of state that "we consider it our duty to insist on constitutional government there and will, if necessary . . . take charge of elections and see that a real government is erected." Secretary of State [Robert] Lansing responded by upping the ante, suggesting that the entire Caribbean region receive U.S. tutelage, again blending a security rationale with an assumption of Latin American inferiority: "Within this area lie the small republics of America which have been and to an extent still are the prey of revolutionists, of corrupt governments, and of predatory foreigners. Because of this state of affairs our national safety, in my opinion, requires that the United States should intervene and aid in the establishment and maintenance of a stable and honest government." In this way, Washington's early-twentieth-century leaders grafted a new belief in the need for hegemony onto the pre–Civil War belief in Latin American inferiority. It was no longer simply that Latin Americans were inferior, but that their inferiority threatened U.S. security—everything from a cutoff of vital supplies and transit routes to the establishment of military bases by powerful European rivals.

After that, the decades passed quickly—the Roaring '20s, the Great Depression, another World War, and then the Cold War, while one significant corner of the minds of U.S. officials remained frozen in time. In 1832 a U.S. envoy had written that Argentines "have all the vices of men and all the follies of children, without the virtues or the sense of either," and so he closed the U.S. legation in Buenos Aires and went home. More than a century later, as the Eisenhower administration was coming to a close, the minutes of a meeting of the National Security Council indicate that "Mr. Allen Dulles pointed out that the new Cuban officials had to be treated more or less like children. They had to be led rather than rebuffed. If they were rebuffed, like children, they were capable of doing almost anything." Soon the U.S. embassy in Havana was also closed.

The generation of officials who padlocked the embassy in Argentina did not share the hegemonic vision of the generation that severed relations with Cuba, and so subsequent policies toward these two governments were quite different. But both generations compared Latin Americans to unruly children—immature, emotional, and needing supervision. To our generation this comparison seems hopelessly quaint, so politically incorrect that readers will not be surprised to discover that in 1832 Minister Francis Baylies knew next to nothing about Argentines, and that in 1959 CIA Director Allen Dulles was uninformed about Cubans. What we have here, we tell ourselves, are two more examples of John Quincy Adams's uninformed prejudice.

But however much we might wish it were otherwise, this prejudice remains today at the core of any explanation of United States policy toward Latin America. It was especially evident during the spasm of U.S. attention to Central America in the 1980s, and can be seen most clearly in the writings of Jeane Kirkpatrick, whose articles in *Commentary* magazine served as the intellectual foundation for the Reagan administration's policy. The first of Ambassador [to the United Nations] Kirkpatrick's two articles developed the distinction between totalitarian and authoritarian regimes, and provided the rationale for continuing U.S. support of Latin America's anticommunist authoritarian governments; the second explained the region's importance to U.S. security, emphasizing the global balance of power. Laced into both articles is the assertion that Latin Americans are pathologically violent. "Violence or the threat of violence is an integral part of these political systems—a fact which is obscured by our way of describing military 'interventions' in Latin political systems as if the system were normally peaceable. Coups, demonstrations, political strikes, plots, and counterplots are, in fact, the norm." To Kirkpatrick, the particularly vicious Salvadoran civil war reflected the fact that "El Salvador's political culture . . . emphasizes strength and machismo and all that implies about the nature of the world and the human traits necessary for survival and success. Competition, courage, honor, shrewdness, assertiveness, a capacity for risk and recklessness, and a certain 'manly' disregard for safety are valued."

Since Ambassador Kirkpatrick never visited El Salvador before writing about its political culture, her views had to come from some source other than direct observation. Their precise origin is unknown, for she mentioned no sources and provided no citations, but since her ideas obviously flowed from the 1940s tradition of national character analysis, she probably relied heavily upon the work of the leading contemporary exponent of that tradition, Howard Wiarda, who at the time was her colleague at the American Enterprise Institute in Washington. Wiarda's writings contained precisely Kirkpatrick's argument, cloaked in academic regalia, and, like Kirkpatrick, Wiarda used his view of Latin American culture as the foundation for policy advice. "El Salvador has had a long tradition of political violence," he wrote; indeed, "*machetismo*, or the butchering of one's personal and political foes, is a way of life. Such endemic, persistent violence is very difficult for Americans to understand or come to grips with. The entire political culture—governance, challenges to it, the circulation of new and old groups in and out of power—is based on the display and use of violence."

Like Kirkpatrick, Wiarda never conducted research in El Salvador. His ideas are also of second-hand provenance and, although their exact pedigree is uncertain, they are remarkably similar to those of the preceding generation of scholars who pursued Ruth Benedict's national character approach to cultural analysis. They especially resemble the ideas of historian Richard Morse, who contended that "Latin America is subject to special imperatives as an offshoot of postmedieval, Catholic, Iberian Europe which never underwent the Protestant Reformation." Like Kirkpatrick and Wiarda, Morse then jumps ahead several centuries to identify the contemporary product of this background: "human laws are frequently seen as too harsh or impracticable or inequitable or simply as inapplicable to the specific case. Hence the difficulty of collecting income taxes; the prevalent obligation to pay fees or bribes to officials for special or even routine services; the apathy of metropolitan police toward theft and delinquency; the thriving contraband trade at border towns; the leniency toward those who commit crimes of passion—all the way down to the nonobservance of 'no smoking' signs on buses and in theaters."

Morse never tells his readers the origin of these ideas, but every word he wrote could have been written by John Quincy Adams. Viewed in historical perspective, it seems clear that contemporary national character analysts borrow their ideas about Latin America from the early-nineteenth-century Anglo view of Hispanic culture, then adapt that view to the special circumstances of their day. Kirkpatrick's special contribution was to simplify—to discard the academic mumbo jumbo that only confuses fast-reading Washingtonians—and to highlight the cultural commitment to "*machismo* and all that implies." Then, knowing where Washington focuses its attention, she drew out the implications for U.S. policy: we may respect human rights here in the United States, she wrote, but the Carter administration should never have expected Latin Americans, heir to a violent culture, to share the same values: "Hurried efforts to force complex and unfamiliar political practices on societies lacking the requisite political culture, tradition, and social structures not only fail to produce desired outcomes; if they are undertaken at a time when the traditional regime is under attack, they actually facilitate the job of the insurgents."

The history of U.S.–Latin American relations is overflowing with this type of thinking. Perhaps the best example is that of George Kennan, the intellectual father of containment, whose only exposure to Latin America was a hopscotch tour of the region's capitals in 1950. His trip report focused on Latin Americans' "exaggerated self centeredness and egotism" and their "pathetic urge to create the illusion of desperate courage." Written by a lame duck in the Truman-Acheson State Department, Kennan's report received little attention, but one cannot help but wonder how much of early Cold War policy toward Latin America was influenced by these ideas while Kennan was serving as director of State's Policy Planning Staff (1947 to 1949) and as Counselor (1949 to 1950). What we need not wonder is the origin of his beliefs about Latin Americans: just as Kirkpatrick could not possibly have uncovered the secrets of Salvadoran political culture without stepping foot in the country, Kennan could not have learned enough in his whirlwind visit to justify his analysis of Latin American personality. Instead, he modernized the thinking of John Quincy Adams, adding the Freudian argot popular at the time.

The Kennans and the Kirkpatricks are crucial to an understanding of United States policy toward Latin America, simply because every administration seems to have a quota for this type of person—like JFK's Richard Goodwin, who revealed that prior to helping formulate the Alliance for Progress, "I had never set foot south of the border (aside from one orgiastic night just beyond the Texas border during the campaign which had little to do with high policy, but which an exceptionally imaginative psychiatrist might conclude had planted the seed of my love affair with Latin America)." However shallow they and their knowledge of Latin America may be, it is important to know what this type of official believes, because their beliefs often determine policy.

XI

The Global Economy

Over the last two centuries, Latin America's relationship with the global economy has been manic, full of exhilarating upswings and, more often, devastating downturns. Latin America's integration into the global networks of investment, production, and trade—in a word, the *capitalist* network—took several centuries to be achieved. Some might say it is an ongoing process even today. This chapter takes a look at some of the defining moments in the development of Latin America's relationship with the global economy, focusing especially on the problem of the region's persistent dependency on the exportation of raw materials to more advanced economies.

The pattern of dependency was established long ago under colonial rule. After all, the Spanish and Portuguese colonies in the Americas had but one main purpose: to enrich the mother countries. After independence the new governments of the region found it difficult to break with the traditional export model of development that had been established under colonialism. During the heyday of classical liberalism from the 1870s to the 1920s, the export model dominated completely. Liberals from Domingo Sarmiento to Justo Sierra believed deeply in modernizing their countries' infrastructures (things like railroads, deep-water ports, and the latest mining equipment) so that more raw materials could be produced, transported to the coast, and then shipped to the industrializing core of the global capitalist economy. The famous export boom of the late 1800s and early 1900s, which included a wide range of agricultural and mineral products from every corner of the region, was the engine that drove Latin America's first great experiment with liberalism. This massive flow of primary products built some vast fortunes among those lucky enough to be its beneficiaries but also unleashed a terribly disruptive set of forces on Latin American workers.

The export engine came to a screeching halt when the Depression hit in 1929. As we saw in previous chapters, the global economic devastation of the 1930s opened the door to new experiments in nationalism and populism—not just in Latin America but in Europe and North America as well—because the legitimacy of the old way of doing things had been shattered. During the years of depression and world war, the Latin American populists embraced a different model of economic development no longer based solely on exports. In some cases, they embarked on the *nationalization* of industries, which meant the takeover of strategic, foreign-owned businesses by Latin American governments. Nationalization, based on the concept of economic nationalism, resulted in the formation of many new state-owned industries like Mexican Petroleum (or PEMEX), which was created by President Lázaro Cárdenas in 1938. In other cases, the populists pursued a policy of economic development known as import substitution industrialization (ISI), which attempted to stimulate the growth of industrial manufacturing enterprises in Latin America. While ISI was not very successful in the long run, it did represent a significant departure from the traditional liberal model of development.

During the Cold War, social revolutionaries like Che Guevara and Salvador Allende took the economic development policies of the populists a step further. The social revolutionary states and movements of the 1960s and 1970s advanced a fundamentally different vision of economic development in Latin America than any that had come before, one that, at the very least, restricted the rights of private property owners to operate their businesses in the global free market. At the most extreme, Cuba's revolutionary government "socialized" the means of production and eliminated private property altogether. U.S. government officials and business leaders, ardent defenders of the private enterprise system, combated such ideas ferociously. What they wanted was for Latin America to return to its traditional liberal model of raw materials. When push came to shove, it was clear the U.S. government would work to overthrow Latin American governments that did not follow its lead.

As we will see below, a combination of U.S. pressure and internal Latin American developments resulted in the emergence of *neoliberalism* (a newly revitalized classical liberalism), which was implemented in many countries beginning in the 1980s, often under military rule. Then when the Cold War ended, many of the civilian governments that took over in the 1990s were even more fervent neoliberals than their military predecessors. They pressed hard for reforms in fulfillment of the International Monetary Fund's prescriptions for "structural adjustment" and the demands of the so-called Washington Consensus, which usually included selling state-owned enterprises (called *privatization*, undoing the earlier process of nationalization), reducing state spending in the public sector, actively courting foreign investment, and aggressively exploiting untapped primary resources.

But then something unexpected happened. At the end of the last century, Latin American politics took a drastic turn to the Left, away from neoliberalism and back toward the economic nationalist and revolutionary socialist experiments of the previous era. The new Left turn was brought about in no small part by changes in the region's relationship with the global economy. Latin America thus currently finds itself in a new period of experimentation with alternative models of economic development, including many new forms of regional economic integration such as the Union of South American Nations (UNASUR/UNASUL), which is modeled on the European Union. But has this current wave of leftist activism really changed Latin America's traditional dependency on exports? By the end of this chapter, students will be able to provide a nuanced answer to that question.

QUESTIONS FOR ANALYSIS

1. Why has the exportation of raw materials played such a leading role in Latin America's economic development?
2. Is the Chinese demand for Latin American raw materials sustainable? What might cause China's demand to decline?
3. What impact is regional economic integration having on Latin America's relationship with the global economy?

1. Neocolonial Economics ~ Celso Furtado*

In the closing decades of the nineteenth century, the volume and variety of goods flowing from Latin American countries to the more advanced economies of Europe and North America was staggering. This great export boom generated tremendous wealth for some, but it was not shared by all. It also deepened the region's dependent position with regard to the industrializing core of the global economy, which contributed greatly to the rise of neocolonialism. That, at least, was the argument put forward by structuralist economists like Celso Furtado in the 1960s and 1970s who were critical of the traditional liberal model of development. In the following selection, Furtado, an influential Brazilian economist, takes us inside the great export boom for a closer look. Furtado's structuralist analysis of the region's path of economic development represented the major school of thought in Latin America at that time. What do you see as the pros and cons of expanding exports?

Latin American countries began to enter the channels of expanding international trade in the 1840s. The primary product-exporting economies involved in this process can be divided into three types: (a) economies exporting temperate agricultural commodities (like those grown in Europe or the United States); (b) economies exporting tropical agricultural commodities; (c) economies exporting

*From Celso Furtado, *Economic Development of Latin America: Historical Background and Contemporary Problems*, trans. Suzette Macedo (New York: Cambridge University Press, 1976), 47–51. © 1976 Cambridge University Press. Reprinted by permission of Cambridge University Press.

mineral products. In each case, foreign trade helped to shape a distinctive economic structure whose characteristic features should be borne in mind when studying its subsequent evolution.

The first type is represented essentially by Argentina and Uruguay. In this case, exportable agricultural production was based on the extensive use of land and was destined to compete with the domestic production of countries undergoing rapid industrialization. Extensive use of good agricultural land made it possible to achieve high profitability from the start. On the other hand, the very extensiveness of the agriculture practiced and the sheer volume of freight involved necessitated the creation of a widespread transportation network which indirectly led to the rapid unification of the domestic market, focusing on the major ports of shipment. These countries display the characteristics of regions referred to earlier as constituting an expanding frontier of the industrializing European economy.

This frontier, to which European agricultural techniques were transplanted in the early stages, soon became an important center for developing new agricultural techniques of its own. Both the techniques of farming vast open spaces and of large-scale transportation, storage, and shipment of cereals originated in the United States. In sum, the countries in this group, precisely because they competed with the domestic production of countries at a more advanced stage of development and with regions of recent European settlement enjoying a high standard of living, were from the start integrated into a productive sector of the world economy characterized by continuing technological advance. Throughout the phase of expansion in their foreign trade, these countries achieved high rates of growth.

The second type, represented by countries exporting tropical agricultural products, involves more than half the Latin American population. It includes Brazil, Colombia, Ecuador, Central America, and the Caribbean, as well as large regions of Mexico and Venezuela. Countries in this group entered international trade in competition with colonial areas and the slave-holding region of the United States. Sugar and tobacco remained typically colonial products until the last years of the nineteenth century. It was the rapid expansion of world demand for coffee and cacao from the mid-nineteenth century that enabled tropical commodities to play a dynamic role in integrating the Latin American economy into world trade during the period under consideration. The direct impact of the structural changes in the British economy was much less, since the British market continued to be abundantly supplied by colonial regions where labor was plentiful and wages were low. The role of dynamic center fell to the United States and, to a lesser extent, to the European countries. On the whole, tropical commodities were of little significance as a factor in development, although they did involve the opening up of large areas for settlement. On the one hand, their prices continued to be influenced by the low wages prevailing in colonial regions, which had long been traditional tropical commodity producers. On the other, they did not usually require the creation of a complex infrastructure; in many regions traditional means of transport continued to be used. Finally, since they were produced in areas lacking the capacity to develop new techniques for themselves, tropical products tended to remain within the framework of the traditional economies. Nonetheless, in certain regions, tropical export agriculture did manage to play an important role in development. The most notable instance is probably that of the coffee region of São Paulo, in Brazil. Here the physical and chemical qualities of the soil permitted extensive coffee planting. The relatively high productivity of labor, the vast size of the area planted, and the use of European immigrants who demanded monetary wages favored the creation of a modern infrastructure and the emergence of a domestic market. The special nature of this case becomes evident when we recall that at the end of the nineteenth century the São Paulo highlands supplied two-thirds of the total world coffee output.

The third type of economy, represented by countries exporting mineral products, includes Mexico, Chile, Peru, and Bolivia. Venezuela entered this group in the 1930s as an exporter of petroleum. The lowering of freight rates for long-distance transport and the rapid expansion of the mechanical industries, by creating an international market for industrial metals, brought about a radical change in Latin American mining. In the first place, precious metals, notably silver, rapidly lost their importance. Secondly, small-scale mining operations of the artisan or quasi-artisan type were gradually replaced by large-scale production controlled by foreign capital and administered from abroad. The considerable rise in the world demand for non-ferrous metals coincided with major technical advances in production methods which permitted or required the concentration of production in large units. This process of concentration carried out initially in the major producing country—the United States—soon spread to other areas, where local producers were marginalized by American organizations with heavy financial backing and the technical "know-how" required to handle low-grade ores.

The three decades preceding the First World War were a period of rapid economic development and some social change in Latin America as a whole: in Mexico, where the Porfirio Díaz administration created the conditions for a large inflow of foreign capital directed mainly into mineral production; in Chile, whose victory in the War of the Pacific against Bolivia and Peru enabled her to monopolize the sources of nitrate; in Cuba, where, even before independence was attained in 1898, the country's increasing integration into the United States market had brought about a dramatic expansion in sugar production; in Brazil, where the spread of coffee over the São Paulo highlands and the influx of European immigrants hastened the collapse of the slave economy; finally, in Argentina, where the economy and society underwent drastic changes under the impact of the great wave of immigration and the penetration of substantial foreign capital.

A closer look at the three largest countries reveals the importance of the changes that occurred during this period. In Mexico, the population increased from 9.4 million in 1877 to 15.2 million in 1910. In the last of the nearly three decades of the Porfirio Díaz administration (1900–1910), the annual average growth rate of the real per capita product was 3.1 percent. During this decade the production of minerals and petroleum, the colony's basic export sector, grew at an annual rate of 7.2 percent, that is, twice as fast as manufacturing production and nearly three times as fast as agricultural production. In Brazil, the population increased from 10.1 million in 1872 to 17.3 million in 1900. In the last decade of the nineteenth century, the rate of population increase in São Paulo was over 5 percent a year, while for the country as a whole it was under 2 percent. Nearly all the 610,000 immigrants entering Brazil during this decade went to the state of São Paulo. Between 1880 and 1910, the total length of railways increased from 3.4 to 21.3 thousand kilometers. Coffee exports, which were around 4 million 60-kilogram bags in 1880, rose to almost 10 million in 1900 and to over 16 million on the eve of the First World War, a total seldom surpassed in later years. In the same period, exports of cacao rose from 6,000 to 40,000 tons, and rubber exports from 7,000 to 40,000 tons. However, it was in Argentina that the changes brought about in this phase were most marked. Between the periods 1890–1904 and 1910–1914, Argentina's population doubled, increasing from 3.6 to 7.2 million; the country's railway network was extended from 12.7 to 31.1 thousand kilometers; cereal exports rose from 1,038,000 to 5,294,000 tons, and exports of frozen meat rose from 27,000 to 376,000 tons.

In sum, during the neocolonial period, Latin America became an important contributor toward trade and a key source of raw materials for the industrialized countries. In 1913, the Latin American share in world commodity exports had reached the following levels:

Product	Percentage
Vegetable fibers	6.3
Livestock products	11.5
Cereals	17.9
Fruit and vegetables	14.2
Sugar	37.6
Rubber, furs, hides, and leathers	25.1
Coffee, cocoa, and tea	62.1

2. Reagan in Cancún, or the Third Conquest of Latin America ∼ Greg Grandin*

We now jump ahead to the closing decades of the twentieth century. According to historian Greg Grandin, when Latin American governments opened their doors

*From Greg Grandin, *Empire's Workshop: Latin America, the United States, and the Rise of the New Imperialism* (New York: Metropolitan Books, 2006), 185–90. © 2006 by Greg Grandin. Reprinted by permission of Henry Holt and Company, LLC.

to neoliberalism, it represented what he calls a "third conquest" of the region by outside forces, comparable to those of the sixteenth and nineteenth centuries. This new conquest was led initially on the U.S. side by President Ronald Reagan (1981–1989), whose election victory in 1980 signaled a major shift in U.S. government policy with regard to the global economy. Reagan embraced a highly conservative* economic philosophy that made him an orthodox free trader and deregulator of industries. In 1981, he took that message to an international meeting held in Cancún, México. In the selection, Grandin begins by pointing out how Reagan's economic policies went against the "developmentalist" recommendations of the UN Economic Commission on Latin America and its most prominent economists, Raúl Prebisch and Celso Furtado, whose ideas on the economics of developing nations were extremely influential in the 1960s and 1970s. President Reagan set in motion a process that would be carried forward under his successors in the 1990s and the early 2000s.

Reagan unveiled the outline of this new system at the International Meeting on Cooperation and Development, held in Cancún, Mexico, in late 1981. At the time, discussions of the international economy were still permeated with the language of developmentalism. Throughout the preceding decade, third-world leaders had expanded on ideas elaborated by the Argentine economist Raúl Prebisch, who headed the U.N. Economic Commission on Latin America, to propose a radical restructuring of the terms of global trade. Their vision of a New International Economic Order included increasing financial assistance to developing countries, negotiating the transfer of first-world technology and industry to poor nations, lowering tariff barriers to third-world manufacturing, recognizing each state's full sovereignty over its natural resources and economic activities (which would legitimate industrial expropriations and nationalizations), and setting just prices for ten core commodities—cocoa, coffee, tea, sugar, hard fibers, jute, cotton, rubber, copper, and tin. A majority of third-world countries called for the establishment of new international institutions, such as an affiliate to the World Bank that would help make energy costs more manageable for non-OPEC countries, and began to organize themselves as a single bloc to press their interests on the floor of the U.N. General Assembly.

. . . But the economic ground under such proposals had already evaporated. "Trade, not aid," is how Reagan's Treasury secretary Donald Regan said development would take place, backed up by a 15 percent cut in U.S. foreign assistance. In a run-up speech to the Cancún meeting in Philadelphia, Reagan chided those who "mistake compassion for development and claim massive transfers of wealth somehow will produce new well-being." Reagan agreed with his critics that "development is human fulfillment" but lectured that such development would be

---

*Conventional definitions of "liberal" and "conservative" in the political culture of the United States can be confusing. In terms of economic philosophy, Reagan's conservatism was really a return to classical liberal principles.

achieved not through regulation or re-distribution but by "free people" building "free trade." The *Boston Globe* urged the president to avoid repeating in Mexico such "doctrinaire one-liners and homespun homilies about the virtues of free enterprise, the necessity of self-reliance and the need of underdeveloped countries to emulate the methods of American capitalism."

But homespun became the core of America's economic policy in the third world. In Cancún, Reagan rejected outright the call to create new institutions and establish fixed commodity prices, along with other nonmarket mechanisms to promote third-world industrialization. Development, he said, would come about by "stimulating international trade, opening up markets," and rolling back regulations to "liberate individuals by creating incentives to work, save, invest, and succeed." Without a "sound understanding of our domestic freedom and responsibilities . . . no amount of international good will and action can produce prosperity."

This was a radical break with past U.S. policy, one that had been based on the strategy that the Cold War would be won by providing a more equitable and successful model of development than did the Soviet Union. In contrast, Reagan in Cancún exalted the unrestrained market as both the end and the means of reform, laying out a vision of the world not as a kind of global welfare state but as a competitive arena. Success was the responsibility not of a community of nations but of each nation alone. Rather than encouraging nations to travel together on a "path to equity," as Raúl Prebisch called on the world's leaders to do, the new system would have winners and losers. And since throughout the previous two decades a generation of Latin America's democrats and economic nationalists had been exiled, executed, or tortured into silence by U.S.-backed military regimes, there were few left to argue.

Compelled by the debt crisis, one country after another implemented a program that was the mirror opposite of what was called for in the nonaligned movement's program for a New International Economic Order. They slashed taxes, drastically devalued their currencies, lowered the minimum wage, exempted foreign companies from labor and environmental laws, cut spending on health care, education, and other social services, did away with regulations, smashed unions, passed legislation that allowed up to 100 percent repatriations of profits, cut subsidies designed to protect national manufacturing, freed interest rates, and privatized state industries and public utilities. Rather than fostering unified efforts to set commodity prices and force fairer terms on the industrialized world, as poor countries were just beginning to do, the debt crisis forced a race to the bottom to attract foreign capital. It was every nation for itself.

In Latin America, the sale of state enterprises was one of the largest transfers of wealth in world history. In the second half of the nineteenth century and early part of the twentieth, Latin America experienced what some historians have described as a "second conquest." The first was, of course, the plundering of American gold and silver by the Spanish and Portuguese. The second entailed the initial phase of U.S. corporate expansion, as extractive firms like United Fruit Company, Standard Oil, and Phelps Dodge turned to the region as a source of raw materials and agricultural products, coming to control most of the continent's railroads, electric companies, ports, mines, and oil fields. "When the trumpet blared everything on earth was prepared," wrote the Chilean poet Pablo Neruda, capturing the Job-like scope of this dispossession, "and Jehovah distributed the world to Coca-Cola Inc., Anaconda, Ford Motor and other entities."

The third conquest, beginning full scale in the early 1980s, was no less epic. Railroads, postal service, roads, factories, telephone services, schools, hospitals, prisons, garbage collection services, water, broadcast frequencies, pension systems, electric, television, and telephone companies were sold off—often not to the highest but to the best-connected bidder. In Chile, everything from "kindergartens to cemeteries and community swimming pools were put out for bid." Between 1985 and 1992, over two thousand government industries were sold off throughout Latin America. Much of this property passed into the hands of either multinational corporations or Latin America's "superbillionaires," a new class that had taken advantage of the dismantling of the state to grow spectacularly rich.

In Mexico, even as the average real minimum wage plummeted, the number of billionaires, according to *Forbes*, increased from one in 1987 to thirteen in 1994 and then nearly doubled the next year to twenty-four. Much of this wealth was concentrated during an orgy of "unprecedented corruption," as a PBS documentary described the privatization program of Carlos Salinas, the Mexican president who sold off over a thousand state industries, many of them to his political cronies. Today, the assets of Carlos Slim Helú, whose acquisition of Mexico's national telephone system catapulted him into the rank of Latin America's richest man, equal that of the seventeen million poorest Mexicans.

Free marketeers today single out state industries as hothouses of corruption and waste yet, as historian Mark Alan Healey and sociologist Ernesto Semán observe, a "vast web of bribes, subsidies, deals and swindles" accompanied the selling off of Latin American "state assets, involving many top government officials and major corporations like IBM, Citibank, and Telefónica"—all winked at by Washington and the IMF. In Argentina, the government agreed to absorb much of the debt of the privatized companies, many of which, such as Aerolíneas Argentinas, were disassembled and had their profitable assets resold. Much of the money from these transactions, write Healey and Semán, "vanished into a tangle of private accounts and offshore banks"—a disappearing act, it should be added, made possible through the magic wand of the financial deregulation that went with privatization. Even Pinochet, despite his reputation for severe rectitude, used his close ties with Riggs Bank and other U.S. financial houses to squirrel away millions of illicit dollars in hundreds of accounts and offshore shelters.

In Chile, public enterprises were sold at roughly 30 percent below value on terms, according to one economist, "extremely advantageous to the buyers," many of whom had close connections with the Chicago alums and with military officers. In Bolivia, between 1995 and 1996, the government auctioned off the oil company, the telephone system, the national airline, and the electric company. Much of the national railroad was dismantled and sold for parts. The following year, the World Bank informed Bolivia that future debt relief was dependent on unloading its water company as well, which it duly did to Bechtel. Nearly overnight, families getting by on barely sixty dollars a month were told that their water bill would average fifteen dollars a month, a 200 percent hike. Bolivians were even outlawed from capturing rainwater for their personal use. The whole deal disquietingly echoed the fate of the Caribbean nation in Gabriel García Márquez's *Autumn of the Patriarch*, which suddenly found itself no longer an island, having had its surrounding sea sold off to dark-suited U.S. businessmen.

3. China's New Role ~ Adrian H. Hearn and José Luis León-Manríquez*

Beginning in the 1980s, the People's Republic of China under Deng Xiaoping embarked on a radical new path away from Maoist communism toward a form of state-run modernization that accepted the supremacy of capitalist markets. In the new China, the Communist Party maintains political power in a one-party system while the economy has gradually been opened to foreign investment and competition. China, in short, became more deeply integrated into the global economy, as both a producer of manufactured goods and a consumer of raw materials. Today it is the world's second-largest national economy. In the following selection, Australian sociologist Adrian Hearn and Mexican international affairs expert José Luis León-Manríquez focus our attention on the history of China's relations with Latin America since the Cold War. Notice their emphasis on China's insatiable desire for fossil fuels and their suggestion that the current commodities boom might be pushing Latin America into a "raw materials corner."

It is an undeniable fact that China has emerged as an essential actor in the international relations of Latin America, filling the vacuum left by the United States during the administration of George W. Bush (2000–2008) and (to a somewhat lesser extent) Barack Obama (2008–). Washington's concern with the global "war against terrorism," military actions in Afghanistan and Iraq, the nuclearization of North Korea and Iran, and the need to rebuild the strained Atlantic Alliance have together relegated Latin America to the status of low priority. While China's

*From Adrian H. Hearn and José Luis León-Manríquez, eds., *China Engages Latin America: Tracing the Trajectory* (Boulder, CO: Lynne Rienner, 2011), 1–3, 9–11. © 2011 by Lynne Rienner Publishers, Inc. Used with permission of the publisher.

growing presence in the region does not appear to follow a political strategy aimed at superseding or replacing the United States, it is clear that sooner or later Mao Zedong's footsteps in James Monroe's backyard will pose substantial challenges to US interests.

China's involvement in Latin American politics during the Cold War stemmed from its government's aspiration to transform what it viewed as an unfair international system. Beijing's foreign policy doctrine was based largely on the theory of the three worlds. This conceptualized the two superpowers, the United States and the Soviet Union, as members of the first world; the developed capitalist countries like Japan, Canada, and those in Europe as the second world; and the wide range of developing countries in Africa, Asia, and Latin America, as the third world. According to this view, China belonged to the third world, and its foreign policy should reflect sympathy toward fellow members. Notwithstanding Chinese support for Maoist movements in Latin America, none of these was able to undertake a successful revolution.

In the early 1970s, US rapprochement with China breathed new life into Beijing's regional ambitions. Although Washington did not establish relations with Beijing until 1979, the Nixon administration (1969–1974) undertook a discreet but protracted campaign of bilateral dialogue, providing Brazil, Chile, Mexico, and other Latin American countries with justification to open embassies in Beijing in the first half of the 1970s. Their initial focus was political and cultural rather than economic, and China responded by shelving its attempt to spread socialist revolution in Latin America in favor of developing new intergovernmental links. A priority for China was to build alliances for coordinated action in the United Nations on issues relevant to developing countries, which it managed to do with Chile under Salvador Allende and Mexico under Luis Echeverria. In August 1973, Beijing signed Protocol 2 of the Treaty of Tlatelolco, which bans the production, storage, and transportation of nuclear weapons in Latin America, and in the 1980s China supported Latin American attempts to achieve a negotiated settlement to the Central American conflict under the Contadora Group. In turn, Mexico and the bulk of South American countries supported Beijing's "One China" policy.*

The 1990s witnessed radical changes in the international system. The end of the Cold War in 1989–1990 and the demise of the Soviet bloc fostered more pragmatic, less ideologically conditioned approaches to international relations. From the 1970s onward, most Latin American countries embraced neoliberalism, and from 1978, China began experimenting with marketization. Accordingly, by the 1990s, the emphasis of Sino-Latin American engagement had undergone quite a remarkable shift from political to economic affairs. Adapting itself to changes in

---

*A policy of the People's Republic of China (PRC) that declares that there is only one China even though there are two Chinese governments, the PRC and the non-Communist Republic of China, which is based on the island of Taiwan.

the international system, China implemented a series of new policies of foreign trade that looked to maximize profits over the long term within the prevailing international system. On this basis, Beijing's diplomatic strategy has come to emphasize three elements: the peaceful rise of China as a regional and world power, the concept of a multipolar world, and the vision of international organizations as a primary instrument of foreign policy.

Since 1990, China has undertaken a serious effort to send its exports to markets beyond East Asia, and these exports are becoming increasingly sophisticated. Medium- and high-tech products, including electronics, automobiles, and ships, now represent 53 percent of Chinese exports to Latin America. This trend poses a formidable challenge to Latin American economies, which have experienced strong pressure to downgrade the sophistication of their exports as Chinese demand for raw materials grows. Public opinion across the region exhibits growing concern about both the wisdom of reliance on commodity exports as a basis for development and about the capacity of local businesses to compete with China.

Energy resources, raw materials, and foodstuffs have become acute bottlenecks for the continuity of China's economic growth in the twenty-first century. Owing to its huge territory, massive population, and current developmental predicament, China demands large quantities of commodities that are produced by South American countries. As León-Manríquez notes, China has become the main consumer of raw materials worldwide, buying 40 percent of cement, 31 percent of coal, 30 percent of iron, 27 percent of steel, 25 percent of aluminum, and 20 percent of copper sold on world markets. China is the second-largest consumer of fossil fuels after the United States, and as long as 97 percent of its economy remains propelled by carbon and petroleum, China's quest for oil will inevitably expand beyond the Middle East, Russia, Africa, and the Caspian Sea basin, into Latin America. The region's trans-Pacific oil exports are currently modest, but China's recent $20 billion loan to Venezuela and $7.1 billion investment in Brazil, noted above, indicate strong potential for expansion.

The worldwide "commodity boom," driven largely by Chinese demand starting in 2003, inflated the international price of oil, copper, pig iron, soy, fish flour, and many other commodities. Most South American countries were blessed by this trend: Argentina, Brazil, Uruguay, and Paraguay acquired considerable sums of hard currency by exporting soy complex (soy beans and soy oil); Chile and Peru benefited from higher copper prices; and Ecuador and Venezuela obtained fine returns from petroleum exports to China. These conditions created an atmosphere of high expectations for the future of economic relations, symbolized by China's establishment of free trade agreements with Chile (2006) and Peru (2009). The global financial crisis that gripped the world in late 2008 precipitated a significant fall in international commodity prices, but China's appetite for oil, raw materials, and food has nevertheless remained a central factor in South America's foreign trade.

During the first decade of the 2000s, bilateral trade grew so swiftly that China became either the second- or third-largest trading partner for most Latin American countries, and the region's main Asian partner. Meanwhile, Latin America has become China's fifth-largest trading partner after the European Union, the United States, Japan, and South Korea; and if current patterns persist, it will displace South Korea within two to three years. Although the value of trade has surged, six out of ten selected Latin American countries (seven including Cuba, whose recent data remain undisclosed) reported trade deficits with China in 2009. Statistics reported by China indicate that these deficits were substantially more modest than reported by Latin America, and in two cases (Argentina and Venezuela) nonexistent.

According to the Chinese government, Sino-Latin American trade sky-rocketed from US$10 billion in 2000 to a precrisis peak of over $143 billion in 2008. As noted above, the trend underlying this trade is the exchange of Latin American raw materials for Chinese consumer goods, and consequent anxiety from manufacturers about their capacity to compete with Chinese imports. While commodity exports have earned Latin America fast cash, some economists argue that the neglect of more labor-intensive and value-adding sectors is pushing the region into a "raw materials corner."

---

4. The New Left and the Global Economy ~
Steven Levitsky and Kenneth M. Roberts*

It did not take long for the promoters of neoliberalism in Latin America to run into serious obstacles in their plan to transform the region's economies. By enacting the tough, disruptive reforms described by Grandin in the previous selection, neoliberal governments hurt a lot of people in their quest to change macroeconomic conditions. As the painful reality of structural adjustment set in, new political leaders arose throughout the region to give voice to those dissatisfied with the new direction. Beginning around 1998 with the election of Hugo Chávez, the controversial (and recently deceased) leader of Venezuela's twenty-first-century socialist revolution, leftist leaders won elections in country after country, resulting in what is called Latin America's new Left turn. In the following selection, U.S. social scientists Steven Levitsky and Kenneth Roberts argue that the new Left turn was made possible by changes in Latin America's relationship with the global economy. Notice how they also credit the China-driven commodities boom for the success and high approval ratings of many leftist governments.

*From Steven Levitsky and Kenneth M. Roberts, eds., *The Resurgence of the Latin American Left* (Baltimore: Johns Hopkins University Press, 2011), 2–3, 4–5, 9–11. © 2011 The Johns Hopkins University Press. Reprinted with permission of The Johns Hopkins University Press.

The rise of the Left was a stunning turn of events in a region where political and economic liberalism—buttressed by U.S. hegemony—appeared triumphant at the end of the Cold War. With the collapse of the Soviet bloc, the demise of statist and socialist development models, and the rise of the so-called Washington Consensus around free market or "neoliberal" economic policies, U.S.-style capitalist democracy appeared to be the only game in town in the 1990s. The debt and inflationary crises of the 1980s had discredited state-led development models, while neoliberal reforms deepened Latin America's integration into global trade and financial circuits, thereby narrowing governments' policy options. The reform process was directed by technocrats who claimed a mantle of scientific expertise for free market policies that were backed by the U.S. government, the World Bank, and the International Monetary Fund (IMF). With labor movements in retreat and revolutionary alternatives seemingly foreclosed, historical rivals to liberalism from both populist and leftist traditions accepted market reforms. In the eyes of many observers, then, the Left had "all but vanished" in post–Cold War Latin America.

By the late 1990s, however, the neoliberal consensus had begun to unravel. Although the free market model succeeded in controlling inflation, in much of the region it was plagued by anemic growth, periodic financial crises, and deepening social and economic inequalities. These problems created new opportunities for the mobilization of opposition, some of it channeled into the electoral arena by parties of the Left and some stoking the mass protest movements that toppled promarket governments in Ecuador, Argentina, and Bolivia.

Latin America's left turn was far from a uniform experience, however. New left governments varied widely: in Brazil, Chile, and Uruguay, institutionalized leftist parties maintained the relatively orthodox macroeconomic policies and liberal democratic constitutions they had inherited from nonleftist predecessors; in Venezuela, however, a populist outsider used plebiscitary means to rewrite the constitutional rules of the game, and he launched a statist and redistributive project that broke sharply with the Washington Consensus. Argentina, Bolivia, Ecuador, Nicaragua, and Paraguay fell in between these two poles, combining different types of policy and regime orientations in distinct ways.

Before proceeding, it is necessary to clarify what is meant by "the Left." This is no easy task. Historically, the Latin American Left was conceived in ideological terms as movements of socialist, and particularly Marxist, inspiration. The Left was associated with a relatively well-defined alternative to capitalist models of development, one that emphasized public ownership of the means of production and central planning as opposed to market allocation of basic goods and services. Differences within the Left were largely strategic, related to the choice between revolutionary and democratic paths to socialism. By the 1980s, however, the crisis of Marxism as an ideological referent and of socialism as a development model compelled the Left to redefine itself. Many leftists began to conceive of their project as an open-ended process of social transformation—one of "deepening" democracy—rather than a predetermined endpoint. In terms of public policy, leftist platforms grew more moderate and ambiguous as historically left-of-center parties that won national power almost invariably watered down or abandoned their preexisting platforms. Many, in fact, felt obliged to adopt neoliberal stabilization and adjustment policies. Those that remained in opposition, such as the PT [Workers Party] in Brazil and FA [Broad Front] in Uruguay, often maintained a more leftist profile, although this tended to be based on little more than a rejection of neoliberalism. At the beginning of the 2000s, then, "What's Left?" remained an open question in Latin America, in terms of both programmatic content and the identity of political actors.

For the purposes of this study, the Left refers to political actors who seek, as a *central programmatic objective*, to reduce social and economic inequalities. Left parties seek to use public authority to redistribute wealth and/or income to lower-income groups, erode social hierarchies, and strengthen the voice of disadvantaged groups in the political process. In the socioeconomic arena, left policies aim to combat inequalities rooted in market competition and concentrated property ownership, enhance opportunities for the poor, and provide social protection against market insecurities. Although the contemporary Left does not necessarily oppose private property or market competition, it rejects the idea that unregulated market forces can be relied on to meet social needs. In the political realm, the Left seeks to enhance the participation of underprivileged groups and erode hierarchical forms of domination that marginalize popular sectors. Historically, the Left has focused on class differences, but many contemporary Left parties have broadened this focus to include inequalities rooted in gender, race, or ethnicity—although, as Deborah Yashar notes, the Latin American Left has been slow to address these non-class-based inequalities.

The initial wave of leftist victories at the turn of the century was rooted in two key economic developments: the market-oriented reforms of the 1980s and 1990s and the 1998–2002 economic crisis. The left turn is commonly viewed as a backlash against neoliberal reforms, as the unleashing of market forces exacerbated economic hardship and insecurity for many Latin Americans and the withdrawal of states from key areas of social protection eroded their ability to meet social demands. Indeed, levels of social inequality increased throughout much of Latin America during the 1990s.

Yet it was not necessarily neoliberalism per se that drove voters to the Left. There is little evidence of widespread public opposition to market-oriented policies during the 1990s; although privatization policies faced significant opposition, other elements of the Washington Consensus, such as free trade and foreign investment, enjoyed broad public support. Moreover, where neoliberal reformers were deemed to perform well—in particular, where they stabilized hyperinflationary economies—they were often reelected.

The 1998–2002 economic downturn is thus critical to explaining the initial wave of left victories in Latin America. After experiencing modest growth between 1990 and 1997, most Latin American economies stagnated or sank into recession in the late 1990s. As a whole, Latin America experienced negative per capita growth between 1998 and 2002, and poverty and unemployment rates increased throughout the region. By 2002, 60% of families in the region reported that an adult member of their household had been unemployed in the previous year.

The economic crisis benefited the Left in two ways. First, as is often the case in democracies, it hurt incumbents across the region. Incumbent parties lost the presidency in 14 of 18 Latin American countries between 1998 and 2004. Since many of these parties were right of center, rotation in power could be expected to benefit the Left. Second, the downturn eroded public support for the economic status quo embodied in the Washington Consensus. Support for neoliberal policies like privatizations started to wane in the late 1990s; by 2004, more than 70% of survey respondents across the region expressed dissatisfaction with the performance of the market economy.

The 1998–2002 crisis thus benefited the Left by both weakening incumbents and eroding public support for the promarket policies they pursued. After 1998, voters in much of Latin America were inclined not only to support opposition parties but also to vote for candidates who promised an alternative—however vaguely defined—to neoliberalism. This dynamic was clearly at work in Venezuela in 1998, Brazil and Ecuador in 2002, Argentina in 2003, Uruguay in 2004, and Bolivia in 2005. Although there is little evidence of a broader shift to the left in terms of political identities or ideological self-placement, the 1998–2002 downturn clearly created an opening for left-of-center alternatives.

If the 1998–2002 economic crisis helped trigger the wave of left-wing victories, two changes in the external environment helped extend it over the course of the decade. The first was the post-2002 global commodities boom. As a result of soaring commodity export prices, economic growth rates in Latin America averaged 5.5% a year between 2004 and 2007, the highest in decades. The export boom contributed to the left turn in two ways. First, just as economic recession hurt right-of-center incumbents in the early 2000s, high growth benefited left-of-center incumbents in the mid and late 2000s. Left incumbents were reelected in Brazil (2006, 2010), Chile (2006), Venezuela (2006), Argentina (2007), Bolivia (2009), Ecuador (2009), and Uruguay (2009), thereby extending the left turn.

Second, the export boom allowed left parties to actually govern on the left. Whereas balance-of-payments and fiscal constraints induced even left-of-center Latin American governments to adopt conservative policies during the 1990s, improved fiscal and trade balances after 2002 provided left governments with new resources and policy latitude. Current-account surpluses and increased revenue flows reduced governments' dependence on the United States and international financial institutions, allowed them to avoid the kinds of fiscal and foreign exchange crises that had plagued populist and leftist governments in the past, and provided resources to invest in the types of social welfare policies traditionally associated with the Left. For the first time in decades, left-of-center governments were able to offer material benefits to popular constituencies—and to do so, moreover, without challenging property rights or adopting highly polarizing redistributive measures. The commodities boom thus permitted the adoption of statist policies and new social programs by governments that, under different circumstances, might have opted for orthodoxy.

Finally, it is likely that regional diffusion or demonstration effects contributed to the left turn in the latter part of the decade. The political success of Chávez, [Ricardo] Lagos [of Chile], Lula [da Silva of Brazil], and [Néstor] Kirchner [of Argentina] in the early years of the wave helped break down the 1990s-era belief that left government was not viable. By the second half of the decade—when it became clear that left governments could maintain economic stability, avoid regime breakdowns, and even gain reelection—the perception of increased viability may have encouraged other leftists (such as [Rafael] Correa [of Ecuador] and [Fernando] Lugo [of Paraguay]) to pursue the presidency and induced voters to take a chance on the Left in countries like El Salvador and Paraguay where conservative parties had traditionally governed.

The resurgence of the Left in the 1998–2010 period may thus be attributed to a variety of factors. Inequality and democracy generated favorable conditions for the growth of leftist parties, but the 1998–2002 economic crisis, which eroded public support for conservative incumbents and the neoliberal policies they had implemented, played a major role in the initial wave of left victories, and the post-2002 commodity boom provided left parties with the resources and the policy space needed to govern on the left.

5. New Organizations of the Global Economy ⁓ BRIC Summit*

Brazil has become the dominant economic power in Latin America today. Its growth is indicative of dynamics experienced more broadly in the region. This chapter's final selection comes from an April 2010 meeting in Brazil of one of the many new organizations of the global economy, the Brazil-Russia-India-China or BRIC organization (now called BRICS since South Africa joined). This was the second BRIC summit of the heads of state of the four major "emerging market economies," as they are called in the selection. The communiqué that was issued at the end of the meeting, which is excerpted below, outlines a long list of specific demands for reform that these countries want to see in the UN, the IMF, and

---

*From "2nd BRIC Summit of Heads of State and Government: Joint Statement," BRICS Information Centre, University of Toronto, April 15, 2010, www.brics.utoronto.ca/docs/100415-leaders.html.

many other areas related to economic and social development. As you read it, remember that it is more of a vision statement than a description of existing reality. How serious these countries are about reducing poverty and controlling climate change is still an open question. Nevertheless, the statement does provide some insights into the changing state of the global economy in the twenty-first century. Notice the statement's commentary on the 2008–2009 global economic crisis. In what ways did that crisis undermine the ability of the advanced economies to dictate to emerging ones?

We, the leaders of the Federative Republic of Brazil, the Russian Federation, the Republic of India and the People's Republic of China, met in Brasília on 15 April 2010 to discuss major issues of the international agenda as well as concrete steps to move forward the cooperation and coordination within BRIC.

We have agreed on the following:

Common Vision and Global Governance

1. We share the perception that the world is undergoing major and swift changes that highlight the need for corresponding transformations in global governance in all relevant areas.

2. We underline our support for a multipolar, equitable and democratic world order, based on international law, equality, mutual respect, cooperation, coordinated action and collective decision-making of all States.

3. We stress the central role played by the G-20* in combating the crisis through unprecedented levels of coordinated action. We welcome the fact that the G-20 was confirmed as the premier forum for international economic coordination and cooperation of all its member states. Compared to previous arrangements, the G-20 is broader, more inclusive, diverse, representative and effective. We call upon all its member states to undertake further efforts to implement jointly the decisions adopted at the three G-20 Summits.

4. We express our strong commitment to multilateral diplomacy with the United Nations playing the central role in dealing with global challenges and threats. In this respect, we reaffirm the need for a comprehensive reform of the UN, with a view to making it more effective, efficient and representative, so that it can deal with today's global challenges more effectively. We reiterate the importance we attach to the status of India and Brazil in international affairs, and understand and support their aspirations to play a greater role in the United Nations.

5. We believe the deepened and broadened dialogue and cooperation of the BRIC countries is conducive not only to serving common interests of emerging market economies and developing countries, but also to building a harmonious world of lasting peace and common prosperity. We have agreed upon steps to

---

*The Group of Twenty, an organization that brings together the finance ministers and central bank directors of the world's largest economies to coordinate policies.

promote dialogue and cooperation among our countries in an incremental, proactive, pragmatic, open and transparent way.

International Economic and Financial Issues

6. The world economic situation has improved since our first meeting in June 2009, in Ekaterinburg [Russia]. We welcome the resumption of economic growth, in which emerging market economies are playing a very important role. However, we recognize that the foundation of world economic recovery is not yet solid, with uncertainties remaining. We call upon all states to strengthen macroeconomic cooperation, jointly secure world economic recovery and achieve a strong, sustainable and balanced growth. We reiterate our determination to make positive efforts in maintaining domestic economic recovery and promoting development in our own countries and worldwide.

8. We are convinced that emerging market economies and developing countries have the potential to play an even larger and active role as engines of economic growth and prosperity, while at the same time commit to work together with other countries towards reducing imbalances in global economic development and fostering social inclusion.

10. Despite promising positive signs, much remains to be done. We believe that the world needs today a reformed and more stable financial architecture that will make the global economy less prone and more resilient to future crises, and that there is a greater need for a more stable, predictable and diversified international monetary system.

11. We will strive to achieve an ambitious conclusion to the ongoing and long overdue reforms of the Bretton Woods institutions. The IMF and the World Bank urgently need to address their legitimacy deficits. Reforming these institutions' governance structures requires first and foremost a substantial shift in voting power in favor of emerging market economies and developing countries to bring their participation in decision making in line with their relative weight in the world economy.

13. Recent events have shattered the belief about the self-regulating nature of financial markets. Therefore, there is a pressing need to foster and strengthen cooperation regarding the regulation and supervision of all segments, institutions and instruments of financial markets. We remain committed to improve our own national regulations, to push for the reform of the international financial regulatory system and to work closely with international standard setting bodies, including the Financial Stability Board.

International Trade

14. We stress the importance of the multilateral trading system, embodied in the World Trade Organization, for providing an open, stable, equitable and non

discriminatory environment for international trade. In this connection, we commit ourselves and urge all states to resist all forms of trade protectionism and fight disguised restrictions on trade.

Development

15. We reiterate the importance of the UN Millennium Declaration and the need to achieve the Millennium Development Goals (MDGs). We underscore the importance of preventing a potential setback to the efforts of poor countries aimed at achieving MDGs due to the effects of the economic and financial crisis. We should also make sustained efforts to achieve the MDGs by 2015, including through technical cooperation and financial support to poor countries in implementation of development policies and social protection for their populations.

16. The poorest countries have been the hardest hit by the economic and financial crisis. The commitments regarding the aid to the developing states, especially those related to the MDGs, should be fulfilled, and there should be no reduction in development assistance. An inclusive process of growth for the world economy is not only a matter of solidarity but also an issue of strategic importance for global political and economic stability.

Agriculture

17. We express our satisfaction with the Meeting of Ministers of Agriculture and Agrarian Development in Moscow, where they discussed ways of promoting quadripartite cooperation, with particular attention to family farming. We are convinced that this will contribute towards global food production and food security. We welcome their decision to create an agricultural information base system of the BRIC countries, to develop a strategy for ensuring access to food for vulnerable populations, to reduce the negative impact of climate change on food security, and to enhance agriculture technology cooperation and innovation.

Fight against Poverty

18. We call upon the international community to make all the necessary efforts to fight poverty, social exclusion and inequality bearing in mind the special needs of developing countries, especially LDCs, small islands and African Countries. We support technical and financial cooperation as means to contribute to the achievement of sustainable social development, with social protection, full employment, and decent work policies and programmes, giving special attention to the most vulnerable groups, such as the poor, women, youth, migrants and persons with disabilities.

Energy

19. We recognize that energy is an essential resource for improving the standard of living of our peoples and that access to energy is of paramount importance to economic growth with equity and social inclusion. We will aim to develop cleaner, more affordable and sustainable energy systems, to promote access to energy and energy efficient technologies and practices in all sectors. We will aim to diversify our energy mix by increasing, where appropriate, the contribution of renewable energy sources, and will encourage the cleaner, more efficient use of fossil fuels and other fuels. In this regard, we reiterate our support to the international cooperation in the field of energy efficiency.

20. We recognize the potential of new, emerging, and environmentally friendly technologies for diversifying energy mix and the creation of jobs. In this regard we will encourage, as appropriate, the sustainable development, production and use of biofuels. In accordance with national priorities, we will work together to facilitate the use of renewable energy, through international cooperation and the sharing of experiences on renewable energy, including biofuels technologies and policies.

Climate Change

22. We acknowledge that climate change is a serious threat which requires strengthened global action. We commit ourselves to [achieving] a comprehensive, balanced and binding result to strengthen the implementation of the United Nation Convention on Climate Change and the Kyoto Protocol.

Terrorism

23. We condemn terrorist acts in all forms and manifestations. We note that the fight against international terrorism must be undertaken with due respect to the UN Charter, existing international conventions and protocols, the UN General Assembly and Security Council resolutions relating to international terrorism, and that the prevention of terrorist acts is as important as the repression of terrorism and its financing.

Alliance of Civilizations

25. We affirm the importance of encouraging the dialogue among civilizations, cultures, religions and peoples. In this respect, we support the "Alliance of Civilizations," a United Nations' initiative aimed at building bridges, mutual knowledge and understanding around the world. We praise the Brazilian decision to host, in Rio de Janeiro, in May 2010, the 3rd Global Forum and confirm our intention to be present at the event, in appropriate high level.

XII

Historical Memory

As the previous chapter on the global economy showed, Latin America today is encountering a world of new opportunities and challenges. But we must also remember that it does so with the weight of many centuries of history bearing down on it, transmitting deeply engrained patterns of thought and behavior, forms of organization, and ways of doing things. As students of history, we must constantly ask ourselves how the past affects the present. This final chapter of the book looks into the relationship between Latin America's past and present by focusing on the concept of historical memory.

For more than a century, the relationship between history and memory has been studied by scholars in various disciplines: sociology, psychology, philosophy, history, and the arts. One of the things that scholars in all of these fields agree upon is the idea that history is related to *collective* rather than individual memory. While individual memories may produce unique narrations of life experiences, by themselves they lack the external validation processes that are required for history. Historical memories are instead produced by the collective memories of social groups. These groups can be entire nations (though not necessarily nation-states) or small communities, as long as they share a sense of identity and a means by which to transmit their collective memories of the group's past from one generation to the next. Not all collective memories are historical memories. The transmission of collective memories in institutional settings like schools, as well as intimate ones like family holiday observances, is a key part of the process of generating historical memories.

Historical memory has recently become its own field of study. The aftermath of the Second World War, with its incomprehensible revelations about systematic genocide, did much to promote the study of historical and collective memory in postwar Europe and the Americas. Spain's experience with the recovery of historical memories of the Civil War (1936–1939) and the dictatorship of Francisco Franco (1936–1975) also advanced the cause of memory studies. In Latin America, the historical memory approach has mostly been utilized for the purpose of reexamining the history of the Cold War, during which the region was polarized by the movement toward social revolution. As we saw in a previous chapter, the social revolutionaries were, for the most part, crushed by the national armed forces of the region that worked closely with the U.S. government to carry out their elimination. The repression of revolutionaries and those that sympathized with them by Latin American military regimes did not let up until the end of the Cold War. At that time (the early 1990s), the region underwent a transition to civilian, democratic rule that created a new state-sanctioned, public space for the discussion of the recent past. It is the historical memories of the period of military dictatorship that emerged in the Cold War's wake that commands our attention in this chapter.

The concept of historical memory has been taken up enthusiastically by Latin Americans in a number of intriguing ways. One area where this can be observed is in the cinematic arts. Chilean filmmaker Patricio Guzmán's 1997 film *Chile: Memoria Obstinada* (*Chile: Obstinate Memory*), for example, documented the awakening of a generation of young Chileans to the suppressed memories of the Pinochet dictatorship (1973–1990). U.S. filmmaker Pamela Yates's 2012 film *Granito: How to Nail a Dictator* is also constructed around the concept of historical memory, in this case the memory (as captured surreptitiously on film) of the roughly three-year period in the early 1980s in which the Guatemalan Army waged a genocidal war against the rural Mayan population in several of the country's administrative departments. *Granito* followed up on Yates's 1983 film *When the Mountains Tremble*, which featured the narration of a young Guatemalan Mayan woman named Rigoberta Menchú, who went on to win the Nobel Peace Prize in 1992 for her work on behalf of the rights of indigenous people. An excerpt from Menchú's famous testimonial is included in this chapter, as well as a critical analysis of that same testimonial.

The historical memory approach in modern Latin America has not been confined strictly to the arts, however. An even more urgent application of the approach can be observed in the legal processes that were established in Chile, Guatemala, and several other Latin American countries in the 1990s and the early 2000s to uncover the truth about the recent past and identify pathways to national reconciliation. These truth and reconciliation commissions (as they were known), working on behalf of national governments, collected testimonies from thousands of individuals who were affected in some way by the violence of the Cold War period. What they found brought them face to face with the human potential for evil. The chapter includes two examples of the work of these commissions.

In some Latin American countries, such investigations have led to the prosecution of former military commanders for crimes against humanity. In other places, amnesty laws and other forms of legal protection have been given to the persons revealed to be responsible for such crimes. The case against Chile's General Pinochet, which started in London in 1998, involved multiple levels of competing legal jurisdictions. At the present moment, a judge in Guatemala is hearing motions to decide whether the trial of General Efraín Ríos Montt will move forward on the charge of genocide.

The attempt by Latin American scholars, artists, lawyers, and jurists to recover the historical memories of an extremely painful, conflictive period of the region's history thus raises the question of whose memories constitute the historical memory of the nation. As we will see below, memory studies show that there are always multiple "memory frameworks" (to use a term coined by historian Steve Stern, whose work on historical memory in contemporary Chile is excerpted in the chapter) contending with each other in an effort to establish a position of dominance. By the end of this chapter, students will gain a deeper understanding of the way struggles over collective memories of the recent past are shaping the present moment in Latin America.

QUESTIONS FOR ANALYSIS

1. What is official history? How are official master narratives perpetuated?

2. What are the arguments for and against using *testimonios* such as Rigoberta Menchú's as sources of history?

3. What does this chapter's dark content tell us about the problem of race and nation building that we explored in a previous chapter? What about the problem of nationalism?

1. Memory, Truth, and Justice ~ Elizabeth Jelin*

In the following selection, Argentine social science researcher Elizabeth Jelin reviews the basic workings of historical memory. In so doing she reviews some key moments in the history of modern Latin America from the perspective of memory studies. In this excerpt from a chapter called "Political Struggles of Memory," her particular interest is in the way official historical narratives were created in the nineteenth century and then re-created in the dictatorships of the twentieth century. Balancing the analysis is her related discussion of the emergence of alternative historical narratives, which came about as a result of the opening of Latin American societies during the transition to democracy of the 1990s. Jelin also points out that the emergence of such historical counternarratives raises fundamental questions about the role of the state in providing justice to victims of human rights violations that were committed by agents of the state.

*From Elizabeth Jelin, *State Repression and the Labors of Memory*, trans. Judy Rein and Marcial Godoy-Anativia (Minneapolis: University of Minnesota Press, 2003), xiii–xvii, 26–30. Originally published in Spanish in *Los trabajos de la memoria*, © 2002 by Siglo XXI. English translation © 2003 by the Social Science Research Council. Reprinted by permission of the University of Minnesota Press.

The past is gone, it is already de-termin(at)ed; it cannot be changed. The future, by contrast, is open, uncertain, and indeterminate. What can change about the past is its meaning, which is subject to re-interpretations, anchored in intentions and expectations toward the future. That meaning of the past is dynamic and is conveyed by social agents engaged in confrontations with opposite interpretations, other meanings, or against oblivion and silence. Actors and activists "use" the past, bringing their understandings and interpretations about it into the public sphere of debate. Their intention is to establish/convince/transmit their narrative, so that others will accept it.

Thus, research about this issue does not consist of "dealing with social facts as things, but of analyzing how social facts become things, how and why they are solidified and endowed with durability and stability." What is involved is the study of the processes and actors that intervene in the tasks of constructing and consecrating memories. Who are these actors? Whom do they confront and with whom do they engage in dialogue in the process? Different social actors, with diverse connections to past experience—those who lived through specific periods or events and those who inherited them, those who studied them, and those who expressed them in different ways—strive to affirm the legitimacy of "their" truth. They engage in struggles for power, searching often to legitimate their current positions through claiming privileged links to the past, asserting continuities or ruptures. In these processes, agents of the state have a central role and special weight because of their power in relation to establishing and developing an "official history/memory." Thus, attention has to be placed on the conflicts and disputes over interpretations and meanings of the past, and on the process through which some narratives displace others and become hegemonic.

One of the central symbolic operations in the processes of state formation—in Latin America throughout the nineteenth century, for example—was the elaboration of the "master narrative" of the nation. This involved advancing one version of history that, together with patriotic symbols, monuments, and pantheons to national heroes, could serve as a central node for identification and for anchoring national identity.

What purpose do these official memories serve? They are more or less conscious efforts to define and reinforce feelings of belonging that aim to maintain social cohesion and defend symbolic borders. At the same time, they provide the reference points for framing the memories of groups and sectors within each national context.

Like all narratives, these national stories are selective. Establishing a group of heroes requires obscuring the actions of others. Emphasizing certain characteristics as indicators of heroism involves silencing others, especially the errors and missteps by those who are defined as heroes and must appear "immaculate" in that history. Once these official canonical narratives, historically linked to the process of political centralization in the process of nation-state building, are established, they come to be expressed and crystallized in the history textbooks passed on in formal education. At the same time, they become the targets of diverse efforts at reform, revisionism, and construction of alternative historical narratives. Because the master national narrative tends to be the story of the victors, there will be others who—whether in the form of private oral stories or as practices of resistance to power—will offer alternative narratives and meanings of the past, threatening the national consensus that is being imposed.

If the state is strong and its policing includes control over ideas and freedom of expression in public space, alternative narratives take refuge in the world of "private memories." At times, these narratives are silenced even in the sphere of intimacy, out of shame or weakness, or they are integrated into practices of more open or clandestine resistance.

In this process of construction of the master narratives of modern nation-states, professional historians have had a central role. Official master narratives are written by professional historians whose link to power is crucial to their task. Over time, antagonistic interpretations and revisions of that memory of the nation or official historical narrative will be produced, be it as a result of open antagonisms and political struggles, of changes in social sensibilities, or of advancement in historical research itself.

The construction of official histories turns to be particularly problematic when dealing with contemporary or recent events, especially when they are marked by deep social and political conflicts. During the dictatorial periods of the twentieth century—Stalinism, Nazism, military dictatorships in Brazil, Chile, Argentina, and Uruguay, Stronism in Paraguay*—public space was monopolized by a dominant political story, where the "good guys" and the "bad guys" were clearly identified. Censorship was explicit, and alternative memories could arise only underground, prohibited and clandestine, thus exacerbating the ravages of terror, fear, and traumatic lapses that generate paralysis and silence. Under such circumstances, the official stories conveyed by the representatives of the regime encountered few challenges in the public sphere.

Generally, the dictatorships' narratives present the military in the role of "saviors" of the nation from a mortal threat (in the Southern Cone in the 1970s, the threat was that of "Communism") and from the chaos created by those who try to subvert the nation. In this context, subsequent military stories may emphasize the achievements of peace (especially prominent in Argentina), of economic progress (in Brazil), or of both (Chile). For example, in 1974, the tenth anniversary of the coup d'état in Brazil was used as an occasion to put into circulation one exclusive story in the public sphere and the school system: the account of the economic success of the military regime—the story of the Brazilian "economic miracle." There was no mentioning of the political system

---

*A reference to the thirty-five-year dictatorship of General Alfredo Stroessner (1954–1989) in Paraguay, which was known for its extremely repressive practices.

or of restrictions of public liberties. Undoubtedly, the ethical and political role and public responsibility of historians and critical intellectuals are of extraordinary significance in such periods.

Political openings, thaws, liberalizations, and transitions give a boost to activities in the public sphere, so that previously censored narratives and stories can be incorporated and new ones can be generated. Such openings create a setting for new struggles over the meaning of the past, with a plurality of actors and agents who express a multiplicity of demands and claims.

The new political scenario is one of institutional change in the state and in state-society relationships. At such times, the struggle plays out between a variety of actors who claim recognition and legitimacy of their voices and demands. The memories of the oppressed and marginalized and the memories about oppression and repression—at the edge, of those who were directly affected in their physical integrity by death, forced disappearance, torture, exile, and imprisonment—emerge, usually with a double intent, that of asserting the "true" version of history based on their memories, and that of demanding justice. In such moments, memory, truth, and justice blend into each other, because the meaning of the past that is being fought about is, in fact, part and parcel of the demand for justice in the present.

These are moments in which stories and narratives that were hidden or silenced for a long time emerge into the public eye. There may be considerable public surprise at the survival (at times for decades) of memories that were silenced in the public world but were kept and transmitted in the private sphere (within family or clandestine social groups), maintained in personal intimacy, even "forgotten" in an "evasive" memory loss (because they might be forbidden, unspeakable, or shameful memories, according to Pollak), or buried in traumatic lapses and symptoms. These conjunctures of political and expressive aperture and "uncovering" provide clear evidence that the processes of forgetting and remembering do not respond in a simple, linear, or direct manner to the passing of chronological time.

Moments of political opening involve a complex political scenario. They do not necessarily or primarily entail a binary opposition between an official history or a dominant memory articulated by the state on the one hand, and a counternarrative expressed by society on the other. Quite to the contrary, multiple social and political actors come to the scene, and they craft narratives of the past that confront each other's, and in so doing, they also convey their projects and political expectations for the future. In these conjunctures, neither is there a single voice on the part of the state. Political transition involves a transformation of the state, a new foundational moment, with new readings and meanings given to the past. At times of political opening, the state itself is crisscrossed by multiple and competing readings, reflecting the variety of meanings of the past that circulate in the societal scenario.

2. Opening Chile's Memory Box ⁓ Steve J. Stern*

For historian Steve Stern, collective memory is like a box of family photos found in a person's home. Inside the box, the photos (or memories) are arranged in various albums (memory frameworks) that give them meaning. The albums, which are constantly being rearranged and fought over, turn the memories into stories or narratives of family history. According to Stern, historical memory works basically the same way at the national level. In the following selection, Stern describes a key moment in the opening of Chile's memory box that played out right after the Pinochet dictatorship ended. The new civilian president, Patricio Aylwin, appointed the Chilean National Commission on Truth and Reconciliation headed by a man named Raúl Rettig (hence it is sometimes known as the Rettig Commission) to investigate more than two thousand cases of death and disappearance of citizens during the early years of the dictatorship. Stern points out the key role played in the process by the Vicaría de la Solidaridad *(Vicariate of Solidarity), a Catholic Church body created to support the families of dead and disappeared persons. What impact did hearing victim testimonies have on the members of the commission?*

The Rettig Commission faced a daunting task as it began work in May 1990. At the time, few useful examples of truth commissions existed for transitions from the violent dictatorships that had spread across most of South America by the mid-1970s. Argentina had a notable truth commission experience, but its circumstances of transition—the military's legitimacy was in tatters after the 1982 Malvinas-Falklands war with Britain—were quite different. Also, Argentina's military rebellions in the late 1980s and its subsequent retreat to "due obedience" and "final stop" laws† had undermined the first democratic government's truth-and-justice policy. Argentina seemed more a warning than an inspiration.

Aylwin had limited the Rettig Commission's mandate. It was to focus on maximal cases—death, disappearance, and torture leading to death by agents of the state or persons in their hire, and deaths by private persons acting from political motive. (Strictly speaking, the former corresponded to international human

*From Steve J. Stern, *Reckoning with Pinochet: The Memory Question in Democratic Chile, 1989–2006* (Durham, NC: Duke University Press, 2010), 67–75. © 2010 Duke University Press. All rights reserved. Republished by permission of the copyright holder, Duke University Press. www.dukeupress.edu/.
†Argentina's Full Stop Law (1986) and Law of Due Obedience (1987) prevented midlevel officers and those below them in the military hierarchy from being tried for crimes committed during the Argentine "Dirty War" of 1976–1983, during which tens of thousands of Argentines were detained, tortured, and killed by the armed forces. Both laws were repealed by the Argentine judiciary in 2005, opening the door to new investigations.

rights law, which focused on violations of the state's basic duty to protect the lives and integrity of its citizens. The latter corresponded to international humanitarian law, which established minimal norms of conduct by anyone, even in war. Including the latter allowed the Commission to take cognizance of and define as violation acts of armed resistance leading to deaths of soldiers or police.) Despite the bounded mandate, the scope and multiple layers of political violence by the state added pressure. At the time, the Vicaría already had specific knowledge of 2,354 individual cases of death or disappearance under military rule. Its count of specifically known political arrests was also huge: 82,429. Even this figure was far less than the real number; a good conservative estimate of political imprisonment under military rule is 150,000 to 200,000. The combined political and economic exile flow had also been massive—200,000 at the lower-end estimates, 400,000 by one Vicaría estimate.

Torture—applying severe bodily pain and mental terror to break down the prisoner's integrity as a human being—was difficult to quantify yet clearly massive. Only a small fraction of torture cases had led to formal legal denunciation under military rule. Problems of evidence compounded the usual problems of fear and unresponsive courts. In most torture cases, physical evidence on the survivor such as maiming, scars, and organ damage faded or disappeared over time and became more difficult to establish in the absence of confirming witnesses. For many victim-survivors, the most lasting and debilitating effects of torture were on mental and emotional health. Despite these problems and a weak rate of legal denunciation, the Vicaría knew of 2,741 specific cases. Translated into estimates, informed by knowledge of the pervasiveness of torture and the numerical scale of arrests, even José Zalaquett—a human rights professional inclined toward conservative methodology in the interests of credibility—thought torture cases would number in the dozens of thousands. The scale of the Commission's work would change drastically if it sought to investigate torture systematically, on a case-by-case basis.

In sum, the number of individual cases to be investigated under the Commission's bounded mandate was large, and the number of persons for whom its report would matter directly, regardless of the Commission's technical scope, was even larger. In 1989, a sixth of the national citizenry (16.6 percent) believed they or a family member had been the direct victim of a human rights violation.

[Inside the Rettig Commission] the realities finally narrated and uncovered were intense and sometimes shocking, even to the experienced. They cut to the core of the human condition—the amazing lows of brutality, violence, and duplicity to which human beings can descend; the ennobling aspect when people act with dignity or ethical clarity amidst extreme fear and degradation; the ultimate issues of mortality, love, and loss that render other issues small. Often it was the oral testimonies by relatives that brought such issues to life.

The presence of social workers on the staff reflected the fact that the hearings with relatives were fundamental to the truth process—not only for fact finding, but also to start the long overdue process of social repair. Most detentions leading to death or disappearance took place before 1977. In other words, most relatives had endured *at least fourteen years* of state hostility and denial of responsibility. Building *convivencia*, and a culture of democracy and human rights, meant recognizing officially that which had gone unrecognized. For the first time in many years, relatives would find a state that would "listen" respectfully to the torment and humiliations they had endured. As the first step of social repair of unjust harm, as the climax of a long struggle to find truth, as the moment of reckoning with the possible death of a disappeared relative, the hearings were potentially cathartic events. Even the making of an appointment was emotionally powerful. Señora Herminda Morales, a veteran of struggle who had searched seventeen years and had joined a hunger strike to find her two disappeared sons, nearly fainted as she made her appointment.

Such circumstances turned many hearings into emotionally intense experiences for family members—and Commission staff and members. Relatives who for years needed to avoid showing weakness before a hostile state could finally expose the deeper meanings of their saga: the treasured "goodness story" that restored the good name of the person killed or disappeared; the humiliation and despair endured when quests for truth met with cruel misinformation and denial; the economic and health toll on relatives, including young children. Since the late 1970s relatives often used a bodily metaphor—the wound that remains open, unallowed to heal—to express memory of military rule as endless rupture.

The metaphor was apt, the health effects physical, mental, and emotional. In the experience of relatives, the line between psychological and somatic afflictions sometimes dissolved. Consider the testimony of the sister of a disappeared person. "My mother succumbed to a gastric cancer as a result of her excessive nervousness, caused without a doubt by the detention and subsequent disappearance of my sister [name]. One of my nephews, who witnessed the arrest of my sister, is in these moments in a psychiatric hospital, specifically [name of hospital]." She believed that "his dementia owes to his having witnessed the detention of his aunt, something that seriously marked his state of mind and emotion." Verbalizing such experiences produced a powerful impact on listeners as well as speakers.

The cathartic aspects of testimony also came through in more unexpected ways. The Commission was considering human behavior and experience at the outer limits of the imaginable. Not all members of a family reacted similarly to such events, not only for the obvious reasons of fear, politics, or personality but also for reasons more profound. The experience itself crossed over into human impossibility. As philosophers, artists, and survivor-witnesses have recognized, situations of "radical evil"—what we call today "crimes against humanity"—test and break the very premises we use to define order, rationality, and ethics. Under the circumstances people invent responses in a world without the usual normative guideposts. They may become deeply confused or ashamed in their own minds. Some of the most powerful truth-telling moments emerged when relatives exposed to each other their own deception or their own regret about the choices made in an impossible context. A staff lawyer could never forget the moment when a woman's appearance coincided with that of her children and their grandparents. To carry on the search for her disappeared husband, she had decided to leave the children to be raised by their grandparents. Without renouncing the search for her husband, she was also overcome by a sense of having abandoned her children. Experientially, she had lost them, too. She asked for and received their forgiveness. The lawyer wept along with everyone present.

Some such moments defied resolution. A staff social worker remembered two children who discovered the truth about their father. After his detention, the family experienced stigma and danger. The young mother—she loved her husband but also wanted to shield her children—moved to another city to live with her parents. She invented a cover story to explain the missing father. He had abandoned them, she said. The children grew up hating their father. Now, in 1990, the children's grandmother—their father's mother—decided that the time had come for the truth. "And she said, 'You are going to accompany me to bear witness for the life of your father,' and she told them . . . who their father had been and took them to the Commission." The youths had to switch from imagining the negligent father to imagining the caring father torn away from them, and then subjected to torture and death. The emotional turmoil of the children and the bitter family conflicts cut in several directions. Such matters would take years to "work through," if they could be worked through at all.

---

3. Human Rights Violations Committed by Government Agents ~ Chilean National Commission on Truth and Reconciliation*

The following selection comes from the report issued by the Rettig Commission in 1991 after concluding the investigative process described above by Stern. The excerpt comes from the section of the report dealing with the events of September 1973, particularly in the capital city of Santiago in the first week after the coup d'état that overthrew Salvador Allende's government. One of the things revealed in the investigation was the Chilean Army's use of soccer stadiums to hold, torture, and execute people who had been detained for their "subversive" activities. One of these stadiums, the Estadio Chile *or Chile Stadium, was the place where*

*From *Report of the Chilean National Commission on Truth and Reconciliation*, vol. 1 (Notre Dame, IN: University of Notre Dame Press, 1993), 201–4.

the well-known Chilean singer, artist, and Popular Unity activist Victor Jara was detained, tortured, and killed by agents of the government. This part of the report summarizes the cases that were heard by the commission. It includes information on Victor Jara's final days as well as those of a pro-Allende lawyer, university student, and factory worker. Notice the references to the government's attempt to create an official history of these cases.

Between September 13–16, 1973, there were a number of deaths and disappearances related to the presence of prisoners in the Chile Stadium.

SOCRATES PONCE PACHECO, 30, an Ecuadorian lawyer who was an active Socialist and the government representative at the INDUMET factory. The official version that the Chilean Foreign Ministry provided on March 27, 1974 stated that "this individual was a government representative at a factory and shot at the armed forces in armed resistance and was killed in the shooting." However, the Commission received credible accounts indicating that Ponce was arrested by police forces on September 11, 1973 at his workplace, and was taken to the Twelfth station.

From there he was sent to the Tacna Regiment on the morning of September 12, and then taken to the Chile Stadium at noon. In the early morning of the 13th, his name was called over the loudspeakers, and army troops took him away.

His body was found near the Chile Stadium, at the corner of Unión Latinoamericana and Alameda, and bore eight bullet wounds according to the autopsy report. His relatives took the body from the Medical Legal Institute. The death certificate states that the date of death was September 12, and thus differs from what his relatives say.

In view of the foregoing, the Commission has come to the conviction that Sócrates Ponce was executed without due process of law by government agents and that thus his fundamental human rights were violated. It bases its conviction on the testimony it took on his arrest and his presence at several sites, and on the documents that explain how he died, all of which make it possible to refute the official version of a supposed shootout.

GREGORIO MIMICA ARGOTE, 22, an unmarried university student and leader at the Technical University who was an active Communist. He was arrested at his house on September 14, 1973, by a military patrol shortly after returning from spending two days under arrest in the Chile Stadium and then being released. Since that day there has been no information on his whereabouts. The Commission has come to the conviction that government agents were responsible for the disappearance of Gregorio Mimica and that in so doing they violated his fundamental human rights. The grounds for that conviction are that he was a politically active student leader, that he had been imprisoned previously in the Chile Stadium, and that since that time there is no indication whatsoever of his fate and his whereabouts.

HERNAN CEA FIGUEROA, 38, a textile worker who was an activist in the Communist party. He was arrested on September 11 at the TextilProgreso factory where he worked. From there he was taken with other arrested workers to the Chile Stadium. On September 15 he became involved in an argument with one of his guards and was executed on the spot by policemen. His family found the body a month later at the General Cemetery. The Commission has come to the conviction that Hernán Cea was executed without due process of law by government agents, and that his fundamental human rights were thereby violated. It bases that conviction on the fact that execution arose out of an argument with one of his guards, that he did not attack them, and that no matter what the prisoner might have done, there is no justification for killing him without due process of law.

VICTOR LIDIO JARA MARTINEZ, 40, a popular singer and theater director who was a member of the Central Committee of Communist Youth. A statement by the Foreign Ministry dated March 27, 1974, in response to a note from the OAS (Organization of American States) Interamerican Human Rights Commission, said, "Víctor Jara: Dead. He was killed by snipers who, I repeat, were firing indiscriminately on the armed forces and on the civilian population."

This Commission received many credible reports refuting this official story and leading to the conclusion that what actually happened was quite different. Víctor Jara was arrested on September 12 on the grounds of the State Technical University were he was working as a theater director. He was taken to the Chile Stadium, where he was separated from the other people with whom he had been arrested, and detained high up in the stands together with other people considered to be dangerous. Between September 12–15, he was interrogated by army personnel.

The last day Víctor Jara was seen alive was September 15. During the afternoon he was taken out of a line of prisoners who were being transferred to the National Stadium. In the early morning of the next day, September 16, shantytown dwellers found his body, along with five others, including that of Littré Quiroga Carvajal, near the Metropolitan Cemetery. As the autopsy report states, Víctor Jara died as a result of multiple bullet wounds (44 entry wounds and 32 exit wounds).

The Commission came to the conviction that he was executed without due process of law by government agents, and hence in violation of his fundamental human rights. The grounds for that conviction are that he is known to have been arrested and to have been in the Chile Stadium, that it is attested that he died as a result of many bullet wounds, thus indicating that he was executed together with the other prisoners whose bodies appeared alongside his. The overview to this period provides an account of the various kinds of torture to which Víctor Jara was subjected while under arrest.

4. Testimony of Atrocity ~ Rigoberta Menchú*

The following selection is taken from the sometimes beautiful, sometimes grue-some testimonio, *or testimonial, of the Guatemalan Mayan indigenous rights activist Rigoberta Menchú. In 1984, her famous book,* I, Rigoberta Menchú: An Indian Woman in Guatemala, *which was told to and edited by Venezuelan anthropologist Elizabeth Burgos when she and Menchú met in Paris in 1982, was published in English. Its fame made Menchú an important spokesperson for the Guatemalan revolutionaries. At the time the testimonial was recorded by Burgos, Menchú had been forced to leave Guatemala because of her involve-ment with the guerrillas (in particular the Guerrilla Army of the Poor). She was beginning an international campaign to raise awareness about the Guatemalan Civil War (1960–1992). The early years of the 1980s were an especially horrific chapter in Guatemala's long civil war era. The government of General Lucas García (1978–1982) and the subsequent military regime of General Ríos Montt (1982–1983) ordered counterinsurgency campaigns to clear the guerrillas out of several provinces where their support in the rural Mayan countryside was strong, including Menchú's home province of Quiché. The generals had the firm support of the Reagan administration. In this excerpt, Menchú tells the story of the extremely brutal killing of her brother Petrocinio. Her family and others in the community have been ordered to come to the village of Chajul where the army has announced that numerous captured subversives will be publicly punished. Notice at the end the responses of those persons who view the horrid scene.*

When we reached the village there were many people who'd been there since early morning: children, women, men. Minutes later, the army was sur-rounding the people who were there to watch. There were machines, armoured cars, jeeps, all kinds of weapons. Helicopters started to fly over the village so that the guerrilla fighters wouldn't come. That's what they were afraid of. The officer opened the meeting. I remember he started by saying that a group of guerrillas they'd caught were about to arrive and that they were going to suffer a little pun-ishment. A little punishment, because there were greater punishments, he said, but you'll see the punishment they get. And that's for being communists! For being Cubans, for being subversives! And if you get mixed up with communists and subversives, you'll get the same treatment as these subversives you'll be seeing

---

*From Rigoberta Menchú, *I, Rigoberta Menchú: An Indian Woman in Guatemala*, ed. Elisabeth Burgos-Debray, trans. Anne Wright (London: Verso, 1984), 175–79. Reprinted by permission of the publisher.

in a little while. My mother was just about 100 per cent certain her son would be amongst those being brought in. I was still not sure, though, because I knew my brother wasn't a criminal and didn't deserve such punishments.

Well, a few minutes later three army lorries [trucks] came into the village. One went a little ahead, the middle one carried the tortured people and the third one brought up the rear. They guarded them very closely, even with armoured cars. The lorry with the tortured came in. They started to take them out one by one. They were all wearing army uniforms. But their faces were monstrously disfigured, unrecognisable. My mother went closer to the lorry to see if she could recognise her son. Each of the tortured had different wounds on the face. I mean, their faces all looked different. But my mother recognized her son, my little brother, among them. They put them in a line. Some of them were very nearly half dead, or they were nearly in their last agony, and others, you could see that they were; you could see that very well indeed. My brother was very badly tortured, he could hardly stand up. All the tortured had no nails and they had cut off part of the soles of their feet. They were barefoot. They forced them to walk and put them in a line. They fell down at once. They picked them up again. There was a squadron of soldiers there ready to do exactly what the officer ordered. And the officer carried on with his rigmarole, saying that we had to be satisfied with our lands, we had to be satisfied with eating bread and chile, but we mustn't let ourselves be led astray by communist ideas. Saying that all the people had access to everything, that they were content. If I remember aright, he must have repeated the word "communist" a hundred times. He started off with the Soviet Union, Cuba, Nicaragua; he said that the same communists from the Soviet Union had moved on to Cuba and then Nicaragua and that now they were in Guatemala. And that those Cubans would die a death like that of these tortured people. Every time he paused in his speech, they forced the tortured up with kicks and blows from their weapons.

No-one could leave the meeting. Everyone was weeping. I, I don't know, every time I tell this story, I can't hold back my tears, for me it's a reality I can't forget, even though it's not easy to tell of it. My mother was weeping; she was looking at her son. My brother scarcely recognized us. Or perhaps . . . my mother said he did, that he could still smile at her, but I, well, I didn't see that. They were monstrous. They were all fat, fat, fat. They were all swollen up, all wounded. When I drew closer to them, I saw that their clothes were damp. Damp from the moisture oozing out of their bodies. Somewhere around half-way through the speech, it would be about an hour and a half, two hours on, the captain made the squad of soldiers take the clothes off the tortured people, saying that it was so that everyone could see for themselves what their punishment had been and realize that if we got mixed up in communism, in terrorism, we'd be punished the same way. Threatening the people like that, they wanted to force us to do just as they said. They couldn't simply take the clothes off the tortured men, so the soldiers brought scissors and cut the clothes apart from the feet up and took the clothes off the tortured bodies. They all had the marks of different tortures. The captain devoted himself to explaining each of the different tortures. This is perforation with needles, he'd say, this is a wire burn. He went on like that explaining each torture and describing each tortured man. There were three people who looked like bladders. I mean, they were inflated, although they had no wounds on their bodies. But they were inflated, inflated. And the officer said, that's from something we put in them that hurts them. The important thing is that they should know that it hurts and that the people should know it's no easy thing to have that done to your body.

In my brother's case, he was cut in various places. His head was shaved and slashed. He had no nails. He had no soles to his feet. The earlier wounds were suppurating from infection. And the woman compahera, of course I recognized her; she was from a village near ours. They had shaved her private parts. The nipple of one of her breasts was missing and her other breast was cut off. She had the marks of bites on different parts of her body. She was bitten all over, that compañera. She had no ears. All of them were missing part of the tongue or had had their tongues split apart. I found it impossible to concentrate, seeing that this could be. You could only think that these were human beings and what pain those bodies had felt to arrive at that unrecognizable state. All the people were crying, even the children. I was watching the children. They were crying and terrified, clinging to their mothers. We didn't know what to do. During his speech, the captain kept saying his government was democratic and gave us everything. What more could we want? He said that the subversives brought foreign ideas, exotic ideas that would only lead us to torture, and he'd point to the bodies of the men. If we listened to these exotic slogans, he said, we'd die like them. He said they had all kinds of weapons that we could choose to be killed with. The captain gave a panoramic description of all the power they had, the capacity they had. We, the people, didn't have the capacity to confront them. This was really all being said to strike terror into the people and stop anyone from speaking. My mother wept. She almost risked her own life by going to embrace my brother. My other brothers and my father held her back so she wouldn't endanger herself. My father was incredible; I watched him and he didn't shed a tear, but he was full of rage. And that was a rage we all felt. But all the rest of us began to weep, like everyone else. We couldn't believe it, I couldn't believe that had happened to my little brother. What had he done to deserve that? He was just an innocent child and that had happened to him.

After he'd finished talking the officer ordered the squad to take away those who'd been "punished," naked and swollen as they were. They dragged them along, they could no longer walk. Dragged them along to this place, where they lined them up all together within sight of everyone. The officer called to the worst of his criminals—the Kaibiles*, who wear different clothes from other soldiers.

---

*The Kaibiles, who wore maroon berets as part of their uniform, were members of a special operations commando unit of the Guatemalan Army that was created specifically for counterinsurgency.

They're the ones with the most training, the most power. Well, he called the Kaibiles and they poured petrol [gasoline] over each of the tortured. The captain said, "This isn't the last of their punishments, there's another one yet. This is what we've done with all the subversives we catch, because they have to die by violence. And if this doesn't teach you a lesson, this is what'll happen to you too. The problem is that the Indians let themselves be led by the communists. Since no-one's told the Indians anything, they go along with the communists." He was trying to convince the people but at the same time he was insulting them by what he said. Anyway, they lined up the tortured and poured petrol on them; and then the soldiers set fire to each one of them. Many of them begged for mercy. They looked half dead when they were lined up there, but when the bodies began to burn they began to plead for mercy. Some of them screamed, many of them leapt but uttered no sound—of course, that was because their breathing was cut off. But—and to me this was incredible—many of the people had weapons with them, the ones who'd been on their way to work had machetes, others had nothing in their hands, but when they saw the army setting fire to the victims, everyone wanted to strike back, to risk their lives doing it, despite all the soldiers' arms. . . . Faced with its own cowardice, the army itself realized that the whole people were prepared to fight. You could see that even the children were enraged, but they didn't know how to express their rage.

Well, the officer quickly gave the order for the squad to withdraw. They all fell back holding their weapons up and shouting slogans as if it were a celebration. They were happy! They roared with laughter and cried, "Long live the Fatherland! Long live Guatemala! Long live our President! Long live the army, long live Lucas!" The people raised their weapons and rushed at the army, but they drew back at once, because there was the risk of a massacre. The army had all kinds of arms, even planes flying overhead. Anyway, if there'd been a confrontation with the army, the people would have been massacred. But nobody thought about death. I didn't think that I might die, I just wanted to do something, even kill a soldier.

---

5. Analysis of Rigoberta Menchú's Testimonial ⁓ David Stoll*

U.S. anthropologist David Stoll did not set out to investigate the truthfulness of Rigoberta Menchú's testimonial. He had gone to Guatemala as a graduate student in the late 1980s to interview survivors of political violence in its Ixil communities (a Mayan subgroup). But his interviews kept raising questions in

*From David Stoll, *Rigoberta Menchú and the Story of All Poor Guatemalans* (Boulder, CO: Westview, 1999), 8–11, 273–74. © 1999 David Stoll. Reprinted by permission of Westview Press, a member of the Perseus Books Group.

his mind about some of the events described in Menchú's acclaimed testimonial. After publishing his book on the Ixil, Stoll returned to Guatemala (particularly the district of Uspantán, where much of Menchú's account takes place) to dig deeper into her story. Eventually he came to the conclusion that, while her depiction of the Guatemalan Army as a brutalizing force that was responsible for barbaric acts like the ones described above was essentially accurate, Menchú's portrayal of the relationship between the guerrillas and the Mayan peasants was problematic. Basically, he argues that Menchú put forward the ideological line or position espoused by the Guerrilla Army of the Poor, with which Menchú was affiliated in the 1980s. In the following excerpt, Stoll explains his uneasiness with reading her testimonial as an eyewitness account of the civil war.

When I began visiting northern Quiché in 1987, to interview peasants about the violence and reconstruction, I had no reason to doubt the veracity of *I, Rigoberta Menchú*. Nor did anyone else as far as I knew. What Rigoberta said about the Guatemalan army, the most important point of the book for most readers, rang true to other testimony. I recall being surprised when a routine atrocity check, described at the start of this chapter, failed to corroborate the immolation of her brother and other captives in the Chajul plaza. Since I was able to corroborate that the brother had died at Chajul, if not in the precise manner described, I did not feel obliged to call a press conference. My interviews were confirming so many of the accusations against the Guatemalan army that the problem seemed minor.

Only after becoming very familiar with what peasants had to say did I realize that their testimony was not backing up Rigoberta's in two significant ways. Not at issue was the record of the Guatemalan army—in that respect her picture of the violence was true enough. Nor were the feelings of peasants toward the army. Most seemed just as bitter toward it as she was, even if they spoke in low tones because they were still under military occupation. What most peasants did not share with Rigoberta was, in the first place, her definition of the enemy. Unlike *I, Rigoberta Menchú*, which describes the guerrillas as liberation fighters, my Ixil sources tended to lump soldiers and guerrillas together as threats to their lives. Instead of being popular heroes, the guerrillas were, like soldiers, people with guns who brought suffering in their wake.

"They look for trouble, not the needs of the family," an ex-combatant told me, explaining why he accepted a government amnesty. "Both the guerrillas and the army like trouble. But we're a civilian population; we just want to cultivate our maize." An Ixil civil servant said, "It's not a problem between the people and the guerrillas, nor between the army and the people, but between [the army and the guerrillas]. . . . They're using us as a shield because, when there are confrontations, the army sends patrollers [Ixil militiamen] to fight. And when the guerrillas attack, they bring civilians to fight with other civilians."

Obviously, the contrast with Rigoberta's testimony could be one of time. She was telling her story in 1982, at the height of revolutionary mobilization, when more peasants supported the guerrillas. Back then, many more peasants might have echoed her statements. Perhaps I was simply arriving too late to hear how they felt, and how they might express themselves in the future. Yet my interviews with Ixils also raised a second, more troubling contrast with Rigoberta's portrait of the violence that could not be explained as the result of disillusion with once popular guerrillas.

The peasants of *I, Rigoberta Menchú* have been pushed to the wall by plantation owners and soldiers hunting down dissidents. Her village has little choice but to organize for self-defense and look to the guerrillas for help. The insurgency therefore springs from the most basic need of peasants, for their land. This is the socioeconomic explanation for insurgency, the immiseration or oppression thesis, which is how guerrilla organizations and their supporters customarily justify the cost of armed struggle. If the people face ever worsening conditions, then they have no choice but to confront the system, whereupon the guerrillas show up to provide leadership.

These were not the prewar conditions I heard about in my interviews with nearby Ixils. Certainly they were living under a military dictatorship, some ladinos* had evil reputations, and at least a few Ixils were eager to become guerrillas at an early date. But this was not a population that could defend itself only by force. Instead, Ixils were learning to use local elections and the courts. The 1960s and 1970s were for them, as for many Guatemalan peasants, an era of modest gains. The first armed groups in their accounts were usually guerrillas, whom many blamed for the subsequent arrival of soldiers. Army kidnappings began not in reaction to peaceful efforts by Ixils to improve their lot but to guerrilla organizing and ambushes. If anyone ignited political violence in Ixil country, it was the Guerrilla Army of the Poor. Only then had the security forces militarized the area and turned it into a killing ground.

Had nearby Uspantán been different? Or was *I, Rigoberta Menchú* voicing a rationale for insurgency that did not really come from peasants, that instead came from someone claiming to speak for them? No one had ever interviewed Rigoberta's old neighbors to compare their stories with hers. In June 1989 I went to Uspantán for the first time. My visit confirmed the basic outline of *I, Rigoberta Menchú*—that she came from the village of Chimel and that her father, mother, and younger brother died early in the violence. Yet a single day in Uspantán raised other problems with Rigoberta's account. At this point I did what any sensible graduate student does with a controversial discovery. I dropped the subject and scuttled back to my doctoral dissertation. It was only later, back in the United States, that I realized that I would have to face the au-

---

*Nonindigenous Guatemalans, including mestizos who identified with the Hispanic side of their heritage.

thority of Rigoberta's story. An unimportant discrepancy, over how her brother died in Chajul, was the first sign of a more significant one: the considerable gap between the voice of revolutionary commitment incarnated by Rigoberta and the peasant voices I was listening to.

Rigoberta's 1982 story, produced while she was on tour for the revolutionary movement in Europe, had become the most accepted perspective on the relation between Guatemalan guerrillas and peasants. In the late 1980s and early 1990s, the aura around Rigoberta's version of events extended far beyond her hometown, to encompass the entire war in the western highlands. Any analysis that contradicted her claims and those of the revolutionary movement that she validated was sure to raise hackles. In the solidarity and human rights milieu, as well as in much of the scholarly community, many still felt that Rigoberta's account deserved to be interpreted literally, as a monument to the popular roots of the guerrilla movement in its northern Quiché heartland. Or if the story had to be taken with a grain of salt, it was not the business of a North American anthropologist to confront it.

Actually, there were two arguments against challenging Rigoberta's 1982 account. One was pragmatic. Since her testimony had generated international pressure, which was finally forcing the government to negotiate with the guerrillas, it might not be the best time to question its credibility. This was an argument I could not dismiss. It was one of the reasons I decided to withhold my findings, in the hope that a peace agreement would be signed. I was less impressed with the second argument—that an anthropologist did not have the right to contradict Rigoberta's story because that would violate the right of a native person to tell her story in her own way.

Anthropologists have long collected life histories from people. Ordinarily we do not dwell on whether the results are true or not. The very idea of refuting a life story sounds journalistic. More important is the narrator's perspective and what this tells us about the culture. Aside from being a life story, however, *I, Rigoberta Menchú* was a version of events with specific political objectives. It was also the most widely hailed example of *testimonio*, the Latin American genre that has brought the lives of the poor into scholarship in their own powerful words. Everyone concedes that testimonies reflect personal viewpoints. But advocates also regard them as testimony—reliable sources of information and representative voices for entire social classes. "My story is the story of all poor Guatemalans," Rigoberta said, and her claim has been taken very seriously, by everyone from supporters of guerrilla movements to the Nobel Committee.

That Rigoberta turned herself into a composite Maya, with a wider range of experiences than she actually had, is not a very serious problem. Certainly, it should be known that her 1982 testimony is not a literal account of her life. Yet she was explicit that this was the story of all poor Guatemalans. On reflection, that could never be the story of one poor Guatemalan. Her narrative strategy is easy to defend because her most important claims, about the Guatemalan army's killings, are true. Rigoberta was dramatizing her life like a Hollywood scriptwriter might, in order to have an impact. Still, factuality is a legitimate issue for any narrative claiming to be an eyewitness account, especially one that has been taken as seriously as Rigoberta's. Even if she should not be held to the same standard as a UN observer, [I] have suggested the importance of comparison with other forms of evidence. Where Rigoberta's account is seriously misleading is in its depiction of the social background of the killing, in particular, why it started around her home. Uspantán is not a microcosm for the entire war, but through Rigoberta's story it has been widely construed as archetypal. Moreover, what happened there illustrates the fate of tens of thousands of victims. Clarifying how the killing started in Uspantán is therefore germane on a broader scale.

Perhaps causality was a secondary issue in 1982 when the killing was at its height, but it was still an important one. It is even more so now that truth commissions are publishing reports and Guatemalans are trying to put the violence behind them. If identifying crimes and breaking through regimes of denial has become a public imperative in peacemaking, if there is a public demand for establishing "historical memory," then *I, Rigoberta Menchú* cannot be enshrined as true in a way that it is not. If you take Rigoberta's story at anything like face value—if you argue, sure, some points are exaggerated but it is basically accurate—you have been led astray about the conditions facing her people, what they wanted, and how political killing started in her area.

---

6. Memory of Silence ~ Guatemalan Commission for Historical Clarification*

In 1994, the Guatemalan government and the umbrella group for all of the country's revolutionary guerrilla organizations signed on to a United Nations plan to negotiate the ending of Latin America's longest-running civil war. At the behest of the UN General Assembly, the Guatemalan Commission for Historical Clarification (CEH, the Spanish acronym used in the excerpt) was created to help facilitate the process of national reconciliation by bringing the truth of the civil war to light. As was the case in Chile, the Guatemalan Commission interviewed thousands of victims of human rights abuses, combed through thousands of pages of reports by human rights NGOs (nongovernmental organizations), and talked with high-ranking political officials and military officers. Using the definition of genocide that was spelled out by the United Nations in the wake of World War II, the commission came to the conclusion that genocide had been committed against the Mayan population in some provinces (including Quiché) by the Gua-

*From *Guatemala: Memory of Silence; Report of the Commission for Historical Clarification; Conclusions and Recommendations*, accessed May 1, 2013, http://shr.aaas.org/.

temalan Army in the early 1980s. The following selection is from the conclusion to the commission's report. The climate of "extreme cruelty" and "terror" that the report describes should make us think again about the impact of Rigoberta Menchú's testimonial on the shaping of historical memory in Guatemala.

Acts of Genocide

108. The legal framework adopted by the CEH to analyse the possibility that acts of genocide were committed in Guatemala during the internal armed confrontation is the Convention on the Prevention and Punishment of the Crime of Genocide, adopted by the United Nations General Assembly on 9 December 1948 and ratified by the Guatemalan State by Decree 704 on 30 November 1949.

109. Article II of this instrument defines the crime of genocide and its requirements in the following terms: ". . . genocide means any of the following acts committed with intent to destroy, in whole or in part, a national, ethnical, racial or religious group, as such:

a) Killing members of the group;

b) Causing serious bodily or mental harm to members of the group;

c) Deliberately inflicting on the group conditions of life calculated to bring about its physical destruction in whole or in part;

d) Imposing measures intended to prevent births within the group;

e) Forcibly transferring children of the group to another group."

On this basis, the two fundamental elements of the crime are: intentionality and that the acts committed include at least one of the five previously cited in the above article.

110. After studying four selected geographical regions (Maya-Q'anjob'al and Maya-Chuj, in Barillas, Nentón and San Mateo Ixtatán in North Huehuetenango; Maya-Ixil, in Nebaj, Cotzaland Chajul, Quiché; Maya-K'iche' in Joyabaj, Zacualpa and Chiché, Quiché; and Maya-Achi in Rabinal, Baja Verapaz), the CEH is able to confirm that between 1981 and 1983 the Army identified groups of the Mayan population as the internal enemy, considering them to be an actual or potential support base for the guerrillas, with respect to material sustenance, a source of recruits and a place to hide their members. In this way, the Army, inspired by the National Security Doctrine, defined a concept of internal enemy that went beyond guerrilla sympathisers, combatants or militants to include civilians from specific ethnic groups.

111. Considering the series of criminal acts and human rights violations which occurred in the regions and periods indicated and which were analysed for the purpose of determining whether they constituted the crime of genocide, the CEH concludes that the reiteration of destructive acts, directed systematically against groups of the Mayan population, within which can be mentioned the elimination of leaders and criminal acts against minors who could not possibly have been military targets, demonstrates that the only common denominator for

all the victims was the fact that they belonged to a specific ethnic group and makes it evident that these acts were committed "with intent to destroy, in whole or in part" these groups (Article II, first paragraph of the Convention).

112. Among acts aimed at the destruction of Mayan groups, identified by the Army as the enemy, "killings" deserve special mention (Article II.a of the Convention), the most significant of which were the massacres. The CEH has verified that in the four regions studied, between 1981 and 1983, agents of the State committed killings which were the most serious acts in a series of military operations directed against the non-combatant civilian population. In accordance with the testimonies and other elements of evidence collected, the CEH has established that, both regular and special Army forces, as well as Civil Patrols and military commissioners, participated in those killings characterised as massacres. In many cases, the survivors identified those responsible for directing these operations as being the commanders of the nearest municipal military outposts.

113. The analysis of the different elements used by the CEH, proves that in the above-mentioned cases, the aim of the perpetrators was to kill the largest number of group members possible. Prior to practically all these killings, the Army carried out at least one of the following preparatory actions: carefully gathering the whole community together; surrounding the community; or utilising situations in which the people were gathered together for celebrations or market days.

114. In the analysis of these events in the four regions, the CEH has established that along with the killings, which in themselves were sufficient to eliminate the groups defined as the enemy, members of the Army or of Civil Patrols systematically committed acts of extreme cruelty, including torture and other cruel, inhuman and degrading actions, the effect of which was to terrorise the population and destroy the foundations of social cohesion, particularly when people were forced to witness or execute these acts themselves.

115. The CEH concludes that, among those acts perpetrated with the intent to destroy, in whole or in part, numerous Mayan groups, are included many actions committed which constituted "serious bodily or mental harm to members of the group" (Article II.b of the Convention). The resulting destruction of social cohesion of the group, typical of these acts, corresponds to the intent to annihilate the group, physically and spiritually.

116. The investigation has also proved that the killings, especially those that were indiscriminate massacres, were accompanied by the razing of villages. This was most significant in the Ixil region, where between 70% and 90% of villages were razed. Also, in the north of Huehuetenango, in Rabinal and in Zacualpa, whole villages were burnt, properties were destroyed and the collectively worked fields and harvests were also burnt, leaving the communities without food.

117. Furthermore, in the four regions which were the object of this special investigation, people were also persecuted during their displacement. The CEH

has established that in the Ixil area, displaced persons were bombed. Similarly, those who were captured or gave themselves up voluntarily continued to be the object of violations, in spite of being under the Army's absolute control.

118. The CEH concludes that some of the acts mentioned in the two previous paragraphs constitute the "deliberate infliction on the group of conditions of life" that could bring about, and in several cases did bring about, "its physical destruction in whole or in part" (Article II. c. of the Convention).

119. The CEH's analysis demonstrates that in the execution of these acts, the national military structures were co-ordinated to allow for the "effective" action of soldiers and members of Civil Patrols in the four regions studied. Military plan Victory 82, for example, established that "the mission is to annihilate the guerrillas and parallel organisations"; the military plan Firmness 83–1 determined that the Army should support "their operations with a maximum of PAC members, in order to raze all collective works. . . ."

120. The above has convinced the CEH that acts committed with the intent to destroy, in whole or in part, numerous groups of Mayans were not isolated acts or excesses committed by soldiers who were out of control, nor were they the result of possible improvisation by mid-level Army command. With great consternation, the CEH concludes that many massacres and other human rights violations committed against these groups obeyed a higher, strategically planned policy, manifested in actions which had a logical and coherent sequence.

121. Faced with several options to combat the insurgency, the State chose the one that caused the greatest loss of human life among non-combatant civilians. Rejecting other options, such as a political effort to reach agreements with disaffected non-combatant civilians, moving of people away from the conflict areas, or the arrest of insurgents, the State opted for the annihilation of those they identified as their enemy.

122. In consequence, the CEH concludes that agents of the State of Guatemala, within the framework of counterinsurgency operations carried out between 1981 and 1983, committed acts of genocide against groups of Mayan people which lived in the four regions analysed. This conclusion is based on the evidence that, in light of Article II of the Convention on the Prevention and Punishment of the Crime of Genocide, the killing of members of Mayan groups occurred (Article II.a), serious bodily or mental harm was inflicted (Article II.b) and the group was deliberately subjected to living conditions calculated to bring about its physical destruction in whole or in part (Article II.c). The conclusion is also based on the evidence that all these acts were committed "with intent to destroy, in whole or in part" groups identified by their common ethnicity, by reason thereof, whatever the cause, motive or final objective of these acts may have been (Article II, first paragraph).

123. The CEH has information that similar acts occurred and were repeated in other regions inhabited by Mayan people.

About the Editor

James A. Wood is associate professor of Latin American history at North Carolina Agricultural and Technical State University. He has published several articles on the political and social history of nineteenth-century Chile and is the author of *The Society of Equality: Popular Republicanism and Democracy in Santiago de Chile, 1818–1851*, which was published by the University of New Mexico Press in 2011.